CORNELIUS SHIELDS
ON SAILING

"The Contenders," the etching used in the endpapers of this book, is by Y. E. Soderberg. The competitors for the 1962 America's Cup are *Weatherly* (17), *Columbia* (16), *Easterner* (18), and *Nefertiti* (19).

With the exception of the photographs on pages 34, 35, 126 (Bermuda News Bureau) and 43 *(The New York Times),* all photographs in this book were taken by Morris Rosenfeld.

A portion of the material in the instructional section of this book appeared in the chapter contributed by Cornelius Shields to *The Experts' Book of Boating,* edited by Ruth Brindze, © 1959 by Prentice-Hall, Inc., Englewood Cliffs, New Jersey.

PRENTICE-HALL INTERNATIONAL, INC., *London*
PRENTICE-HALL OF AUSTRALIA, PTY., LTD., *Sydney*
PRENTICE-HALL OF CANADA, LTD., *Toronto*
PRENTICE-HALL OF INDIA (PRIVATE) LTD., *New Delhi*
PRENTICE-HALL OF JAPAN, INC., *Tokyo*
PRENTICE-HALL DE MEXICO, S. A., *Mexico City*

*To Do Do, with love and appreciation
for her great patience*

Acknowledgments

Several individuals have been very helpful to me on this book. I would like to thank Maitland Edey of *Life*, John Rendel and Steve Cady of *The New York Times* for their comments on the manuscript; John E. Walsh, John Duffett and David L. Goodrich for their aid in the preparation of the material; Bruce Aldridge for his diagrams; Everett B. Morris of *The New York Herald Tribune* for his concurrence in the chapter on racing; William E. John, Jr. for his assistance on the matter of rigging and fixtures; Helen Ward for her invaluable proofreading and editing, and Alexander Bryan for his review of the biographical chapters.

Contents

Introduction

This is the first time that Corny Shields has ever invited me to precede him. This covers quite a period of time, too, as some of my earliest memories and most indelibly inscribed lessons in tactics and strategy were learned from the "Gray Fox of Long Island Sound," as he has been affectionately called for many years. I am flattered and delighted at the opportunity for our lifelong (for me) friendship ashore and competitive jousting afloat (on the golf course, too, but that's another story) has been most meaningful and rewarding.

There have been a sizable number of keen students of the boat racing game—Harold Vanderbilt, Arthur Knapp, Bill Luders, Bill Cox, Briggs Cunningham, Herman Whiton, Ted Hood, George O'Day, Albert and Ernie Fay, my brother Bob, to name just a few—but none who have made a more thorough study of all the many facets. There is little, from the hull and sails through crew and rig or tactics and weather, that Corny has not given careful thought and attention. This devotion to detail and masterful dedication to achieving the maximum possible results is famous.

The greatest testimonial to Corny Shields and what he has stood for must necessarily be the manner in which he ran the International One-Design Class, and the Sound Interclub Class before it, during his active years. He was obsessed with keeping these fine arenas competitive on a man to man basis at the highest possible level. The strictest control was maintained over sails, gear, haul-outs, and the like so that no one could buy an advantage. He also waged a perpetual campaign to bring to this battlefield men or women, young or old, who were of championship caliber. As soon as such a sailor won an important series or title in good competition, a most persuasive phone call from Corny was soon to follow. Incidentally, lack of a boat or of the financial ability to obtain and campaign one was never an obstacle to this type of prospect. When necessary, Corny could always form a syndicate for the purpose or persuade some elder statesman to help out a deserving youngster.

With all his dedication to the one design principle, however, when Corny turned his hand to the cruising boats or the open design six or twelve meter classes, he was as resourceful and ingenious as anyone—to this I can attest, with scars to show. Many have also said over the years how much he has contributed to both the frostbite fleet and the junior sailing program at the Larchmont Yacht Club. These I have not had the opportunity to witness personally, but their records speak most eloquently.

I think back over my happy years in sailing, and find so many of the great memories intertwined with the Shields family. Aileen Shields sailing Bob's and my International *Susan* in her first try at a "big" boat in "big" competition and winning by a mile; Aileen crewing for me on *Susan* in Bermuda in my first try at international team racing abroad; playing golf with Corny while Doe Shields visited and shopped with my Patricia during our honeymoon; the hard fought *Vim-Columbia* duels during the 1958 America's Cup Trials; a friendly foursome in a driving rainstorm at the climax of that series with George Hinman and Bubbles Havemeyer, members of the selection committee; his experienced hand helping Corny, Jr. and *Columbia* in 1962 during the trials; the appreciation for the way the *Weatherly* crew turned out to a man—designer, engineers, and all, to lend a hand when *Columbia's* rig went over the side.

I've wandered afield, though. All who read this book will profit therefrom as I have, for, as Corny stresses, there isn't a day when we can't learn something new about this wonderful sport. I wish it had been written twenty-five years ago so that it might have been a little easier to learn many of the secrets that Corny reveals here. I know you'll enjoy this most fascinating and informative volume, which while it has come a bit late for me shall be required reading for my three young sons.

BUS MOSBACHER

Part One

1. There's More To Gain Than a Trophy

When I was a youngster, just old enough to wander around by myself, I lived on the St. Mary's River in Sault Ste. Marie, Ontario. The river, which links Lake Superior with the other Great Lakes, was a fascinating place to me. Two or three miles across, it lay between low, sparsely-populated banks.

I used to spend hours exploring the water's edge, watching the great 400- and 500-foot ore boats steaming past. As was the custom on the lakes, the ore boats had pilot houses almost on their stems, and stacks in their sterns. Some were of "whale-back" design, with such low freeboard that the hulls looked very much like submarines. There were other boats to study and wonder at, too—the little sloop belonging to my two older brothers, other yachts, various power craft coming and going. And I liked to watch the water itself—to see the beautiful sparkle of the morning sun on it.

One morning, down at the water's edge, I found a log two or three feet long. It had been run lengthwise through a saw, and a third of it was sliced off, leaving a kind of ship's deck. I doubt that anyone else would have given that log a second look, but it was to become my first "boat."

I hauled it out of the water and shored it up as I had seen real boats shored at the shipyard. I cleaned it, painted it, and put masts and little liferails on it. I spent hours admiring it, and came to love it. With my child's imagination, I could transform it into the beautiful America's Cup racer *Reliance,* or into the magnificent ocean liner *Majestic,* on which my mother and older sisters had just returned from Europe. Most of the time, though, it remained simply my boat, a thing of beauty as children have always found magical delight in their own simple objects—broken dolls or sticks that become, for them, racing cars or airplanes.

The kind of feeling I had for that first boat has stayed with me all my life. The boats, of course, have changed, but the emotion is basically the same: a blend of pride and hope and gratitude. As the boats have changed, so has my relationship to them. From a child building a toy, I've moved through an active, rewarding lifetime on the water: an apprenticeship in the fundamentals of sailing; then the first, tentative steps in racing; then years of active campaigning against the keenest rivals in the world of yachting. I've been racing boats for over half a century, and I'm certain there's no one who has received more pleasure than I from my sport.

Scattered throughout the house and in my library are silver cups and trays engraved with names and dates—trophies I've won. The trophies won by my son and daughter are on the shelves, too, for I am most fortunate in having them share my interest in racing.

Each of these trophies has a special meaning for me. The sight of one of them recalls the details of the race which I won: what the weather was like, the names and faces of my competitors, the direction of the wind, the spectacle of heeled-over boats driving for the starting line, the order of finish. Just as some golfers can replay a long-ago round stroke by stroke, so I can recapture most of the races which have been so large and fulfilling a part of my life. The trophies are there to stir my memory, to keep the past alive.

In the library is the Mallory Cup bowl I won in 1952, for the first North American Sailing Championship. No victory ever meant more, or demanded more of me. Seven of the finest skippers in the country competed and I won by the breadth of a mast. Then there's the bowl that signifies my victory in the Atlantic Class Championship in 1931. I'm particularly proud of that one, for the racing presented special challenges: I'd had no experience with these boats, and we sailed in Narraganset Bay waters that were brand new to me.

My first and last trophies are at home, too. The first is a pewter mug with a glass bottom. I won it when I was twelve—not for sailing, but for swimming. I remember bicycling home after the race to proudly show my prize to my mother. A thunderstorm broke when I was half-way home, and I tucked the mug under my shirt so it wouldn't get wet. The last trophy is a mahogany box for storing flat silver. I won it in 1961, in what amounted to a "comeback" race for me.

The awards Aileen and Corny—my daughter and son—have won mean even more to me, for they rekindle the joy any parent feels at the accomplishments of his children. Here is the evidence of how well they profited from the long, pleasant hours we passed together as they were growing up, hours spent learning the tactics and skills that make for successful sailing. In truth, these cups won by the children mean *most* to me, for watching a child grow up is the happiest occupation I can imagine.

Also important to me are the races I did *not* win, for each taught me a lesson. Perhaps a particular race was lost because I anticipated the starting-gun. Thereafter, I tried to improve the organization and timing of my starts. Perhaps another was lost because a competitor outsailed me to windward. This showed I needed to study the boat's trim and rigging and sails—and, more important, to improve my own capacity to get the most out of her, to take full advantage of the qualities that had been designed and built into her.

So I realized early in my career that to make a mistake once can be valuable for the learning it involves; it is the way to learn. But to make the same mistake twice is inexcusable.

There are other things more precious than trophies that I've gained from yacht racing. This sport has the most wholesome environment of any. The fresh, invigorating air, the gentle warmth of the sun, the pleasant physical activity—all have a wonderfully healthy effect on mind and body. There is no locker room atmosphere in yachting, and it remains the only major sport free of professionalism. To my mind, these characteristics help explain why it is the fastest-growing sport in the world.

Working around a small boat is a wonderful way to keep fit—not too violent for the chap past 30 who might be out of shape, but still demanding enough to be beneficial to the youngsters. If you own a boat, you'll spend a lot of time in the water, scrubbing the bottom, and physical therapists agree that swimming is superb for toning up all your muscles. It seems incredible to me that when a person voices concern about physical fitness, he exposes himself to being considered an eccentric. Yet the direct and important relationship between bodily health and general well-being is a known and accepted fact of life. If you race boats, you automatically keep fit, and you have a lot of fun doing it.

I have always held that a man will carry over into life the same attitudes toward competition that he shows in yacht racing. Even more important—especially in the development of children—is that proper training in competition will enrich the individual and help to mold a sound character. We encounter competition in every department of living, and the person who competes poorly will be tremendously handicapped in the attempt to achieve his goals.

The man who's a poor loser at yacht racing will be a poor loser at anything, but the man who accepts defeat gracefully in racing will do so in life—and this is valuable, for none of us can win always.

It is more difficult still to learn how to accept success with good taste and humility. The human tendency is to boast of prowess and good fortune, to grow superior, and to ignore the role chance plays in our triumphs. But nobody in the racing fleets will let you get away with that kind of boorishness for very long. Sooner or later, someone will take the wind out of your sails, both literally and figuratively, and you'll wind up at the tail of the class with a more realistic estimate of yourself.

This sort of education is good because it teaches sportsmanship. The world's principles of behavior are not much different, and if we learn only this code of competition from sailing, we have added to our lives.

I think we're poorer in some respects today than were our ancestors, despite our great material comforts. We're poorer because we've lost contact with the greatest things of all: nature, the elements, the seasons. Through sailing, it's possible to get back to these fundamentals for a time. We can learn a great deal from them, and can draw pleasure and stimulation and solace from them. The days I've spent sailing boats have been among the happiest and most richly rewarding of my life.

2. A Look Astern

In Sault Ste. Marie, I didn't spend all my time on shore, building "boats." I also went sailing—when my older brothers, Lou and Paul, took me. The memory of one such sail is still very much with me.

On a lovely, clear day in July 1903, when I was eight years old, Lou and Paul took their sloop, *Virginia,* out on the St. Mary's River. We left the mooring and beat upwind. I was sitting on the weather quarter, watching the sails and the sky and the water. The breeze began to make up and Paul, who was steering, didn't ease her at all, but let her have her head. She heeled over until the lee rail was buried. The weather side, with me on it, rose higher and higher until I was looking straight down into the water, sliding to leeward and grabbing desperately for a hand-hold.

I knew the boat was going over, and I was afraid. Though I had only heard the words used by the grownups, and barely understood what they meant, I muttered under my breath, over and over, "Luff her, you damn fool, luff her!"

I can hear those frightened words as if I'd spoken them today. They must have eased her eventually, because they sailed back to the dock, where they unceremoniously dumped me and left me to walk home. Probably they were disgusted with my chicken-heartedness, but in truth I was badly scared in that hard breeze.

Now, some uncomfortable experiences simply arouse a youngster's curiosity, while others build up a lifelong dislike. About this time, I was introduced to horseback riding. The first time up, I was jogging along minding my own business, watching the world go by at eye level for a change, when my mount threw me and bolted for the barn. I have entertained a dogged dislike for horses ever since, and have never ridden again. With boats, though, it was different. Fortunately—for otherwise I would have missed a world of pleasure—that frightening sail didn't make me hate the sport at all. Three years after that day of panic and shame, I tasted, for the first time, the full measure of excitement a boat can provide. My fears were forgotten from that moment on, and I soon discovered that I liked sailing best when the wind blew hardest.

I still feel that way. A sailboat is meant to move in a wind, and the more wind, the more lively she becomes. For me, the wonderful sensation of sailing a boat hard is without equal. Perhaps I've been compensating ever since, trying to live down that initial disgrace, but I know I've always done better in a good, strong breeze, and on the day of a race it can't blow too hard for me.

I was born in St. Paul, Minnesota, in what turned out to be a good yachting year, 1895. It was the year *Defender* beat *Valkyrie III* and kept the America's Cup in the United States, and it was also the year the beautiful little sloop *Ethelwynn,* designed and sailed by W. P. Stephens, beat England's *Spruce IV* in the first race for the Seawanhaka Cup. There is some sort of prophetic coincidence here, for both of these famed yachting prizes were to play an important part in my life.

My father, who had started working as a waterboy on James J. Hill's Great Northern Railroad and had risen to become its vice-president, moved the family to Bristol, Tennessee, where he became president of the Virginia Iron, Coal and Coke Company. Fortunately for my future as a sailor, we didn't stay long in landlocked Bristol, but in 1900 moved to the beautiful harbor city of Sydney, Nova Scotia, where my father became president of the Dominion Iron and Steel Co.

We lived a little to the west of Sydney, where two bays form a *Y* that cuts into the Sydney Peninsula. The house was set back a few hundred yards from the water and had an immense lawn running down to the water's edge. We had several boats, I remember; a canoe, some rowing boats, a launch, and my father also had an interest in a big cruising cutter, the *Dione.*

It was a wonderful place for a boy to learn to love the water, for the tradition of the sea was very strong in Nova Scotia. Both Paul and Lou became fond of sailing while we lived there. My father first bought them a little 18-foot ketch-rigged sailboat, something like the Block Island boats, and then later commissioned Herick Duggan, who designed boats as a hobby, to do the drawings for a lovely little fin-keel sloop about 28 feet overall. She had a gaff rig and mahogany hull, and was christened *Virginia*. We took delivery of her after we moved to Sault Ste. Marie, Ontario, where my father had gone to become president of the Lake Superior Corporation.

Despite the story at the beginning of this chapter, I have fond memories of *Virginia*, for it was aboard her, some years later, that I acquired a true awareness of the beauty of sailing and developed a passion for boats.

In 1904, my father died. Because I was so young—only nine when he died—I had never been as close to him as my older brothers and sisters; my feeling for him was rather one of great respect and admiration. This was partly because of the times: the father of that era wasn't as free and easy with his children as the father of today. Also, because of the large size of our family, he had little time to spare. Without question, parents are more conscious of their children as personalities today than when I was a boy, and we are luckier for it. I know I've gained immeasurably from the sharing and interchange with my children, and have learned a great deal from them.

After my father's death there was no reason for us to stay in Ontario. My oldest sister, Katherine, was married and living in New York, so in 1906 my mother bought a house in New Rochelle, where she could be close to family and friends. My other two sisters, Alice and Cornelia, assisted my mother in bringing me up. They couldn't have been better "guardian angels." My appreciation, love and affection for them continues to this day. *Virginia* was shipped down, and we found a mooring place for her in New Rochelle Harbor. Paul and Lou were occupied with their careers, so the boat spent most of the time at the mooring.

New Rochelle was a wonderful place for a boy to grow up, and I spent my time swimming in Long Island Sound, tramping along the harbor shore, and doing the thousand things that interest a boy. I sailed only once or twice with Paul on *Virginia*, and a few times I crewed for Fred Gade or Bob Mahlstedt on their Bugboats, the predecessors of the Star class. I loved the water, but there were many other things I liked to do just as well as sail. I was certainly not prepared for the radical change that would soon come over me; shortly, I was to undergo an experience that would make sailboats a part of my life forever.

One day I was sailing off New Rochelle harbor with Sterling MacKintosh aboard his Larchmont Interclub. It is over half a century since that day, but I've never forgotten it. It was about eleven o'clock, and the weather was clear and beautiful. The wind was blowing 10 or 15 knots from the northwest, and we were beating into it. I was preoccupied and interested in what was going on around me.

"I've been steering all morning," Sterling said. "Would you like to take the helm for a while?"

This was the first time I'd ever been offered a helm. I'd never asked to steer, either, for I'd simply never felt the inclination—I was content just to look on while others did the actual boat-handling.

But we changed places, and it didn't take 20 seconds before I was hit by a welling-up of emotion so strong that it's almost indescribable. It was like a theater curtain going up. Suddenly, I was tremendously happy. Perhaps what I experienced is similar to what happens to a glider pilot when he's set free from the tow and soars for the first time. Transmitted through that tiller was the *feel* of having control over a living, energetic thing. The emotion was far more exalted and complex than the simple thrill of command. I felt a great exhilaration, and for the first time really sensed the full joy of sailing, rather than the mere motion of the boat.

It was one of the greatest experiences of my life, and I will be forever grateful to Sterling for having given it to me. Never, before or since, has anything opened up to me so spectacularly.

I kept the helm for the balance of the hour. Then we went about and came in for lunch. Food was the last thing in the world I cared about: I couldn't wait to pick up the sails and get out to *Virginia*. I sailed her for the rest of that day, and for years after, until I sold her, it was a rare day when I missed the delight of sailing her all day long. From the first time I took the tiller, I never again worried about capsizing. When you handle a boat yourself, you learn instinctively what she'll take, and your confidence grows.

During the next few years, I came to love the water in the way that's natural to a sailor. Occasionally, I crewed for local skippers during races, but for the most part I spent my time aboard *Virginia*, absorbing all she could teach me. My mother, who hadn't sailed much in the past, often went out with me. While I handled the sheets and tiller, she would sit up on the forward deck, leaning against the mast, and she would sing. This always made me nervous, for she wasn't the world's best swimmer. (She'd taught herself to swim—in an unusual and frightening way. She always said she *knew* she could do it, and one day, when I was in my early teens, she simply jumped off the end of the dock into fifteen feet of water and proved her point.) I remember one sail when we ran into a thunderstorm. My mother persuaded me not to go back into the harbor. She was sure we'd be perfectly safe, and said she assumed I could handle a boat in rough weather. When the storm broke, I discovered her down under the deck, taking her shoes off—"just in case we go over," she said.

Without my realizing it, these days were preparing me for the time when I'd be a racing skipper. And racing is the aspect of sailing that has gripped me the hardest.

I'm supposed to be a "competitive" person; at least, I've always enjoyed competitive sports and matching skills with others. When I was at school in New Rochelle, I organized a swimming race because I thought I was a pretty good swimmer, and a bicycle race because I thought I was a pretty good cyclist. I won the swimming meet and was presented with the pewter mug I mentioned before—the first trophy I ever won—and I lost the bicycle race dismally. I kept on with my swimming, and later was successful in prep school competition, but the sport that continued to attract me more and more as I grew older was sailing.

I sailed my first race as a skipper in 1909, and from the start it was a comedy of errors. The race was held off Stamford, Connecticut, and I had to sail the 12 or 13 miles up there from New Rochelle. Some friends had said they would crew for me, but in the morning they didn't appear, so I left without them. The *Virginia* was a sizable boat for one person to race, especially one with my limited experience, but I was all fired up and vowed I'd take part, no matter what.

My trip up the sound went badly from the outset. The wind was from the northwest, and it was strong, hitting 20 knots in the gusts. As I was leaving the harbor, the battens in the mainsail broke. A few miles further on, off Larchmont, the bobstay fitting let go; then the backstay parted and the tiller broke off at the rudderhead.

The last was too much; I knew I wouldn't be able to race without repairs. I patched things up, sailed back to the harbor, and rowed to the shipyard. The man at the yard fixed the tiller, and I rove a new backstay, repaired the bobstay with wire, and borrowed a set of battens. Two hours

21

later, I was reaching back up the sound. There was a wonderful breeze, and late or not, I was determined to compete.

So *Virginia* and I came up to the committee boat and went roaring across the starting line, ready for a battle to the death. *Virginia*, though noble and proud, was past her maidenhood, and though I would have fought the man who said so, with strain she tended to weep at the seams. She had been lightly built to save weight, and the years had dealt somewhat harshly with her. Because I loved the boat so, she and I kept the secret between us. My habit was to steer her with one hand, and, bail her out with a bucket with the other hand.

The course was a reaching start east to the "Cows," the light buoy off Stamford, then a jibe with another reach out into the middle of the sound, and finally a beat home to the weather mark. Well ahead, I could see the group of boats that had started on time. *Virginia* was fin-keeled and flat-bottomed, which made her fast on a reach. Crouched low in the cockpit, I strained my eyes ahead. It looked as though we were gaining on the fleet—perhaps we could still beat one of the stragglers.

Turning the last mark, I trimmed the sheets for the beat to windward. A race is not lost til the finish; on we sailed, intent on catching someone.

Then, suddenly, I realized that *Virginia* was almost half-full of water. Bucket in one hand, tiller in the other, it was a question of keeping her going while at the same time keeping her from swamping.

If we had roared across the starting-line, we more or less wallowed across the finish line, nearly awash like a rock at half-tide. "Who won?" I shouted to the race committee as I went by. "How did the race come out?"

"What class are you in?"

"Special Class 'R'." I answered the hail as proudly as Commodore Perry signaling "We have met the enemy and they are ours."

"There are no other class 'R' boats out today," they called. "You're the only one."

The ignominy of it! The shame of it! I had won my first race by a sail-over. I was broken-hearted, but nonetheless the sail had been glorious, and now I was blooded, after a fashion. I set to work with the bucket. Ten minutes later *Virginia's* bilges were dry and I started for home.

Between 1910 and 1913 I went away to school at Loyola in Montreal. I was always an indifferent student, and like most boys of fifteen I couldn't wait for classes to end so I could go outdoors and find something interesting to do. I lived only for the summer holidays, when I could get back to sailing. Long before, probably from the time of my first race, life had taken on an important meaning for me, and I was impatient with anything that interfered. My drive to excel had found its natural expression—I was convinced that some day I'd be a champion racing skipper.

It's interesting to me that I never doubted I could become a champion. I just knew I had the capability. It's difficult to explain this without sounding boastful, but the truth is more important than any wish I might have to appear in a good light.

It's been my privilege to know many outstanding athletes including Ben Hogan, Jack Dempsey, Sam Snead, and Andy Bathgate. I've questioned these men about their experiences. I wanted to learn if this sense of calling, which amounted almost to a feeling of predestination, was a common one. Without exception, I found that at one time or another they all knew with absolute certainty that they could reach the top. Indeed, I think that without such self-confidence it would be impossible for anyone to attain championship status.

Having found my element, I wanted to sail constantly, to learn all I could about the tremendously pleasurable and intricate business of racing. I soon realized the poor *Virginia* had to go. I needed to get into a really active, competitive class, where I could test myself against top skippers.

In 1913, feeling like a traitor, and with horrible pangs of nostalgia, I sold *Virginia*. The Larchmont Interclub one-design boats were my ideal class. I happened to think of a family friend who lived in Niagara Falls and owned such a boat, which he kept in Larchmont but sailed very little. I got in touch with him and asked if he'd be willing to charter his craft. We made a deal; I would care for the boat and race it, and he would have it when he came to Larchmont to race. In the latter event, I would serve as his crew. There would be no charter fee.

She was everything I expected and I was proud to be a member of this popular class. I did not do well, but it was always the equivalent of winning in my opinion if I could be in the first five or maybe on occasion beat some of the top skippers at the start or across the finish line.

I had a wonderful, constructive summer and got much enjoyment out of having this beautiful boat to sail. The summer included one experience, in particular, that I have thought about many times since. One day I unfortunately touched a heavy gas buoy and badly scarred the topsides—so much so that I was afraid it might necessitate a new plank. The boat was insured, which permitted me to have her repaired at the famous City Island Yard of Robert Jacobs, who had built the boat several years previously. Jacobs personally seemed to take great interest in my concern for the boat and saw that she had every attention. It was reassuring to learn from the boss painter whom he had summoned to examine the damage that it could easily be repaired with no replacement of the plank. This man, too, was extremely kind to me and appeared to be interested in my racing activities, as I presume he would have with any youngster. He soon became aware of my love for the water and sailing of this boat in particular.

I was in the yard the entire two days that the boat was on the enormous marine railway. She looked dainty there—almost like a toy boat in the surroundings of the great big sloops and yachts. Before I left, the painter said with great seriousness, "Some day you will be sailing one of these America's Cup yachts."

Even though I realized he was being generous in his comments to a youngster, I thought it was one of the nicest compliments I could imagine. I have always remembered his remark, and I am sure that, at the time, it gave me the confidence that some day I really would sail a cup yacht.

The following season I bought an Interclub and named her *Barbara*, after Paul's little daughter. The next three years were spent learning from good men in good boats. At that time the club was running only one race a weekend, and I didn't feel that was sufficient. I was able to persuade several of the Interclub skippers into coming out on Sundays for informal races so we could sharpen our techniques. Also, some of the younger members of the class held scrub races on weekdays. These informal races were invaluable for all of us. On my part, they built up a feeling of confidence and helped me to go on the offensive instead of sailing purely defensive races. I soon learned that in certain tactical situations it's preferable to sail a defensive race—for instance, when you have the highest point standing in the fleet and choose to cover the rival nearest you in standing. But as a general rule you can't sail tentatively and defensively if you want to win. You must sail purposefully, with a spirit of attack. Your competitors must always be aware of your threat, and the only way they'll remember your boat and name is if you sail against them aggressively.

During the first two years of my ownership of *Barbara*, I won a few races and lost many more, but eventually the rigorous training paid off. In 1916, sailing *Barbara*, I won the championship of the Yacht Racing Association of Long Island Sound. The same year, I sailed Gordon Hammersley's New York 30, *Okee,* in the annual New York Yacht Club Cruise. This was the first time I'd competed outside the sound, and the *Okee* was the biggest boat I'd raced. (The 30's, one of the great classes in yachting history, measured 30 feet at the waterline and 44 feet overall.) We finished the cruise with the highest point score.

Regularly, every day I went out sailing. The beach at New Rochelle was a fine place to swim, and I used to moor *Barbara* there and swim to shore. Once in a while I would take friends out, and we'd spend an afternoon lazily poking around the sound.

On one of these trips, I met a young girl with lovely brown hair and a wonderfully sunny disposition. Her name was Josephine Lupprian—her friends called her "Doe." When I first saw her, I said to myself "I'd certainly like to get to know *her* better." But that looked impossible, because she was always surrounded by many admirers. "All the same," I thought, "perhaps luck will come my way."

The years 1914 to 1916 were fateful ones for a youth passing from boyhood into manhood—but I suppose this time of transition is fateful no matter what the years. The world, too, was going through its own period of upheaval. When on April 6, 1917, the United States went to war, I was 22.

Like everyone, I wanted to serve—and I wanted to serve at sea only. I enlisted in the naval reserve, and was sent to Seagate, near the Bensonhurst section of Brooklyn, where I became a chief petty officer. A short while later, competitive exams for officer's training were announced, and I was lucky enough to pass. After training, I was commissioned an ensign in the naval reserve.

At about this time, the United States decided to increase the complement of the regular navy. The regulars were already on active duty, and most of us felt we stood a better chance of getting into things if we were regulars. (As it turned out, this wasn't the case: the reserves saw as much action as the regulars.) There was also a matter of prestige involved—it was considered a mark of honor to wear the silver anchors of the regular navy.

Nothing is done in the service without an examination first, so the reserves from all over the country were tested, and 400 of us were chosen to attend the U.S. Naval Academy at Annapolis.

During the following four months, I worked harder than I ever have in my life. My indifferent scholarship caught up with me, and I had to keep at my books from the first light of morning until late at night. Seamanship and boat-handling were easy for me, but my lack of grounding in mathematics made navigation extremely difficult and gunnery seemingly impossible. I worked with the other cadets, especially one fellow—Al Wolf —whenever I could, until my mind was a seething tangle of mathematical formulas, gun-laying tables, intercepts, trajectories, and equally esoteric terms. Unfortunately, firing a gun in the navy isn't just a matter of drawing a bead and pulling the trigger.

The day our grades were finally posted, I felt like a king. I had scored 100 percent in boat-handling, 3.8 out of a possible 4 in navigation, and done well in the other subjects. Somehow, by the grace of God, I had scraped by in gunnery. Now, silver anchors and all, I was an ensign in the United States Navy. (Such are the inequities of life that a year after I earned these coveted symbols, they were issued to all officers, regardless of branch.)

The tension and anxiety weren't over yet; we still had to sweat out our assignments. We were all afraid we'd be saddled with desk jobs, or else assigned to battleships or service ships. We didn't want battleships, because the navy had few of them, and they were kept moored so far up the York River, in Virginia—out of reach of enemy attack—that we were sure the war would be over before they could put out to sea.

When our orders were finally issued, I'd worked myself into such a state that my hands actually shook as I tore open the envelope. Again, I was lucky. I had been assigned to the armored cruiser *Montana*.

Although everyone wanted to draw destroyers—the most gloried and dashing of ships—an armored cruiser was the next best thing. The *Montana* subsequently became one of the most active ships in the navy. Armored cruisers were used as capital ships-of-the-line, and the *Montana* made sixteen trips across the North Atlantic escorting the troop ships that carried the American Expeditionary Force to France. We would assemble at Hampton Roads, Virginia, at Halifax, Nova Scotia, or at New York, and steam eastward to within 100 miles of the Irish coast, where we would turn our sea-weary charges over to the British escort destroyers.

Although their forays had lessened somewhat as Germany became hard pressed by the Allies, German U-boats were still a constant threat in the

North Atlantic. In order to avoid exposing our vulnerable troop ships to attack, the convoys usually kept to the more northerly routes. There, the weather was our greatest enemy.

My introduction to convoy work was an eye-opener. The very first trip, we went through the worst storm to hit the North Atlantic coast in years. We were off Halifax harbor, and slowly, majestically, our convoy came into sight, ship after ship, steaming into the fairway. There were about 40 altogether, and among them was a beautiful, new, 30,000 ton Dutch liner. She passed us as we fell back to take up our station at the rear of the convoy, and I read the name *Justicia* on her stern. She was the biggest ship I'd ever seen, and was really an impressive sight.

About the third day out of Halifax, the wind and seas made up. Everything movable aboard the *Montana* was secured, and all the hatches and ventilators were battened down. As the day passed, the seas got worse, and the ship got sloppier and sloppier. The majority of the crew was laid low with seasickness, and the ship was so crowded that ratings and messboys were sleeping in the companionways. With the ventilators battened down and the blowers off, not a breath of air moved belowdecks, and the smell was overpowering.

As a boy, I'd had trouble with severe headaches and a delicate stomach. When I mounted the ladder to the bridge to take over my first trick as a junior watch officer, I hoped I wouldn't get sick. I was so preoccupied with the problem that I forgot the pride of standing a junior bridge-watch on an armored cruiser. I wasn't sick, however, and managed to keep functioning.

By evening, conditions had worsened, and all attempts at maintaining stations were abandoned. The convoy scattered, and each ship was left to slog it out alone. At one point, I spotted what appeared to my inexperienced eyes to be a little navy steam-launch rolling her bottom out and making very heavy weather of it. I couldn't imagine what a vessel that small would be doing out there, and took a look at it through the glasses. It wasn't a launch, of course—it was the huge *Justicia*. She was simply dwarfed by those monstrous seas.

After battering us for three days, the storm finally moderated. It had blown full hurricane strength, with winds up to 100 miles per hour recorded at the height. The *Montana* bore the scars of the struggle. Her forward deck had been sprung, and the forecastle metalwork was a mass of twisted wreckage.

Oddly enough, I was never again bothered by seasickness.

I was lucky to have good friends aboard the *Montana*. One of them was Drake Sparkman, with whom I'd grown up in New Rochelle. (Drake later became head of the noted design and brokerage firm of Sparkman & Stephens, and was instrumental in getting many fine yachts for me to sail.) Another was a chap named Thomas Kilkenny, a true Irish wit, a marvelous storyteller, and one of the most popular men aboard.

I recall one of Kilkenny's stunts with particular vividness. Every fourth day, as an exercise, the junior officers had to turn in a number of positional reports, called the "day's work," to the navigating officer. Some junior officers resented the task, for it left them little time for themselves. Kilkenny got into the habit of slipping into the chart house before 8:00 A.M. and copying the navigator's positions from the charts, altering the latitudes and longitudes a little. His "day's work" consisted of the time it took to steal the positions.

One day he changed the figures a little more than usual. The navigating officer was a bristly little fellow with a toothbrush mustache. He stepped out of the chart room and sent up a shout. Kilkenny came running, imagining, I suppose, that he was going to be shot for treason or stealing military secrets.

"Kilkenny," the navigating officer said severely, "what's the matter with you? You're two minutes out in your noon fix, and two miles in error."

"Oh, hell, sir," Kilkenny said with relief, "you can *see* that far."

Kilkenny had a natural aversion to work and was somehow able to make a living doing the things he liked. After the war he built a beautiful junk in Hong Kong and sailed it through the Mediterranean and Red Seas. Later, in Hong Kong, he built the famous schooner *Safong* to a Sparkman & Stephens design and sailed her to this country. He was a wonderful, free-and-easy fellow with a great zest for living. He died a few years ago, and the world is a gloomier place without him.

When the war ended, I was as eager to get out of the navy as I had been to get in. For one thing, I wanted to get started in business. I was also eager to resume my racing. Most important of all, I feared that if I stayed in the navy, I might be shipped to China or some place equally distant from New Rochelle, where Doe was still living. She and I had been seeing a good deal of each other, and I wanted that pleasant state of affairs to continue.

For the time being, however, the navy had other ideas. The reserve officers were released within two weeks of the Armistice, but we regulars were retained. I had made lieutenant (jg) aboard the *Montana,* and was detached from her and ordered to report aboard the U.S.S. *Prairie,* a destroyer tender.

As it turned out, my tour aboard the *Prairie* was far from onerous. We went first to Guantánamo, Cuba, for fleet maneuvers, and then to Trepassey, in southeastern Newfoundland. Our assignment there—my last in the navy—proved to be both exciting and historic. The *Prairie* served as a tender for the famous N.C. flying boats, assisting in the preparations for the navy's attempt at the first transatlantic flight. On May 19, 1919, I watched as the three heavily-laden aircraft labored aloft against 30-mile-an-hour winds, then circled overhead and winged off to the eastward, against the sun. Two of them were forced down in the water short of their goal in the Azores—fortunately without loss of life—but the third, the N.C. 4, made the crossing to the Azores successfully, and then went on the Plymouth, England.

A month later, I received my discharge. Thanks to Paul, it didn't take me long to settle back into civilian life. He was in the real estate business in Great Neck, Long Island, New York, and lived there. I moved in with him, and helped with the selling end of the business. I was eager to get back into sailing; I felt I had a lot of time and lost experience to make up if I were to reach my goals. Also, I had to make some decisions about the future.

I had been able to save very little from my navy salary, and the small amount that had been left to me by my father was not sufficient to begin housekeeping. So my Larchmont Interclub, *Barbara,* went on the market, and I used the proceeds to buy an engagement ring for Doe. That was one part of the future I wanted definitely settled.

I resumed sailing in the newly-formed Victory Class with a borrowed boat, the *Alert,* and was pleased to find I hadn't lost my proficiency. If anything, the time away from racing had been beneficial, because I was eager and more aggressive. I was able to capture the Victory Class championship in both 1920 and 1921.

By this time Paul had left the real estate business and was working for the investment firm of Merrill, Lynch. It wasn't long before he became a partner and hired me to sell securities. I wasn't of much use for a while, but as I learned more about the business, I was better able to pull my own oar.

My chief responsibility as a fledgling salesman was to secure new customers. I put together a sales talk that I thought would convince any intelligent listener to turn his money over to us for investment right on the spot. My problem now was to find listeners, intelligent or not.

I had exhausted all of the leads I had been given, both because they were few in number and because I was so eager the first few weeks. The only thing I could think of was to simply walk in on people cold, like a magazine salesman, and hope that I could convince them. If I had no luck, it was because I was a poor salesman. At least it would give me a chance to practice my talk on a lot of unsuspecting victims. I could take the rough edges off my salesmanship, tighten up my presentation, find out what questions I'd have to answer, and learn how to deal with people.

I began canvassing the better office buildings from top to bottom, always insisting I had to see the man in charge. Now, it's a difficult job to ring a doorbell and *give* something away; it's harder still to ring and sell something for a trifle, and it's almost impossible to ring and separate a stranger from a large sum of money. I came to know the buildings I'd chosen almost as well as their janitors knew them. I was ushered firmly out of some offices, and I had valuable talks with interesting people in others. And, believe it or not, I did a little business. Some accounts were small and some were large, but I was proud of each one, because it showed I could do it. I also got the world's fastest course in human psychology. When I went back to selling from leads, it was fairly easy.

In 1921, Percy Chubb and four British yacht clubs donated a trophy, the British-American Cup, for team races in six-meter-class yachts. The races were to be held alternately in Great Britain and the U.S. The first year, the series was held in Cowes, England, and the British trounced the Americans by a score of 117 to 88 points. In 1922, the U.S. challenged for another series, to be held at Oyster Bay, New York.

I wanted desperately to be on the American team, for this was my first chance to take part in an international yachting event. I sailed the six-meter *Viva* as hard as I could in the trials, but in one race she lost her mast because of a defect in the rigging and I was unable to qualify. I had a bad time getting over the disappointment, but I knew there would be other chances. I felt a little better when the Americans won by 111 to 104.

Doe and I were married in New Rochelle on January 21, 1922, and winning the competition against her other suitors was the biggest success I ever had. When we returned home from our honeymoon in Lake Placid, I took stock of my resources. I had returned to work none too soon: I had exactly twenty-five cents left in my pocket. We moved into a small apartment in New Rochelle and began our life together.

In 1923, Paul decided to go into business for himself, and I went with him. We left Merrill, Lynch, rented an office at 27 Pine Street in downtown New York, and in May the investment firm of Shields & Company began operation.

As with any new business, our greatest need was to find customers, so I continued as a salesman. I had unlimited confidence in our company. I knew that our management would bring in a good profit with a minimum of risk for our clients if they would only trust us. With this belief always with me, I went out and burned shoe leather.

That summer, I sailed Joseph Dunbaugh's beautiful New York 30, *Countess*, and was able to win a class championship for the fourth time. Apart from that, these were lean times for an aspiring sailing champion. I had new responsibilities, a bride, and a new job with a new firm. I had no boat of my own, and I resigned my membership in the Larchmont Yacht Club because I couldn't afford the $100 annual dues. Nevertheless, I had other things to cheer me: I was young, healthy, happy in marriage, and an incurable optimist.

3. *The Competitive Spirit*

I think that a man who believes he has special talent in a sport should make every effort to meet his competitors, and actively seek opportunities to test his skills against the skills of others. This applies to any sport you can name: tennis, golf, track—and, of course, yacht racing. Throughout my racing career, I always sought to meet top skippers in any kind of boat, anywhere, at any time.

Not long ago, a friend asked me if there was any particular year of racing I considered the most rewarding. My answer was that every year was a big year—I loved them all. This same friend did some calculating, and came up with an estimate of the number of races I sailed since I started. The total was in the neighborhood of 8500. I can no longer recall the details of all of them, but at the time each had a special importance for me, and brought me fresh pleasure and knowledge.

Through the 1920's and 1930's, I crowded as much racing as I could into every month. Sometimes, this took careful planning. For example, when I sailed in overnight races aboard the boats of friends, I always arranged to be left off, on Sunday mornings, as close to my home in Larchmont as possible, so I could get back to my International, *Aileen*, for the afternoon's racing. We might have had a strenuous night, but I never missed those Sunday races. I used to be teased about that habit, but it seemed to me as natural as eating or sleeping.

Since sailing had become such a large part of my life, I had strong hopes that our children would also want to follow the sport. When Aileen was born, in early April, 1925, I told myself she would certainly want to grow up around boats. We got her off to an early start: she was baptized toward the end of the month, and right after the ceremony Doe and I tucked her into the car and drove down to City Island, where we carried her around while we explored the yacht yards. This was a trip we took every Sunday in the off-racing season; it seemed perfectly natural for our three-week-old daughter to be with us.

From then on, Aileen was continually exposed to boats and the water, and, as I'd hoped, she loved every bit of it. Doe and I had a busy time with her when she was an infant; long before she could even dog-paddle, she developed the habit of crawling down the beach and into the water. I was forever running after her and pulling her out. As she grew up, I took her out sailing more and more; by the time she was four, she was regularly aboard the boat. The next step was Junior Racing, and she and her little friends would go out and sail for the fun of it, not taking the competition very seriously.

As all children do, Aileen gave us a number of bad scares. She and some friends would go off for a short sail in a dinghy and not return for several hours, while we scoured the Sound for them. It frequently turned out that they'd gone down to Glen Cove, roughly seven miles away—which amounts to an ocean voyage for young children.

Aileen's love of sailing kept up unabated until she was fourteen, and then, suddenly, out of the blue, she didn't want to sail any more. She came to me one day and announced her decision: she was through with boats.

I was stunned by this—she seemed to love the water so much. I asked her why she didn't want to sail any more.

She said she wanted to try something else for a while.

I asked her what she had in mind.

"Well," she said, "horses look interesting. I think I'd like to ride a horse."

I told her that was fine, and that I'd make arrangements for her to ride. I said she could do as much of it as she liked, and added that I'd miss her in the boat.

For two years after our conversation, she poured her interest into rid-ing, not boats. Perhaps this was because she'd been overexposed to the

water. Maybe I expected too much of her, and had taken for granted she would feel the same enthusiasm and depth of interest that I felt. Whatever the reason, she stuck with her riding, ignoring sailing, and got to be a rather proficient horsewoman.

Then, as abruptly as she'd left sailing, she came back to it. The summer she was sixteen, she phoned me in my office, roughly two weeks before Larchmont Race Week. She told me she wanted a boat, and had to have it by the race week. I was delighted, of course, and I said I'd see what I could do. After she hung up, I phoned around and was eventually able to charter an Atlantic for her.

Aileen sailed well that week, and from then on she continued, her interest as keen and intense as it had been before. A few years later, we bought her an Atlantic, and not long after that she won the Atlantic Class Championship. Then, in 1948, when she was 24, she became the Women's National Sailing Champion.

As I said, I don't really know why Aileen turned her back on sailing during those two years when she did. I guess many children go through periods of change like that. You might expect that my son Corny experienced a similar loss of interest, but he has sailed avidly every year of

In her first race, *Dauphin* leads other 6 meters at the start, 1924.

his life, and it certainly looks as though he plans to continue. He has just added the 1963 International One-Design Class World Championship to his many other championships.

Aileen is still sailing, too. She's now Mrs. Alexander Bryan, of Middlebury, Connecticut, and has four children—two boys and two girls. Alex's company builds the Sailfish, Sunfish, Catfish, and Aileen is regularly out on one of those lively little craft, more often than not with a child or two for company.

In 1925, a new class of 28 one-design boats, the Sound Interclubs, was founded by John B. Shethar. Joseph Dunbaugh asked me to sail his Interclub, and did Doe and me the great honor of naming her *Aileen*. I sailed her the next summer, too, and in 1927—thanks in part to the fact that Shields & Company was prospering—I was able to buy her. Her hull was white; I had her painted light green, the color I've used on all my boats since. The Interclub class, incidentally, was probably the first major class in which boats were painted a variety of colors. Hulls used to be either white or black, but we had blue, yellow, grey, and red boats among us.

The Interclubs were lively boats, and we had ten years of spirited racing in them, during which I won the class championship a number of times. John Shethar sold his boat and dropped out of the class after the second season, and I was selected as class chairman.

I have always believed strongly that a successful class must attract the best possible skippers. In part, this belief is founded on selfishness—if I were fortunate enough to win a race, I wanted to know I had beaten the best skippers there were. Over the years, I worked hard at persuading top-flight sailors to join the Interclubs. Among the early competitors were Sam Wetherill, Hobey Ford, Ralph Manny, Carroll Alker, Gordon Raymond, Bill Luders, Egbert Moxham, Bill Cox, Arthur Knapp, Lorna Whittlesey, Bus Mosbacher, and my brother Paul. We felt that these men were among the very best racing skippers in the country.

Down through the Interclub fleet, too, there was a high level of ability. This is where the praise belongs for making a racing class really successful. The middle-of-the-fleet skippers, who turn up Saturday after Saturday out of love of the water and racing, keep the rest of the fleet on its toes and make the challenge tougher and tougher every week. Without them, competition—and the fun that goes with it—would die.

As in any class, there were the habitual also-ran's in the Interclubs—boats that never seemed to be well sailed, and that always trailed far back in the fleet. Despite their lack of success, the skippers of these boats still enjoyed themselves, and they often amused the rest of us. I remember especially a boat we'll call the *Frisky*.

The *Frisky* was regularly in last place, and as a result she wasn't the easiest boat in the fleet to get a crew for. One race day a young friend of mine, an ardent sailor named Morgan Valentine, arrived at the dock at the last minute, looking for a boat to crew on—any boat. As the last of the Interclubs were leaving for the starting-line, he hailed them, and one swung past the dock. Morgan leaped aboard, happy to have a chance to sail.

His happiness began to dim, however, shortly after the start. The boat dropped steadily back, until Morgan found himself staring balefully at nearly every transom in the fleet.

This state of affairs rapidly worsened, and as the race was ending, Morgan turned to the skipper and moaned "We're going to be last!" Then he had a happier thought, and brightened. "We can't be last," he said; "not while the *Frisky's* out here. We'll beat the *Frisky*, at least."

The skipper glowered at him. "My boy," he said, "you're *on* the *Frisky*."

36

During these years, I was also active in bigger boats, particularly 6-meter boats. In 1924, I skippered Harold Tobey's *Dauphin*, a member of the team that successfully defended the British-American Cup. In 1930, Paul and I sailed Herman F. Whiton's *Cherokee* in the same series; again, the American team won. In 1928, I was asked aboard William Bell's New York 40, *Mistral*, for the New York Yacht Club Cruises.

This last was both a pleasure and a new adventure for me. Life aboard these boats was luxurious, with professional crews and stewards on hand. I gained further experience in offshore sailing, and had an opportunity to practice my coast-wise navigation. Also, I learned how to deal with problems that we never met in the triangular races.

One day, when we were racing up the coast of Cape Cod to Marblehead, we encountered a strange phenomenon: right in against the beach, stretching off into the distance around the bend of the cape, there was a narrow, dark patch of wind. It extended out only 150 yards; beyond, there was glassy calm. If we could get in close to the beach, we could play that breeze to advantage, and we would also avoid having to buck the head tide running through Pollock Rip Slew.

It was hard to get close to shore because of a sandbar running parallel to it. The chart, however, showed an 8-foot gutter crossing the bar at Monomoy Point. We drew 8 feet, and figured that with the half-tide we could just get through.

Our bearings proved to be correct, and we got safely over the bar and into the breeze. Then, all the way around the cape, we hugged the shore, making over a hundred tacks. Occasionally, in the surge of the swell, we touched bottom and had to push off with the spinnaker pole.

The breeze held for us, and we avoided the head tide; the result was that we beat our nearest competitor to Marblehead by four hours—and there were some big boats in the fleet that day. For me, that narrow strip of breeze was a true marvel, one of the most unusual sights I've ever seen.

The year I began racing aboard *Mistral*—1928—I also sailed the 6-meter *Lea*, and earned the privilege of representing the country in the Gold Cup series against boats from England, Italy, Holland, Norway, and Sweden. During this series, one of our opponents, Sven Salen, from Sweden, used a genoa jib. It was the first time the sail had been tried in competition on this side of the Atlantic, and at first the American sailors tended to take it lightly. (For my own part, I completely failed to recognize the sail: the first time I saw it in use, I thought Salen was going to windward with a

The start of the New York 40's during the
1927 New York Yacht Club Cruise.

ballooner.) Salen soon showed us how effective the sail could be, and the Swedish boat won the cup handily.

At this time I became active in the annual competition with the Royal Bermuda Yacht Club, which had been instituted by John Shethar the previous year with the famous Trimmingham brothers, Eldon and Kenneth. In this, we sailed our Interclubs—which were shipped down on the *Queen of Bermuda*—against their RBYC one-designs. The two classes, although materially different in design, were very evenly matched, and the racing was spirited and hard-fought. This series has established a relationship that has meant a good deal to me. I have a great affection for my Bermuda friends.

I remember one incident that occurred during these races in Bermuda. Gordon Raymond, a friend of mine, was sailing his Interclub with a pickup crew made up of 6-meter skippers who had completed their own series the week before. Gordon was a large, powerful man, and a very competent skipper. He was also excitable, and used to let off steam by setting his hat down on the deck and crashing his fist down on it. You could hear the thump half a mile off.

During this particular race, one of the other men in the boat succeeded somehow in winding one of Gordon's fingers in under the wire on a winch. Ignoring what must have been enormous pain, Gordon made a remark that has since become a part of Bermula sailing folklore: "Four skippers in the boat and not a sailor in the crowd—*get my finger out of this winch!*"

This misadventure ended happily, but there are others that do not. Accidents are bound to happen aboard even the best-sailed boats. I've had my share of misfortunes, and I've done my best to learn from them. It's a natural reaction for a skipper to want to fix the blame on a crew member in these cases, and that, I believe, is a mistake. A skipper mustn't chastise his crew unduly. In most cases, the ultimate responsibility is his. If the skipper has a proper regard for his own role, he'll be tolerant of shortcomings and will not get excited or rattled. A skipper's assumption of ultimate responsibility is what makes a boat sail smoothly, and divisions of authority and recriminations only make difficult situations worse. Above all, a skipper must make the final decisions, must retain his authority. If he loses it, trouble is bound to develop.

By 1929, Shields & Company was six years old. The firm had been blessed with real prosperity, particularly in 1928, and was continuing to expand. I was especially eager to open a stock brokerage business to supplement our underwriting and distributing operations. Paul agreed this was a good idea, but felt it could wait until we had taken on experienced personnel to manage the division.

In January 1929, we underwrote a large stock issue, and were surprised to find that the stock acted poorly in the after-market: demand for it wasn't as great as we'd anticipated. We couldn't understand the reason for this. We felt that perhaps there was some economic unrest we couldn't see—or that we might be losing our touch. We decided it was time to take a careful look at the firm's position and our own abilities, and we set about getting our house in order, reducing inventory and selling the equities we'd gained through underwriting.

This period of lessened pressure and self-appraisal seemed like a good time to set up the stock brokerage business, so we hired the personnel we needed and bought a seat on the New York Stock Exchange. By sheerest coincidence, we announced our membership in the Exchange on October 24—Black Thursday. As I've indicated, at the time almost all of the firm's assets were in cash. During the next weeks and months, we picked up many customers from other firms unable to accommodate them. Within the next two years, we took over the businesses of eight distressed firms— some of them sizable operations. Through the entire depression, we had losses in only two years, and they were small.

I don't want to make us sound wiser than we were. By no means did we foresee the full size of the storm that was moving down on the American economy—rather, we experienced a small puff and reacted to it in the most natural manner, by shortening sail. There was, of course, a great amount of luck involved; I'm well aware that Shields & Company has much to be grateful for.

An innovation came to yachting in 1931 that has had far-reaching unexpected consequences. This was the birth of "frostbiting," the flourishing winter sport which has transformed competitive sailing from a seasonal affair into a year-round activity. In my opinion, frostbiting is the greatest single development in yachting in this century. I've sailed in hundreds of frostbite races, and they're among my fondest memories. To my regret, I wasn't present at the actual birth of the sport, but no account of racing in relatively recent years would be complete without a mention of it.

One December afternoon in 1931, a group of sailors got together informally at the Manhasset Bay Yacht Club. (I wasn't there, but heard about the gathering later, the same day.) They started talking about how they hated to be inactive during the winter. Finally, Bill Taylor—who was then the sailing reporter for *The New York Herald Tribune* and who is now an editor of *Yachting* magazine and a Pulitzer Prize winner—suggested that there wasn't really any good reason why they shouldn't race. All they had to do, he said, was get some boats together, bundle themselves up in warm clothes, and go to it. Why not the following Saturday, January 2, at Port Washington?

The idea caught on immediately, and plans were made to get the boats together. They were a mixed lot, brought in from all over the sound: a flat-bottomed boat, a lap-streak 14-footer, a scow, etc. Drake Sparkman lent me a little Ratsey pram he owned. The idea of the competition appealed to me enormously—an America's Cup race wouldn't have excited me more. I set to work getting Drake's pram ready for the big event, and planned how I would keep warm. The greatest problem, I thought, would be with my hands, and I decided to take along two cans of Sterno, which I would burn inside a bucket to keep them from rolling around on the floorboards.

The day before the race, I learned that I would have to go up to Boston on urgent business and would miss the fun. I don't think I've ever been more disappointed. I sent the other sailors—they included Porter Buck, Gordon Curry, Arthur Knapp, Robert Fraser, Bill Dyer and Colin Ratsey—my best wishes, and unhappily took the train.

The racing was thoroughly successful. I have always treasured Bill Taylor's account of it in the *Herald Tribune*, which read, in part:

> The first annual regatta or maybe it was just the first regatta, of the Frostbite Yacht Club was a howling success and was won by several people because of the fact that there were several races. Colin Ratsey and Eugene Kelly, sailing the good ship *Spinnaker*, took the grand prize, but the boats that finished first in the three races were *Dorade*, sailed by Porter Buck and Bob Garland, in the first race, and *Nippy*, sailed by Gordon Curry and Charley Henderson, in the other two.

> The racing had everything that a good Frostbite regatta ought to have. It rained during the first race, rained and hailed during the second, and snowed during the third. There was wind and there were several shipwrecks, though none of the shipwrecks happened during the race.

The idea of Frostbite regattas, of course, is to prove that some people are crazier than others and those who are craziest sail races in eleven-foot open boats in the middle of snowstorms—and enjoy it. When daylight gradually dawned this morning—and it dawned very gradually—the wind was blowing the better part of a gale out of the northeast and it was raining cats, dogs, pitchforks, and all the other traditional things, only colder. The breaking waves dashed high on a stern and ice-bound coast and one by one sailors with chilly blue noses looked out and shook their heads. . .

The week after the first Port Washington race, we raced at New Rochelle, the weekend after at Stamford, etc. These times, thank the Lord, I was able to take part. Enthusiasm for dinghy-racing mounted quickly, and more and more skippers joined us, eager to get out of doors

The start of frostbite dinghy race on Long Island Sound. Corny Shields, Jr. with a nicely-timed start in the extremely dangerous "coffin corner."

43

and to be doing what they loved best. We soon found that except for really poisonous days such as the day of that first race, we could keep comfortably warm in relatively light clothing. We were always busy and active, and no more felt the cold than a skier in competition does. I never had to use the Sterno.

As frostbiting really took hold, those of us dedicated to it found ourselves going to extreme lengths to get competition. I thought nothing of putting my dinghy on a trailer and driving up to Mystic, Connecticut, or Boston, or Marblehead, for a day's racing. This often meant leaving home at 3:30 in the morning and driving back after the races, sometimes through snow and ice. Like dyed-in-the-wool hunters and fishermen, sailors will put up with amazing discomforts for the sake of sport.

While frostbiting was in its infancy, Bill Taylor continued to support it with his wonderful enthusiasm and energy, attracting new people to it and focusing valuable attention on it. Bill has made many contributions to yachting, but to my mind the greatest was his origination and fostering of frostbiting. He is the true "father" of the sport, and sailors everywhere will forever be indebted to him.

As I said, the first frostbite races were sailed in boats of widely varied classes, ranging in length from 10 to 14 feet. There was no standardization as to sail area, displacement, etc. This sort of arrangement has obvious drawbacks. I believe that the most meaningful racing is done in a strictly controlled one-design class, with boats as nearly identical as possible. Under these conditions, the skill of the skipper and his crew is what brings a boat home first, and not some characteristic drawn into the boat by the designer.

In the case of frostbiting, the need for a one-design boat was obvious soon after the sport had caught on. The frostbite skippers, however, disagreed as to what kind of boat they wanted. To resolve the differences of opinion between the various groups, I suggested that an independent selection committee be formed, to which designers would submit drawings. The committee would look over the entries and pick out the boat it liked best, and we would then build ourselves a one-design fleet. The primary restrictions on designs were that the boats would have to measure 11 feet, 6 inches overall and have 72 square feet of sail.

William Crosby, the editor of *Rudder*, announced the contest in his magazine, and soon designs were pouring in from all over the world—

South America, South Africa, New Zealand, Australia, England, and, of course, the United States. The selection committee, of which I was a member, checked all the entries and chose one by Nicholas Potter of Providence, Rhode Island. The boats, which were sturdy, lapstreak craft, were built at the Herreshoff yards in Bristol, Rhode Island, and at George Lauder's yard in Greenwich, Connecticut. We named the class the B.O.'s, for B-One Design; they gave us many pleasant years of racing.

To my mind, frostbiting has done more for small-boat racing than any recent development. It has brought thousands of new people, from across the country, to sailing, and it has taught them valuable lessons in many different areas: sail construction and handling, tactics, the rules of racing, weather, etc. And dinghy racing has materially benefited the more experienced sailors as well by opening up a whole new season. Instead of sailing in only one race a week in summer—as had been the case up until 1930—a skipper can now race the year 'round, sailing in as many as ten races a day on Saturdays and Sundays.

The nature of the boats makes dinghy sailing especially educational. Things happen a lot faster in dinghies than in larger boats, and this difference can teach even the most seasoned veteran a great deal. Dinghies are delicate, and they react rapidly to poor handling, whereas a bigger boat, with its greater momentum, gives the skipper a margin for error; if he fluffs, the boat keeps going.

Dinghy sailing teaches the indefinable quality of "feel," and the importance of proper trim. There's also a lot of fun and instruction in the maintenance of the little boats—in scraping, painting, and varnishing them, and in keeping the rigging and fittings in order. All in all, they are invaluable training tools, as well as constant sources of excitement and satisfaction.

In 1931, my mother died. I felt the loss deeply, for she and I were very close through the years. This was soon to be followed—in 1933—by the death of Louis, my oldest brother. Again, the blow was severe; we had shared much, in sailing, in the firm, and as next-door neighbors.

Of all the competitions I entered in the 1930's, the one I remember most vividly is the 1935 defense of the Seawanhaka Cup, or Seawanhaka International Challenge Cup for Small Yachts, to give its full title. The significance of the cup is well known to yachtsmen. It is among the most eagerly coveted international small boat trophies in the world of sailing, and since 1895 has been raced for by champions from the U.S., Canada, Great Britain, Sweden, and Norway. The competition always had a special appeal for Paul and me, for in our boyhood in Sydney, Nova Scotia, we had watched Seawanhaka cup challengers—one of which later became a winner—sailing in the harbor.

In 1934, Paul decided to enter the trials that would produce a defender to race against the Norwegian challenger for the Seawanhaka Cup, and he commissioned A. E. Luders, Jr., to build a 6-meter, *Challenge,* for him. With two additional crew members aboard, we campaigned her through that summer, and sailed her as part of the American team, which success-fully defended the British-American Cup. Then, after a rugged series of trials during the summer of 1935, we were selected to meet *Norna IV,* owned by Crown Prince Olav of Norway and sailed by a near-legendary figure in international yachting, Magnus Konow. The series was scheduled for mid-September, and the cup would go to the winner of three races out of a possible five.

I had never met Konow, but I'd heard a great deal about him. A tall, slender, powerful man, he was rated as Europe's finest helmsman, and

Cornelius and Paul Shields in *Challenge,* 1935.

he had sailed with particular brilliance in the Olympics. On our way out to the starting-line on the first day of competition—the wind was easterly, I recall, and there was a large spectator fleet out—I sailed *Challenge* in close to *Norna* so I could take a good look at Konow. When I gazed across the water at him, I found that he and his three-man crew were all staring at us out of *Norna's* cockpit, giving us exactly the same cold-eyed sizing-up we were giving them. I still have a photograph of Konow and his crew taken at that moment; whenever I look at it, I'm reminded of the stares prizefighters exchange just before the bell.

The first two races were back-and-forth battles—and we lost them both, by margins of 45 and 8 seconds respectively. *Norna* outsailed us going to windward, and although we managed to regain lost ground downwind, our recovery wasn't sufficient.

At this point, with Konow only a race away from victory, many of the spectators abandoned hope for us. Word was even cabled abroad that it was only a matter of sailing one more race, and then it would all be over.

My brother and I didn't agree. That may sound over-confident, but we felt that *Challenge* was a good boat, and that we could, and would, make her go. The observers might be discouraged, but we couldn't be.

As we were sailing into the harbor after that second defeat, a large lapstreak motorboat pulled alongside us, and one of the founders of the present Pitney-Bowes company, Walter Bowes was there in the cockpit. Bowes was a highly entertaining, lighthearted fellow, whom Paul and I had been running into here and there for years. He hailed us and said he wanted to see us when we got ashore.

There was a somber note in the air as Paul and I walked up the dock toward the Seawanhaka clubhouse. Bowes met us by the flagpole. He looked serious, which was unusual for him.

He announced that he was taking over as our "manager." "Now I don't want you to get discouraged," he said. "This thing is going to turn out all right. You're going to win."

This was the sort of talk I wanted to hear at that moment. I asked Bowes if he realized we needed to take three straight races to win. He nodded. "It's going to be all right," he repeated. "All you have to do is listen to my advice, and you'll win."

I asked him what his advice might be.

"Well," he said, keeping his voice firm, low, and sincere, "the first thing we'll do is bring ashore that genoa jib you've been using, and lay it out by the flagpole here, and then burn it, just to make sure it doesn't appear again." He went on, still talking like a doctor making a diagnosis. After we had burned the genoa, he was going to visit Konow and his crew, and get to work on their morale. While he was at it, he would extend some of his famous hospitality, and see if he couldn't perhaps keep them up half the night in the bar. That was the sum and substance of Bowes program, and he was sure it would be effective. Within three days, he said, we'd be steaming back to Larchmont with the Seawanhaka Cup safely stowed in the lazaret of his motorboat.

I don't need to tell you that we didn't burn the genoa. The rest of Bowes' strategy, however, *was* put into execution. He stood the Norwegians to drinks in the evenings and played what he called "gypsy music" for them on the piano until the small hours of the morning. He also took Konow aside and told him he hadn't won the cup by a long shot. "You don't know what you're up against," he told him. "These fellows are good —really good. You'll see."

We finally got *Challenge* going in the third race. What made the difference was a larger genoa and our new Wilson mainsail. We had refrained from using the mainsail before because the conditions never seemed quite right. While we were maneuvering for the start, however, we passed close by the powerboat from which Bill Luders was watching. He hailed us and asked why we didn't try the sail. I replied that I didn't want to experiment with it because the weather seemed uncertain.

He shot a question back at me: "What are you saving it for?"—obviously implying that if we didn't use the sail in this race, we might never get to use it against Konow.

We had to hustle to set the mainsail before the start, but we were soon glad we had—in the words of a *New York Times* reporter, *Challenge* went "like a winged witch." We led all the way, and beat *Norna* by 40 seconds.

In the fourth race, we got a good start, crossing the line with the gun. Again, we used the new sails, and this time our margin of victory was large —four minutes and six seconds.

We sailed the fifth and final race in a moderate southwest wind, going twice around a windward-leeward course. As she had before, *Norna* outdid us going to windward, and we overtook her on both of the runs. The summary shows how excitingly the lead changed hands: *Norna* ahead at the first windward mark by 34 seconds; *Challenge* ahead at the first leeward mark by 10 seconds; *Norna* ahead at the second windward mark by 18 seconds; *Norna* ahead at the second windward mark by 18 seconds . . . ; then, in the run for the finish, we clinched it. *Challenge* gave us everything she had, and we won handily, with a lead of 2 minutes and 47 seconds.

Paul and I were, of course, pleased by the outcome, and Bowes was delighted that his "managership" had turned the trick. It's possible that, in a way, he had really helped us. I'm not saying that his hospitality and "gypsy music" were what tipped the balance—Konow and his crew were as dedicated as we were ourselves; but Bowes' confidence in us, his certainty that we couldn't lose, somehow supplemented our own confidence, and honed our competitive edge a bit finer.

The greatest part of success in yacht racing—as in anything else—is belief in yourself.

4. A Racing Life

By 1935, the Sound Interclub class, of which I had been chairman since 1927, was ten years old, and our boats had reached what might be called "early middle age." Although they still had many good years of racing left in them, it was plain to me that within a relatively short time the Interclub skippers would want to switch to bigger, faster boats. I thought it would be wonderful to anticipate this—to form a new class while we were still sailing the Interclubs, and then to move all of the skippers over to the new boats without disturbing the splendid condition of racing we had established. This would not be simple to accomplish; it would take work and planning. The first step, of course, was to find the right boat.

In the spring of 1936, Paul and I went down to Bermuda to race *Challenge* against sailors from the Royal Bermuda Yacht Club. The day I arrived, I went to inspect a new 6-meter boat that had just been built for Eldon and Kenneth Trimmingham in Norway by Bjarne Aas, one of the finest designer-builders in Europe. Her name was *Saga*.

The minute I saw *Saga*, I fell in love with her. I thought she was the most beautiful boat I'd ever seen. I loved her shape, her sheer, her dainty transom, and her long, straight counter. The sheer, although a penalty under the 6-meter rule (which encourages high freeboard), gave her great grace and beauty.

When I got back from Bermuda, I couldn't get *Saga* out of my mind. She seemed very close to what I was looking for, and I felt it would be worthwhile to ask Aas to do some drawings of a boat with her beautiful lines. I knew that a one-design class could be built very economically in Norway. With proper care, I could be certain the class was truly one-design, with the boats as nearly identical as possible. This requirement was extremely important to me, for as I've said, it's only in a one-design class that a skipper's real abilities can be measured.

These were good reasons for exploring the idea, and there was still another. I hoped to bring new life into international racing, which had become rather prohibitive in cost. Because of the expense involved, 6-meter boats were sailed only in years when there was a match like the Seawanhaka Cup or the British-American Cup. In off years, there was almost no competition in 6-meter boats. The founding of a new one-design class would give 6-meter skippers a chance to compete more economically and also every year.

I spoke to Magnus Konow about my idea (he and I were still competing against each other, in boats and on the golf course), and he agreed to get in touch with Aas for me. I asked Aas to send me designs for a semi-displacement boat about 33 feet overall, with a 6-foot, 9-inch beam and a small cabin.

When the initial designs came, I knew we had something good. There were some minor changes I wanted, and I thought them through during all-night sessions in my library at home. The cabin seemed too large to me, and I suggested that Aas shorten it by one frame—approximately 12 inches. Also, I wanted a loftier rig and shorter boom, which would suit the boat better for the relatively light airs of Long Island Sound, and which would also, I felt, improve her appearance. With the loftier rig, I suggested we add more weight to the keel. Aas decided that 100 pounds was sufficient. He also agreed to the other changes.

When I'd made reasonable progress, I discussed my idea with Paul and four friends—Egbert Moxham, Magnus Konow, Henry Maxwell, and Frederic Spedden. The plan excited them, and between us we formed a syndicate to underwrite the construction of 25 boats. It was Paul who named the class—the International one-design class.

In my dealings with Aas, I continued to emphasize the great importance of uniformity. The boats had to be identical. During the actual construction, we employed Veritass, a firm of Norwegian maritime surveyors

The beautiful 6-meter *Saga*, "godmother" of the International one-design class. She was designed and built by Bjarne Aas and owned by the famed Bermudian yachtsmen Eldon and Kenneth Trimingham.

similar to Lloyd's, to supervise operations, and stressed the need for uniformity to them, too. These efforts produced gratifying results. For example, when the lead keels were being cast, we had Veritass send each boat-owner a certificate giving the exact weight of the keel. The original specifications called for keels of 4,100 pounds. The certificates showed that the greatest variance from that figure was 25 pounds, a negligible difference.

We announced the formation of the class in the summer of 1935, in a brochure mailed to Interclub owners and other likely prospects. The response was overwhelmingly enthusiastic: the newspapers featured the idea, welcoming the new class; skippers phoned to reserve boats and down payments came in almost by return mail.

As we'd expected, the cost of the first 25 boats was moderate. Incredible as it may seem with Internationals costing $14,000 today, the price-tag for our boats—fully rigged, fully insured, and including sails, a shipping cradle, and the cost of shipping—was only $2670.

It was my idea to have as many Interclub skippers as possible buy Internationals, and this presented a problem. If we sold our Interclubs all at once the bottom would drop out of the market. To avert this, the Interclub owners agreed that none of them would sell for less than $2000. Eventually, all of the Interclubs were sold, and that basic price was not broken in a single case. So you could say that in way, we got our Internationals for $670.

My boat was one of the first four to be delivered. I had decided to name her *Aileen*. (My Interclub was sold to a man who lived on Lake George, but I preserved the name.) She arrived in early December, and I went to Brooklyn to see her lowered in her cradle from the freighter to the dock. If anything, she was even prettier than I'd hoped—especially her under-body: she had a beautiful entrance, midship section, and run. Like all my boats, she was painted light green.

From Brooklyn, *Aileen* was towed to City Island. For the next few weeks, I stopped off at the yacht yard to see her every chance I got, breaking my trips to and from the city. Naturally, I was impatient to take her out.

I finally arranged to sail her the week after Christmas. It was the first time anyone had sailed an International—not even Aas had done so. I don't think I've ever had a more joyous day on the water. As crew, I had Ducky Endt and another friend. The wind was from the northeast, light in the morning and then stronger at mid-day, so we had a chance to try her out under a variety of conditions. In early afternoon, we put into Larchmont harbor and tied up at the Yacht Club dock so family and friends could look at her. They came aboard in groups of four, all brimming over with the same pleasure I was feeling.

The trip back was as satisfying as the morning's sail, despite the fact that the wind softened. The boat was a delight to handle, and balanced perfectly. I felt great satisfaction at this—the planning and hope and care hadn't been in vain.

Yankee, with her double clewed jib, originated and constructed by the famous sailmaker, Prescott Wilson.

We started racing our Internationals the following summer, 1937, keeping our group of skippers together and preserving the high standards of competition that had existed in the Interclubs. Other sailors were soon attracted by the boats and ordered them from Aas, and there has been a steady growth of the class through the years. There are now over 250 Internationals in all, located in Maine, Marblehead, Bermuda, San Francisco, on Long Island Sound—where the Western Sound fleet, under the very able chairmanship of William E. John, now numbers 35—and in Europe (in England, France, and Norway). They are still built exclusively by Bjarne Aas to the original specifications and under the same controlled conditions. I like to think that wherever they are, they have brought many happy hours of sport to the people who sail them.

International yacht racing, soon to be curtailed by the war, continued through the late 1930's. In 1937, Gerard Lambert invited me to sail aboard his J-Boat, *Yankee*, in the America's Cup trials. *Yankee* was no match for the new *Ranger*, owned by Harold Vanderbilt, but I enjoyed working out the starts, in the majority of which we more than held our own. (I had also sailed with Gerard Lambert in 1934, when, in a somewhat parallel situation, his *Vanitie* sailed in practice trials against Vanderbilt's *Enterprise*. I've always admired Lambert's good sportsmanship in entering these competitions even though he knew his chances were slim.)

The same year I was aboard *Yankee*, the Royal Norwegian Yacht Club issued a challenge for the Seawanhaka Cup, and Paul entered his new 6-meter *Rebel* in the hard-fought trials and earned the right to defend the cup. This we again did successfully, winning three straight against *Buri*, owned by O. Ditlev-Simonsen, Jr. The following summer, *Rebel* earned a position on the four-boat team for the British-American Cup; the American team came out the winner by four races to one.

The war, of course, brought great changes to yachting. Those of us who could continued to race our dinghies and Internationals, and there was considerable activity in the western end of the Sound. Almost singlehandedly, Alex Gest, the chairman of the Larchmont Yacht Club race committee, kept competition going during the war years, not only at Larchmont but at other yacht clubs.

As in World War I, yachtsmen made great contributions to the war effort. They distinguished themselves in all theaters, aboard ships of every description. Many of my yachting friends served, and they often told me

55

they'd made the same discovery I had nearly three decades before: that the knowledge they'd acquired through sailing was invaluable to them. The yachting world was able to make a second direct contribution, too, in the tangible form of boats. Many large pleasure craft on both coasts were converted for the rugged and necessary task of antisubmarine patrol.

When sailing had resumed its peacetime pace, the frostbite skippers on the Sound found themselves in a situation similar to the one that had existed in the Interclubs ten years before. Our BO dinghies were eleven years old and had to be replaced—but to preserve the competition in the class, it was essential to move all the skippers into new boats in a body.

I asked Olin Stephens to design a boat with more stability than the BO's, which had always been a bit tender. The new boats were also to be 11 feet, 6 inches overall. I suggested that Olin might use as a guide the lapstreak 10-footers that had served as dinghies aboard his New York 32's.

In Olin's first drawings, the boat—we later named the class the Interclub Dinghies—had a flat sheer aft. I felt she would be prettier, and perhaps drier, with a spring to the sheer in this area. Olin very obligingly swept it up, giving the boat a pleasant, sassy appearance. To my mind, these are the prettiest dinghies ever designed.

The reason for naming them the Interclubs was to attract the dinghy skippers from the Manhasset Bay Yacht Club into the class. I took a scale model to the Manhasset winter meeting in 1945, and though I talked as convincingly as I could about the merits of the new dinghies, I failed to persuade the skippers to make the switch from BO's. I've always thought they missed a good thing: we got our dinghies for only $425, which I consider a bargain. Eighty-five were built the first year, and now there must be approximately 500 in all. (The Larchmont fleet alone numbers 50. The Manhasset sailors finally joined the class a number of years after my talk; there, as in Marblehead, the boats are built of fiberglass.) Every year, the dinghies are being raced and enjoyed more and more.

Prior to the 1940's, I had been pretty much a small-boat man. Most of the larger boats I had sailed on—*Vanitie* and *Yankee*, for example— had been pure racing craft, rather than cruiser-racers. In 1945, however, I decided to explore some new territory, to try my hand in competition in the middle-distance, overnight races which were sailed in cruiser-racers in the sound and up the coast as far as Cape Cod. Through Drake

Sparkman, I arranged a summer's charter of *Persephone,* a lovely-looking yawl built by Francis Herreshoff and belonging to the late Philip Roosevelt.

Persephone was a wonderful boat to sail, and the summer proved to be an arduous one, full of surprising, educational experiences. By the time it was over, I had developed a strong, new appetite.

Three races come back to me with special vividness. The first was from Huntington, Long Island, to Stratford Shoals, and return. Some 35 or 40 boats were entered. We had expected the usual gentle summer night, but found instead that it breezed up steadily throughout the first leg, to the point where finally it was blowing 25 or 30 knots. This wind, against the strong flood tide, built up very sizable seas as we rounded Stratford Shoal light.

In my inexperience, I had chosen not to shorten sail, and had kept both the genoa and the mizzen set. Shortly after we rounded Stratford Shoals, the genoa ripped. I sent some of the crew forward to take in the remains of the sail, which they managed to do despite the short, heavy seas that threatened to wash them off the foredeck. In the midst of this operation, the mizzen blew off, leaving us with only the mainsail.

As if these worries weren't enough, I had two additional concerns: Corny, who was then 12 or 13, was miserably seasick; and *Aileen,* I was sure, was in great danger from the storm. I had taken her to Greenwich before going out on *Persephone,* planning to race her on Sunday afternoon, as was my custom, and had not left her on a mooring, but had her anchored with her 35-pound anchor.

The wind—which, according to Coast Guard reports, reached 50 knots in the gusts—continued all night. It was at its height the next morning, when we crossed the finish line in first place. We learned later that only four boats had gone the whole distance.

We set about tidying up *Persephone,* and discovered that the starboard shroud turnbuckle had developed a deep crack. With only a bit more strain it would have given way, and we would have been dismasted. I swallowed this bit of information and then hastened to Greenwich to check on *Aileen.* She had dragged anchor during the blow, as I had feared, but a few yards from the rocks the anchor had caught on a cable of some sort, and she had safely ridden out the worst of it.

The night had brought two close calls, which were more than enough as far as I was concerned.

The second memorable experience on *Persephone* was the Vineyard Race. Again, it blew hard, and after we rounded the Vineyard lightship the mainmast was put under such a strain that I feared we'd lose it. (I knew that there was real cause for concern: in previous years, *Persephone* had lost two masts.) We dropped the mainsail and continued with the jib and mizzen set. About 2:00 A.M., off Watch Hill, Rhode Island, one member of the crew was hit on the head by the flogging clew of the jib, and at the last instant was saved from going overboard by two other crewmen. I still have nightmares about what might have happened if he hadn't been caught. How would we have found him under those strenuous conditions—and in the dark?

This time, too, *Persephone* was one of a handful of boats that finished. Although we hadn't done well in the final standing, to finish at all was something of an accomplishment.

Then there was the "Case of the Wandering Blinker," as neat a lesson in the foolishness of complacency as you could find. This occurred on a lovely October night, during a second City Island-to-Stratford-Shoals-to-Huntington race. We were beating home in close competition with *Gesture,* Howard Fuller's 57-foot cutter. Conditions were ideal: good visibility, a 10-knot breeze, the air mild. The crew had all gone below to sleep. At one point, the professional hand came on deck, and I asked him to get out the chart and confirm my position for me. He started to do this, but then I recalled that he wasn't particularly adept at navigation, and told him not to bother—I knew where I was. (After all, I told myself, I'd been sailing these waters for years. Besides, I felt I didn't need navigational guidance on such a clear night.)

An hour or so went by, when ahead of us appeared what I was sure was the blinker off Eaton's Neck. I knew that out here we had plenty of water—roughly a hundred and fifty feet of it. The shore would be several miles to leeward.

I glanced in that direction, not expecting to see anything in particular —and there, before my eyes, were what looked like islands. I told myself that my vision was playing tricks on me because I was overtired—there couldn't be islands out here. I was seeing things, that was all.

At this juncture, we hit a rock—and we hit it hard, for we were traveling at a good 6 or 7 knots. The boat staggered, then bumped on for a while, her keel bouncing and scraping. Down below, I heard shouts and the banging of loose gear.

I couldn't have been more astounded. The shock was as great as if a stranger had suddenly struck me in the face for no reason. *My God, I asked myself, what have I hit? There can't be a rock in the middle of Long Island Sound!*

The hatches started popping open and the crew came boiling up from below, wild-eyed and yelling. They piled back into the cockpit. We bumped once or twice more, and then, to my vast relief, we were off and under way again. In a minute or two, everyone had calmed down, and we continued our race with *Gesture,* but failed to catch her. *Persephone,* fortunately, was not damaged; only her keel had hit.

With the aid of a chart and by picking out landmarks, I soon figured out what had happened. We had been headed. The wind had hauled slightly to the west, altering our course without my realizing it. Instead of continuing in mid-Sound, we had veered gradually closer to the Connecticut shore. The light I'd picked up hadn't been the Eaton's Neck blinker, but the blinker on the eastern end of the Norwalk Islands. We had fetched up on one of the reefs that dot that section of the coast.

I learned my lesson that night, and from then on never sailed without making constant navigational checks, even in familiar waters.

The year after chartering *Persephone,* I sailed in my first Bermuda Race. Again, an interesting new area of competition was opened up to me. Until then, I thought there must be something a bit crazy about men who got pleasure out of the very demanding and uncomfortable business of long-distance ocean racing. The only way I ever wanted to travel to Bermuda, I said, was in ease, aboard a stable, substantial liner like the *Queen of Bermuda.* However, when Drake Sparkman told me he could arrange for me to skipper the yawl *Good News,* I was excited at having a chance to try a new form of competition and I decided to do it.

We made a respectable showing, placing second. The winner was my old rival *Gesture;* she caught us in the last 5 or 6 miles, sailing around us in a squall while we, a mile or two away, were becalmed. During this and other long distance races, I formed some opinions of how a boat should be raced offshore; I'll discuss them later.

By 1947, I was intensely interested in sailing large boats, while at the same time I continued to race in Internationals and dinghies. That summer I was aboard Arthur Tickle's *Steel Sylph* in the Annapolis race; the following year, I went to Bermuda as a watch captain on *Stormy*

Weather, owned by Fred Temple. The summer after that, it was Annapolis again, aboard Bill Moore's *Argyle.* Then, in 1950, the magnificent 72-foot yawl *Bolero* was launched, and her owner, my good friend John Nicholas Brown, invited me to race aboard her with him.

To my mind, *Bolero* is structurally the finest yacht of her type ever built. Olin Stephens put strength and solidity into every foot of her, without sacrificing speed and fine handling qualities. I sailed many races on her, and she always performed outstandingly.

I will never forget the last time I sailed aboard *Bolero,* on the final day of the 1955 New York Yacht Club cruise. Our course took us from Marion, Massachusetts, down Buzzard's Bay to Hen and Chickens lightship, and from there to a finish off Padanarum, Massachusetts. The wind blew a full 25 knots, and many other large ocean-going racers chose not to come out at all. (Some of the boats that did come out fared badly, particularly several 12-meter boats, which were over-powered and dropped out.) *Bolero* beat all competitors handily on that rigorous day, and proved conclusively what a powerhouse she was.

I mentioned before that Aileen won the Woman's National Sailing Championship in 1948. This made me extremely proud, of course—but watching her sail for the title was a difficult, uncomfortable business.

Aileen was 24 that summer, and was living at home. The championship finals, ten races in all, were to be sailed at the American Yacht Club, in Rye, New York, in early July. I planned to attend, despite the fact that watching my children compete has always been something of a trial for me. This is difficult to explain. I want to be there, of course, to see them race—in fact, as will be plain in a moment, I can't stay away—but at the same time I honestly suffer when they're racing. I'm sure parents who've sat in the stands while their children played football or field hockey—or whatever—will understand my feelings. You want them to do well so badly that watching them is actually painful.

In my case, there's the added factor of my own sailing experience. I coach Aileen and Corny from a distance. I sail the race for them, so to speak, silently urging them to tack one minute, to slack the main sheet a trifle the next minute. These emotions come over me every time the children race—but I watch them nevertheless.

In the case of the 1948 women's championship, there was an added complication: Aileen didn't *want* me to be a spectator. Shortly before the start of the series, she told Doe that having me there would make her too nervous and jittery. She preferred to have me go to the office as usual while the racing was on.

Doe naturally passed this along to me. I sympathized with Aileen—but I *had* to go watch; my pride in her was such that I simply couldn't stay away. So I hit on a compromise—one which, to be frank, involved a bit of deception.

I told Doe to say to Aileen that since she felt the way she did, I'd heed her wishes. Then I went ahead and made arrangements to watch the races from a friend's power boat.

This worked out satisfactorily, in the sense that Aileen didn't realize, during the races, that I was present. However, it had its drawbacks: whenever the boat I was on got too close to the competitors, I had to go below and watch through a porthole so Aileen wouldn't see me. Also, at dinner in the evenings, I had to pretend that I'd been in the city all day.

Aileen did splendidly, beating the finest women sailors in the country, and after her victory we had a celebration dinner at the American Yacht Club. I told her then about what I'd done, and she forgave me. Now that she has children of her own, I'm sure she understands.

The victory that meant the most to me in all my years of sailing came in 1952, when I won the Mallory Cup in the North American Sailing Championship series. As I've said, every race has been important to me, whether a 600-yard dinghy race or the long haul to Bermuda, but for me this series will always stir a special warmth.

Prior to 1952 there had never been a North American Sailing Championship for men. The first one was organized that year, and Mrs. Clifford Mallory put up a very handsome trophy in memory of her husband, a fine sailor who had made many important contributions to yachting—among them the founding of the North American Yacht Racing Union. The trophy had a most interesting history: it was a large Georgian soup tureen which was presented by the Sultan of Selim to Lord Nelson in gratitude for fighting the Barbary pirates; embossed on it, among other things, were replicas of the transom of *Victory*, Nelson's flagship, and the Nelson family crest. The champion would keep the trophy for a year; the next year it would be competed for again. (In addition, each year's winner would receive a bowl marking his victory; as I said in the first chapter, the bowl I won in 1952 is one of my proudest possessions.)

To select the eight finalists for the championship and the Mallory Cup, the North American continent was split into eight divisions. In each, local selection committees were set up, to which sailors submitted their names. The committees screened the applicants, generally choosing men who had won championships. In my district—Western Long Island Sound —there were, as I recall, 24 skippers on the list after the screening.

Then the actual racing began. We were paired off, taking turns in the various types of boat sailed in the area. I found myself sailing in yachts of every description—and always coming back to my own home territory, the Internationals. For example, I had to race a Victory class champion in Victories, after which he had to race me in Internationals; I had to race a 210 champion in 210's, after which he had to race me in Internationals; the same for Stars, Atlantics, etc. All of this was intensely interesting to me—and demanding as well.

I won against the 23 other skippers, which not only qualified me for the semi-finals, but also earned me the Long Island Men's Championship and the Hipkins Trophy. (Corny, I'm proud to say, won this same trophy in both 1960 and 1961.) In the semi-finals, I raced against the two champions from the eastern Sound and Great South Bay. The competition was spirited and keen; when it was over, I had earned a place among the eight finalists. (It was later estimated, that between 500 and 600 different races were sailed all across the country to pick the eight finalists.)

The finals took place in Mystic, Connecticut, in early September. We raced QA's—Quincy Adams 17's, a class of one-design 26-footers—and we changed boats after every race, so each skipper and crew raced in all eight boats. As crew, I had Corny and Bill "Boots" Le Boutillier, my very able first mate from *Aileen*. This was the first time Corny had been a full member of my crew—although, of course, he'd sailed with me ever since infancy—and he couldn't have been more helpful. I'm convinced I would never have won without his able assistance.

The competition in the elimination races was keen, as I said; but in the eight championship races, the competition was the toughest I've ever encountered. We sailed in both light and heavy weather, in the very strong, 2 to 3 knot tides of Fishers Island Sound. No single skipper ever "took charge." Through the first seven races, I finished third, first, sixth, fourth, fifth, second, and fourth. The result was that going into the eighth and final race, I held a very slim two-point lead over the runner-up, Charles Ill of the Barnegat Bay Yacht Racing Association. To win the series, I had to either beat Ill or finish right behind him; if he put a boat between us, we would be tied on points. (And, I learned after the race, such a point tie would have made him the winner. We each had the same number of firsts and seconds, and we had each beaten the other the same number of times; he, however, had two thirds, while I had only one.)

We had a strong northeaster, 18 to 20 knots, for the eighth race. A good-sized spectator fleet was on hand, with brightly colored burgees and signal flags snapping in the clear air. I was too conservative at the start, and got away in the middle of the fleet. By the time we reached the first windward mark (we were to go twice around a windward-leeward-windward course), I was in fifth place, with Ill ahead of me in fourth.

During the rest of the race, Ill succeeded in moving up into second place, then dropped back into third. In the meantime, I held my fifth position the first time around, and then, on the second downwind run, managed to overtake one boat; when we rounded the downwind mark the second time and started for the finish line, Ill was in third place, and I was in fourth.

That last windward leg to the finish is one that I will not soon forget. As the four of us front-running boats closed in on the finish line, it was plain that Ill was steadily gaining on the second boat—and if he succeeded in passing him, of course, he and I would be tied in points. Ill and the second-place boat approached the finish on different tacks: Ill on port tack, the other man on starboard. With a hundred yards to go, it was evident that although Ill couldn't quite cross the other's bow, he nevertheless had room to cross the line to leeward of him. Ill waited until he could pass the buoy close aboard on the port tack, then went about. A moment later, with the other boat coming in fast on the starboard tack, he shot the line.

In fourth place, we sailed on for several anxious seconds, heading for the line. From our boat, it had been impossible to tell whether or not Ill had caught his man. Finally there were only a few yards to sail, then none —and as we crossed, two guns sounded in the customary salute to the winner of a series. I was still uncertain of the outcome, however, and sailed over to the committee boat for confirmation. They told me Ill had finished third: I was North American Sailing Champion.

At the presentation of prizes, I learned that the margin between Ill's boat and the second-runner was less than the width of a mast.

My racing career came to a virtual end on April 26th, 1956. This was a beautiful, warm day, with a brisk southerly blowing, and I was sailing BO dinghies in the overall Long Island Frostbite Championship, held that year at the Manhasset Bay Yacht Club. We sailed four races in the morning, and I felt fine and did well, alternating for the lead in the series with Arthur Knapp, who, in my book, was the man to beat.

At lunch, I sat between a stranger and Glen MacNary, one of the other skippers. The newcomer, with whom I had a most pleasant conversation, told me his name was Dr. Cortez Enloe. At one point during the meal, Glen said he was surprised I was having only a glass of water. He asked if that was my habit on race days, and I told him it was.

He looked me up and down, smiled, and said: "No wonder you're in good shape." I remember those words vividly, for no more than 45 minutes later my good health cracked wide open.

The fifth race of the day—there were to be eight in all—started right after lunch. A minute or two after I had crossed the line I felt a deep, stabbing pain in the left side of my chest. I knew instantly that this was far more serious than an indigestion pain or a muscular twinge. I had never had any heart trouble before (in fact, I had been examined only two weeks before at a well-known clinic and had been told that I was in excellent condition), but it was plain what had hit me. I remember thinking that I was really in for it now—and in the same instant I decided that I would go on with the race. That decision, I know now, was foolish and dangerous. It came to me instinctively, however; there was no arguing with it.

Through the next two races, the tautness and throbbing continued deep in my chest. Then the fourth race of the afternoon got underway, and at the weather mark I met a competitor. He was on the port tack; I was on the starboard, and therefore, of course, had the right of way. We converged on the mark simultaneously, and I purposely sailed past it a boat length of two, to force him about. He didn't tack, however, and I hit him. There was a scramble as we hastened to recover and continue, and then the pain came surging back, sharper and deeper this time, and I could feel a gushing in my chest and a warm tingling down my left arm. I knew now that I was in real difficulty.

I finished the remaining two reaches and then sailed for the committee boat. Harry Powell, the commodore of the Manhasset Bay Yacht Club, was in the cockpit. I drew up alongside, and told him I had a problem. It was necessary for me to drop out. Could I come aboard the committee boat?

They helped me up over the rail and led me forward, and I lay down on the deck.

The rest of that afternoon is a blur of impressions, some of them distinct, others shadowy. A Coast Guard launch soon appeared, and I was given a shot of morphine—by Cortez Enloe, the doctor I'd met for the first time at lunch. I remember asking him how serious the thing was—if it was really bad, I said, I ought to know. He told me not to worry, but I knew he was jollying me along. Another memory is of a discussion between two Coast Guardsmen: they were supposed to be giving me oxygen, but didn't know how to work the equipment, and got into a lively, confused argument, ignoring me while they figured things out. Strange as it may seem, I thought their conversation was very funny.

I can recall some of my thoughts exactly. For the most part, they concerned the changes this business was going to bring about. I never doubted for a moment that I was going to get well, but I had a suspicion my racing days were over, and that was agonizing. I kept saying to myself, "You're not going to race any more, it's all over, they're going to restrict you now." I had plenty of time for this silent monologue—while we made for the shore, while I was carried in a stretcher up the dock, while we waited for the ambulance, during the ride to the hospital in New York. And that refrain kept coming back again and again: not that I wasn't going to get well, but the realization that from then on I'd be missing the racing, that I'd become a spectator.

Everyone was wonderful to me. From the yacht club in Manhasset—while I lay on a sofa in the ladies' lounge—Dr. Enloe called my close friend and guardian angel, Dr. Harold Lovell. Harold in turn made arrangements for me to be admitted to the Doctors' Hospital in New York, and got in touch with Dr. Milton Raisbeck, a heart specialist who had been giving me routine checkups for ten years. When the ambulance arrived, Clinton Bell, a Larchmont friend, very kindly insisted on riding into town with me. We were held up for an hour on the parkway by a flat tire (the ambulance had no spare, and the driver had to send for one), but for some reason the delay didn't bother me: I recall thinking that the worst of it was that we were keeping Dr. Raisbeck waiting.

Finally, I was tucked away in bed. Just before I dropped off into a drugged sleep, that same persistent, painful thought returned: "You're not going to get any more of it." The thought hurt a great deal worse than the thing in my chest.

I had had a coronary occlusion. It was soon evident to my doctors that with reasonable luck and a sharply curtailed regimen. I was going to be all right. I would have to take it easier around the office, and, as I'd feared, racing was *out*.

During my convalescence, both Dr. Lovell and Doe came to see me every day, and Aileen and Corny kept my spirits up with frequent telephone calls. I'll never forget my first conversation with Corny, who was then going to business school in Boston. After I'd reassured him about my health, he brought up a subject that he had obviously been dying to discuss: the collision with the other boat. He wanted to know if I had registered a protest with the race committee. I told him I had.

"How did it come out?" he asked.

I replied that the matter was forgotten: there couldn't be a race committee hearing because I was in the hospital.

This didn't satisfy him. "You should have gotten it cleared up right there and then," he said. "I'm sure the ambulance driver would have waited for you while you went to the hearing."

I found I enjoyed the hospital routine and the rest I was getting, so much so that I arranged to stay a seventh week, one beyond the normal time, just to make sure the job of convalescence was thoroughly done. Even there, I managed to keep in touch with boats. My room overlooked the East River. Doe brought me my binoculars, and I watched the occasional yachts and the pretty little tugboats coming and going. One day John Nicholas Brown came up the river in his son's boat. He called me on the ship-to-shore phone, and we talked as he went by. Another time, Dr. Enloe and Jim Moore went past in a power boat, towing a fleet of the beautiful, brand-new Resolute sloops, just in from Sweden, up to Manhasset.

I returned home in early spring, and spent the summer lazing around, going out for an occasional relaxed sail, but doing no racing. The inactivity, I discovered, was very trying.

In the fall, I presided at the annual meeting of the International class, and was pleasantly surprised to receive a handsome silver bowl, decorated with the signatures of all of the skippers who had sailed in the class back through the years. The thought behind this was most touching, and I shall always treasure the bowl.

By this time—mid-autumn—I felt thoroughly fit, and decided no harm would come of a race or two. I would do a little frostbiting in the winter, spacing the races and taking care not to get overactive during them, and would race *Aileen* now and then the next season.

When I announced this plan, it met with definite disapproval from everybody—Doe, my doctors, Corny. It was Aileen, however, who really made me understand how foolish the idea was. "Don't do it," she told me. "It won't work out the way you think. If you go out there and race and get beaten, you'll only want to do better the next week. And if you win, you'll feel you have to give the people you've beaten a chance to get even. Pretty soon, you'll be back on the old grind. It's got to be all or nothing."

Those were wise words, and I'm glad to say I've had the sense to heed them. With only three exceptions, I have done no competitive sailing since April 1956. Living with this deprivation has been a trial: there isn't a day when I don't long for the excitement, don't wish that I could race the *Aileen* or my dinghy, *Dainty,* again. I am most grateful for all the years of racing I had, but I'd be telling less than the truth if I didn't add that I envy men who can still do it. And I get very upset when I see them pass up a chance to race—to me, that's a crime, to stay on the beach when you could be racing your boat.

I know I'm going to go on missing it—badly—for the rest of my life.

5. The America's Cup

Since 1956, there have been three occasions when I decided to run whatever health risks might be involved in racing. All were special cases, where my desire to participate was irresistible. These were the 1958 and 1962 elimination trials for the America's Cup, and a special "alumni" race for International skippers.

On New Year's Eve in 1957, Corny and I went to a hockey game in Madison Square Garden. We sat right behind my old friend Richard Maxwell, and at one point Richard turned around and said that Corny ought to think about the possibilities of crewing on *Columbia* in the America's Cup trials. This struck both Corny and me as a wonderful idea, and a day or two later I talked it over with Drake Sparkman, who got in touch with Henry Sears, the head of the syndicate that built *Columbia*. Within a few weeks, Corny had been selected.

Columbia was launched in the spring, and I went out on her maiden sail. I thought she looked fine—well designed and fast. Also, her skipper— Briggs Cunningham—and crew seemed highly competent. There were to be three sets of trial races during the summer against the other contending 12-meters—*Vim, Easterner,* and *Weatherly*—and the series against Great Britain's *Sceptre* would be sailed in early September. From the outset, I was convinced that *Columbia* would prove to be the best boat.

The members of Henry Sears' syndicate knew, that because Corny was aboard, I was intensely interested in *Columbia,* and they very kindly asked me to serve as an adviser. I was to observe the shake-down sailing and the trials with the idea that I might be able to offer some advice on how the boat could be sailed most effectively. Although I was more than happy to do this, Doe and my doctors were concerned that I might be subjecting myself to undue strain. I succeeded in convincing them that I would be careful, and by mid-May I was out on the water.

The Sears syndicate had chartered another 12-meter, *Nereus,* as trial horse for *Columbia.* The plan was to take the two boats out in the sound —we would later do the same thing in the waters off Newport, Rhode Island, where the trials and finals were to be held—and sail them against one another, practicing starts and tactics, changing sails between the two boats to see which benefited *Columbia* the most, and so forth. I was asked to skipper *Nereus,* and welcomed the opportunity. I was secretly worried that I might get over tense, but I kept that to myself. If the pressure grew too great, and was affecting my health, I could withdraw.

We learned a great deal from sailing *Columbia* against *Nereus.* The two boats were evenly matched when they were reaching or running— they were, after all, built to conform to the same rule, and not even a man as good as Olin Stephens, *Columbia*'s designer, can produce any really marked difference in performance on these two points of sailing. Going to windward in light airs, they were, again, fairly closely matched. In a breeze to windward, however, *Columbia* showed she was clearly the better boat. I was pleased by that; it confirmed my faith in her.

In those practice races, I sailed *Nereus* as well and as hard as I could, and I always enjoyed the occasions when we were able to beat *Columbia.* However, for the first time in my life, I had mixed feelings about the competition: I wanted to get beaten almost as badly as I wanted to win. I wanted *Columbia* to prove she was the boat I knew she was. This sensation of divided loyalty was brand new to me. Always before, I'd cared only about the boat I was sailing.

These were long, exciting days, and it was delightful for me to be racing again, even if it was only practice. We went out early, and spent the day experimenting, testing, then discussing what we'd learned. We used walkie-talkies to communicate with *Columbia* and Briggs Cunningham's tender. When we wanted to change sails, for example, we'd signal for a conversation, then talk over the change before making it. In the

69

evenings, through dinner and right up until bed time, we discussed the progress we'd made. I felt these informal conferences, attended by members of both crews, were invaluable.

While I was aboard *Nereus* and *Columbia*, everyone was most considerate of my health. If I tried to exert myself, in even the smallest way, a crew member would get ahead of me and do what I'd started to do. Naturally, I was grateful for the treatment, but it made me a bit uncomfortable to be considered an invalid.

I observed the first series of trials, held in late July, from a powerboat. *Columbia* performed creditably, but not spectacularly. To the delight of many onlookers who had a sentimental attachment to an older boat, *Vim*— very ably sailed by Bus Mosbacher—came through especially well.

Watching from the powerboat was extremely difficult and trying. I was taut all the time, and could feel pain and pressure in my chest. I didn't tell anyone about this; I didn't want others to know as I also knew that if I discussed my difficulties, I'd soon be back ashore.

The author on *Columbia's* first sail, with Briggs Cunningham at the helm.

When the second series of trials started, it was suggested that I get aboard *Columbia*—that way, if I had anything to contribute, I could communicate it immediately. As on *Nereus*, I was given the most friendly, considerate attention, and wasn't allowed to do anything physically demanding. I found that although I still experienced tension in my chest, the situation was considerably easier than it had been in the first series. Though I still felt the strain to a degree, on the whole I was more relaxed and comfortable.

In the second series, *Columbia* again proved she was well designed and fast, but as before, she failed to make a truly impressive showing—one that would prove conclusively that she was the best boat. The other boats, notably *Vim*, were still pressing her hard.

The third and last series of trials began in late August. This time, it was suggested that I start *Columbia* and sail her on the windward leg. By now, I was having a hard time getting to sleep at night, and had lost 10 more pounds—making a total of 35 lost since my attack. I hoped that when I actually got a chance to take the helm, I'd feel even less tense than during the second series, but all the same I was a bit concerned that something might happen to me while we were racing. From my experience in 1956, I knew that if it did, the first thing I'd need would be morphine. I decided it was best to be prepared for any eventuality, however remote, and phoned Harold Lovell, my doctor, in New York.

During our talk, I commented that I wasn't getting enough sleep, and asked for some sleeping pills.

Harold's reply was that if that was the case, I was in trouble and should quit and go home.

We talked that over for a while, and he finally agreed to send me the pills. Then I told him I wanted some morphine, a hypodermic, and instructions on how to use them. (Morphine is the first treatment for a heart attack.)

Harold practically jumped through the phone. His first response was a flat "no." He said this proved I positively had to come home.

We exchanged a good many more words, and in the end I got the morphine and the needle. I rechecked the rules, and found that I was correct in my belief that a boat wouldn't be penalized if a man were taken off for health reasons. So I had solved everything except the question of how to get the injection if I needed it.

This called for careful planning, for if worse came to worse, I wouldn't be in any shape to do the job myself. I remembered that *Columbia*'s professional captain, Fred Lawton, had been a destroyer escort captain in the Pacific during the war—he had probably had experience with morphine.

I didn't want Fred to know I'd brought the drug aboard, but at the same time I had to be sure he would know what to do with it in an emergency. One evening, I drew him into a conversation about the war. I said I presumed that as a ship's captain he had performed many different jobs. I asked if he had ever given medical aid to members of his crew, and he said he had, many times.

Had he ever given morphine injections?

"Often."

That was all I needed to know. For good measure, I pasted Harold Lovell's instructions on the package, and then hid it in my footlocker down below, under some extra clothes.

Fortunately, Fred never guessed the reason for my questions. If he had, and had told the other men on the boat, I would almost certainly have been beached.

In the third series, when I was actually at the helm, the tension in my chest lessened considerably, as I hoped it would. The series started on Labor Day, September 1. We beat *Weatherly* that day, and on September 2 we beat *Easterner*. Then, on September 3, we beat *Weatherly* once more. *Vim* was also the victor in her three races on those days, and as a result the selection committee eliminated *Easterner* and *Weatherly*.

Those two boats provided strong competition, and made the trials an absorbing spectacle for people around the world. To my mind, the handling and organization aboard *Weatherly* were superior to those aboard *Easterner*. *Weatherly's* skipper was Arthur Knapp, Jr., a wonderful competitor in any boat, who is especially talented in light airs and downwind sailing. Unfortunately, *Weatherly* in 1958 lacked power in strong breezes—and it was expected that the cup defense would be sailed in those conditions. (A great many changes, incidentally, were made in *Weatherly* prior to the 1962 America's Cup trials. Among other things, she was lightened considerably, her rig was changed, and she was given a new, reshaped keel. I've always felt that Bill Luders deserved great credit for the success of those modifications. To my mind, Bill is the unsung hero of the 1962 cup defense.)

Getting back to 1958: we now faced the final trials against *Vim,* and I was still confident that *Columbia* was the better boat. Her sails were not, in my opinion, as good as *Vim's*, but she was faster to windward in moderate-to-fresh breezes, and decidedly more powerful in the big southwest seas.

In our match racing with *Vim,* I ran into distressing difficulties. I'd never sailed in competition where tailing was involved. (Tailing is a complicated series of pre-start maneuvers designed to keep your opponent from starting ahead of you.) The result was that I was occasionally boxed at the start. This upset me badly—so much so, in fact, that every single evening since I've gone to bed thinking about the mistakes I made in those particular starts, analyzing them, "replaying" them. That may sound extreme, but it's true. Just as some golfers are haunted by the memories of missed chip shots or putts, so I'm plagued to this day by the lickings I took in those starts.

Vim fought us hard, right down to the wire. On September 4, we won handily over a windward-leeward course. The next day, however, we were beaten by ten seconds; this was one of the times Bus Mosbacher outmaneuvered me at the start, and, in addition, our spinnaker sheet let go in the jibe at the second mark. There was no race on September 6 because of fog, but we went out anyway and practiced. Henry Sears, managing owner of *Columbia* and her navigator, greatly appreciated this weather as it permitted him to practice. He certainly did not need the latter. His accuracy was remarkable.

On September 7, *Columbia* got the heavy breeze she relished, and we crossed the finish line with a lead of a quarter of a mile. But the following day, *Vim* came right back, and after beating us at the start she led all the way. (In this race, *Vim* stayed clamped on our wind, and I tacked *Columbia* 36 times in 42 minutes, trying to shake her loose.) On September 9, it blew hard, and we won decisively, by three minutes.

After the fifth race, it was becoming plain that *Columbia* was the faster boat. Many kind comments appeared in the press to the effect that I'd been responsible for the change—including one by Carleton Mitchell in *Sports Illustrated* which called me a competitor "risking his life . . . for the thing he loves best." *Columbia,* the writers said, was showing more enterprise and life, and was obtaining better results. They also pointed out something I agreed with heartily: that Briggs Cunningham was sailing and racing the boat beautifully.

By this time, the strain on me was severe, and I decided I'd have to get off the boat. Olin Stephens, who had stepped down when I came aboard, resumed his role as relief helmsman.

The last race of the trials was sailed on September 11. The selection

Paul Shields, Cornelius Shields and Cornelius Shields, Jr. on *Columbia,* in an early spring sail, 1961.

committee very kindly invited me to watch it from Harold Vanderbilt's *Versatile.* In a strong breeze, *Columbia* again showed her power, and won the close contest by nineteen seconds.

The selection committee retired for a conference, and when they had made their decision they very generously called me into the main saloon, where the chairman, William A. W. Stewart, informed me that *Columbia* was to be the America's Cup defender; the committee said they wanted me to be the first to know. You may imagine how much the verdict buoyed me up.

The trials had been enormously exciting for everyone involved; unfortunately, what followed—the actual racing for the cup—was, to put it mildly, less gripping. *Columbia,* as we all know, made very short work of *Sceptre,* roundly trouncing her in four straight races. The 1958 America's Cup competition will go down as one of the greatest anti-climaxes in yachting history.

I bring up the subject of *Columbia*'s lopsided victory because it's such a conspicuous example of what can happen when yacht racing becomes a contest between designers and sailmakers, rather than between sailors. *Sceptre,* to be blunt about it, was nowhere near the boat *Columbia* was. The result was that when the two met, there was an overnight collapse of interest in the racing.

To me, that's sad. I hate to see an event as important as the America's Cup racing turn into a fiasco.

What follows may strike many readers as pure, unadulterated heresy.

I'd like to see the America's Cup races become a competition purely between sailors. To accomplish this, the races should be sailed in truly one-design boats, and the skippers and crews should switch boats after each race. If the cup races were sailed this way, a debacle such as that of 1958 would be avoided—the possible differences between sailors are not nearly as great as the possible differences between boats.

There are those who say that the point of the America's Cup competition has always been to allow designers and sailmakers to compete against one another. This is simply putting the emphasis in the wrong place, and I want to see it put where I believe it belongs: on the sailors. Other people contend that racing in one-design boats would rob the competition of some of its glamour. I maintain that the boats can be as glamorous—as beautiful and as big—as the two countries involved care to make them. As long as they're identical, I—and, I believe, a lot of sailors, too—would be happy.

Probably the sort of competition I suggest will never come to pass. If it should, however, we'd have truly fair and interesting racing.

It's the only way to find out who the real champions are.

I repeat: let's put the emphasis where it belongs—on the sailors.

The decision of the America's Cup Committee to conduct all races with modified Gold Cup Courses, producing three windward legs, is excellent. This will provide a better test of the boats, helmsmen and crews. The spectators, too, will see much more interesting racing.

The International one-design class was 25 years old in 1961. During the spring, the class committee, headed by William E. John, originated an exciting idea: they would hold a race for class ex-champions—"alumni." It would be sailed after the close of the regular season, in October. The boats would be provided by Herman Whiton's Small Boat Training Facility and the skippers would draw lots for them at 10:00 A.M. the day of the race.

All through the summer, I thought about that race. I knew it would be unwise for me to sail in it. I also knew that if I mentioned the possibility, Doe and my doctors would come down hard on me, raise a fuss, and try to make me promise not to enter.

On top of all this, I knew I *was going* to sail in that race. That much was certain. Somehow, I would figure out a way to enter without anyone at home finding out—except Corny, who would be part of my crew. For this one afternoon, which would bring together all the men against whom I'd competed in the past with such pleasure, I was going to cheat a little. I just couldn't miss it—it was as simple as that.

Since it had been six years since I'd raced an International, I was afraid I might have lost my touch because of inactivity. I knew that as a warm-up, I should sail in at least one practice race. The problem, of course, was to arrange this without tipping my hand. If my doctors learned my intentions, that would be the end of the alumni race for me.

I chose the "lay-up" race, the last regular competition of the season, for my first warm-up. This was sailed on Columbus Day, October 12. After a good deal of thought, I finally hit on a way to keep word of my sailing from getting back to Doe and my doctors. I went to the race committee and asked them not to list me as skipper. Corny, I said, was going to skipper—I was merely going along as crew. I suspect the committee members guessed what I was up to, but they agreed to cooperate.

The day was sparkling and beautiful, with a steady 10 to 12 knot breeze blowing from the northeast—always my favorite. As we sailed out of the harbor, I was delighted to find that I was feeling none of the tautness or pressure in the chest that had bothered me aboard *Columbia*. On the contrary, I was as composed and relaxed as could be.

There were sixteen other boats out. We got a good start, and going for the windward mark I stayed offshore, as I always had in the past when the wind was easterly. We led most of the way, and beat the second boat by at least 300 yards.

The experience was thoroughly exhilarating and satisfying. Everything fell naturally into place, and it was as though only a week—not six years—had elapsed since I'd last raced an International. A large part of the pleasure was having Corny in the boat; he was a most helpful, ideal crew.

I sailed another trial race the next Saturday, in heavy rain and a 15 to 18 knot wind. This time I was beaten by eight seconds—and didn't mind at all, for the skipper of the winning boat was Corny. Again, there was no comment at home or from my doctors.

I don't think I'll ever forget waking up the morning of the alumni race. All through the previous week, as the day grew closer and closer, I hoped more and more that it would really blow. I wanted one of those perfect northeasters I'd always enjoyed so in the past. That morning, I woke early and went to the window—and there were the conditions I'd been praying for: 25 to 30 knots of wind, right out of the northeast. The weather couldn't have been better if I'd created it myself.

Just before our spinnaker blew out in the International Alumni Race.

There were six other skippers entered: Arthur Knapp, Bus Mosbacher, George Hinman, Bill Cox, Arthur Davis, and Bob Bavier. (Bill Luders was ill, and couldn't take part.) We drew lots for the boats at 10:00 A.M., and I spent the next few hours tuning mine up. By race time, she seemed to me to be completely right.

As crew, along with Corny, I had Dick Ronan and Jack Webb, all very able sailors who had crewed on *Columbia*. Once again, sailing out of the harbor, I felt very much at ease, free of nerves and tautness.

The line favored the leeward end. My start was good, on the gun and at the leeward end, and we were first going toward the Westchester shore. I'd learned in special Larchmont 6-meter races in the 1930's that in this rare weather condition it was disadvantageous to go too close to shore, so I tacked early, which turned out to be the proper move. Thanks in large part to Corny's fine work with the sheets—so important in working the boat through the seas and very hard puffs—we had a substantial lead over the second boat when we rounded the windward mark. (People in the spectator fleet later estimated it at 300 yards.) The wind was now blowing a good deal harder, and it had started to rain. None of this bothered my crew. As we rounded the weather mark, I glanced quickly astern, to see that we were safely clear, and when I looked back, mere seconds later, the crew already had the spinnaker set and pulling beautifully.

I felt secure now. The boat was sailing at maximum hull speed for this strength of wind, there was no one close enough to overtake me. . . .

At this point, when we had gone 100 or 150 yards past the buoy, the spinnaker halyard slipped off the cleat, and the spinnaker went flying out before the boat, flapping wildly in mid-air for a moment and then dropping onto the water. Before anyone could move, it had filled with water—and was torn.

My crew got it up again, but it lasted only a second or two. One instant it was there, pulling the boat along at a terrific rate, and the next it had vanished, the wind widening the tear into a split and then tattering the two halves to ribbons, until all that was left were the two naked luff lines.

I knew then that it was only a matter of time before one of the other boats, all of which had their spinnakers set now, would pass us. We sailed on, doing our best with jib and mainsail, and then, sure enough, when we had covered 40 percent of the 4-mile leeward leg, first George Hinman and then Bob Bavier went by. The other competitors were too far back to catch us, however; we rounded the leeward mark and beat up to the finish, crossing in third place 30 seconds behind Bavier, the second boat.

I was disappointed, of course—and at the same time I was pleased with the way I'd taken the lead and had beaten the other boats to windward. I felt—pardonably, I think—that there was a kind of victory in that, a proof that my absence from racing hadn't hurt my ability. As for losing the spinnaker: I had forgotten my usual reminder to double-cleat the halyards, so the fault was really mine.

All in all, it was a spendid afternoon, and I'll treasure the memory of it for the rest of my life. I'll also remember the ironic postscript: I soon learned that none of my pretense had been necessary. Doe and my doctors knew all along what I was up to. They decided, however, to look the other way and let me have my fun.

In 1960, Paul bought *Columbia* from the Sears' syndicate, with the intention of entering her in the 1962 America's Cup trials. The plan was that Corny would skipper the boat, and I'd offer whatever help I could in the form of comments and suggestions. The decision to buy *Columbia* was Paul's alone. I wasn't entirely in favor of the idea of taking on such a demanding expensive campaign, but I reminded myself that I'd had similar reservations about *Challenge* and *Rebel,* Paul's 6-meter boats. In the end, both of these boats had been highly successful, and Paul's judgment had been vindicated.

We made some changes in *Columbia,* notably on the keel: the second year we had her—1962—we had the lead V'd at the bottom, and had the removed lead placed in blocks in the deadwood. The changes seemed to me to make the boat decidedly faster before the wind, but it was hard to say whether she was improved going to windward—for the simple reason that the other 12's, including *Weatherly,* were also changed materially, so there was no standard of comparison.

We campaigned *Columbia* through the summer of 1961, and when the 1962 season opened we felt our chances of success were good. This seemed confirmed in the early-season sailing, before the observation trials: *Columbia* outperformed both *Weatherly* and *Easterner,* and won the City of Newport Cup.

In the observation trials, with the new Boston boat *Nefertiti* rounding out the fleet, Corny did remarkably well in *Columbia,* I thought. He particularly distinguished himself in his starts, getting the jump on the other skippers time and time again. This was, in part, a result of my sad experience in the 1958 trials. We'd both seen how vital it was to concentrate on tailing, and during the summers of 1961 and 1962 we devoted a great deal of time, thought, and hard work to mastering it. At least once a week, sometimes more often, we'd go out off Larchmont, Corny in one International and I in another, and practice tailing for hour after hour. As I said, the study paid off handsomely. (In Chapter 15, I have set down some of my thoughts concerning tailing.)

Columbia came out of the observation trials with a record of four victories and six defeats. In the final trials, which began August 15, I went aboard as I had in 1958—to advise. My health was good, and I felt only a bit of the tension that had bothered me four years before.

We won the first two races, lost the second two, and won the fifth. Then, on August 21, the selection committee eliminated us and *Easterner.*

To be frank, I felt the committee's decision was premature. *Columbia* deserved more of a chance to show what she could do. The committee

Columbia (#16) and *Nefertiti* (#19). *Nefertiti* is comfortably carrying her huge running spinnaker even though the apparent wind is on the beam. Note her large balloon staysail.

wasn't pressed for time—they had until September 8 to make their final selection. Several more races could have been held before cutting the field to two boats; to my mind, these races should have been held.

I say this because I'm concerned about the possibility that hasty decisions such as the one that eliminated *Columbia* may discourage future yachtsmen from entering cup trials. A great deal of time, effort, and money go into the building and upkeep of a contender, and every contender deserves a really thorough testing before she's eliminated. It's already very difficult to get people to make the effort and enter a boat; hasty judgments will make it even harder, for potential owners will feel reluctant if they fear their boat will be written off after only five or six races.

This is not intended as a reflection on *Weatherly,* the boat that was finally selected and which, as we all know, did such a splendid job of defending against *Gretel,* the Australian challenger. *Weatherly* was definitely the right boat, and she was very ably sailed by Bus Mosbacher, an extremely smart, cool-headed skipper.

As for *Gretel:* I personally didn't believe she was as good as many others did. I felt, in particular, that she was extremely weak in light weather. She was an amazing 23 minutes behind *Weatherly* at the end of the first round of the third light-weather race. She won only one race, of course, and in my opinion she passed *Weatherly* because *Weatherly*'s crew was too conservative in setting their spinnaker; by the time it was drawing, *Gretel* was on top of *Weatherly* and blanketed her. After *Gretel* passed *Weatherly,* *Weatherly*'s spinnaker pole broke, giving *Gretel* more of a lead. When the pole was replaced, however, *Weatherly* closed the gap between them by 150 yards. In wind of 18 to 20 knots, with the boats almost at hull speed, it's difficult to reconcile how so much distance could be gained. To me, this is additional proof that *Weatherly* was the faster boat.

After the tremendous world-wide interest in Twelve Meters during an America's Cup year, it is a sad sight to see them laid up and out of commission thereafter. How nice it would be if the Series could be held in boats built to the requirements of the Cruising Club of America rule. They would provide years of enjoyment and good racing, as well as being candidates for future America's Cups.

6. _Patience_

A few years ago, Ben Hogan came up to Mamaroneck, New York, to play in the U.S. Open at the Winged Foot Club. I've known Ben for many years, so one day just before the start of the tournament, I walked around the course with him while he shot a practice round.

Ben was involved in some demanding business affairs at the time, and after the round we talked about them. He said he was under a good deal of pressure, and wished he could get his business cleared up quickly so he could start to enjoy himself. "I'm 45 now," he told me. "It may be another five or ten years before I get these things settled, and by then I'll be too old to appreciate what I've earned."

Those words struck home, and started me talking. I told Ben he was wrong if he thought he wouldn't enjoy himself later on. If my own case was any indication, the later years of a man's life are the richest and most satisfying. I told him that when I started to slow down, after my heart attack, I found I was really able to savor the things my work had brought me. If possible, I said, I was getting more out of life than ever. Even for a man who is used to living at top speed, I said, the tapering-off process can be remarkably pleasant. I used to think there was nothing to look forward to in old age. Let me assure those who are worried about it that it's delightful.

The things I said to Ben that day still hold true for me. The easier tempo of the life I've led since 1956 continues to keep me happy. I like taking things slowly and living without pressure and tension. My heart attack was a warning that I was trying to do too much.

I'm still active in business and go to the office regularly. But my schedule is more relaxed and sensible, and I leave the grindstone work, the fretting and sweating, to the wonderful group of younger men who are now running the firm. To my delight, I've found my slower pace makes me more effective in business: I have time to think things through, and can focus my efforts where they do the most good. The result is that I look forward keenly to my days in town, and enjoy myself thoroughly when I'm there. I realize I'm fortunate to be able to continue to work under this arrangement—not every man of 66 gets such an opportunity.

Not a day goes by when I don't remind myself how lucky I am that I have other interests to occupy me. This is the most important single factor in making a success of these later years. It doesn't matter what the interest is. It could be collecting furniture, or painting, or gardening, or golf— anything will do, as long as you really care about it and do it as well as you know how. I pity a man who hasn't got this sort of resource to fall back on.

While on vacation one winter, I was playing in a golf tournament at The Breakers in Palm Beach when the New York office called to say that the Chris-Craft Corporation might be for sale. I was asked to make an appointment with Harsen Smith, chairman of the company, whose office was in Pompano Beach, not far down the Florida east coast.

Chris-Craft was (and is) the leading producer of pleasure boats in America. The company was founded in 1922 by Christopher Columbus Smith, a marine mechanic and small-boat designer. Three of Smith's sons and his grandson Harsen Smith were the company's trustees, and Harsen Smith was its chief executive officer.

For several years we had heard rumors that Chris-Craft was planning to sell out, but nothing had ever come of them, so I was neither optimistic about our chances nor enthusiastic about withdrawing from the golf tournament. But I went down to see Harsen Smith in Pompano Beach the next day.

He is a fine fellow, but rather quiet and reserved, and I thought to myself as we began talking how difficult it would be to make a living trying to sell securities to men like him. Time was short, because I had been told that several other companies and banking firms were sitting on Smith's doorstep, notably the Brunswick Corp. It was the plan of Shields & Company to have the NAFI Corporation, a diversified industrial company that we controlled, make the offer to acquire Chris-Craft.

I soon surmised that Harsen Smith himself didn't want to sell Chris-Craft, but that he might be outvoted by the other trustees. During that first meeting we spent a good deal of time discussing power boats and yacht racing. After a while, Smith said, "We should be able to do business, because we have a common love—the water." He also mentioned that we were both members of the same "club"; he was referring to our both having been *Time* magazine cover subjects.

Encouraged by the freeing up of his attitude, I felt at least I was making progress. We talked further about the company and I told him I would very much like to see the company's figures—balance sheet, income statements, etc., to guide us in our bid for the company.

Harsen Smith opened the top drawer of his desk, but made no move to bring out the sheets that I knew must be inside. Instead he spoke of the company his family had built and of its tradition of fine workmanship. If they sold it, it must be to people who would preserve the excellent condition, spirit, and happiness that prevailed in the organization.

I assured Smith that we wanted to keep Chris-Craft intact and that it was our desire to preserve the present management in its entirety; that the company would be run by them, not us, and that it would not become a division of a giant corporation. This obviously impressed him. Nevertheless he continued to open the drawer partially and close it without producing the figures. I sensed his growing enthusiasm for my presentation and at last he produced the balance sheet and income account. I tore off the top part, which contained the company's letterhead, so if by chance the sheets went astray, no one could relate the figures to Chris-Craft.

I knew we had to work fast. Theodore Crockett, our research partner, flew down to Florida that night to study the balance sheet. My brother Paul and two of our senior partners, H. Virgil Sherrill and Macrae Sykes, conferred with Chris-Craft's lawyers in Detroit. After several days of negotiation in Michigan, Florida, and New York, we finally settled on a price of $40 million for Chris-Craft. It was a great accomplishment for us, since we were competing with many firms that were much larger both in the banking and industrial fields.

Obviously I knew that Brunswick was eager to acquire a boat manufacturer to add to its varied line of leisure-activity products. As a director of Owens Yacht Company, second only to Chris-Craft in the industry, I thought I might persuade the four Owens brothers to sell their company. I told Paul after our second meeting at Pompano that if we were successful in closing the Chris-Craft deal, I was going to try to sell Owens to Brunswick.

Several days later, on a bleak, snowy Sunday after Virgil Sherrill had been successful in his final Chicago negotiations and I had returned to New York, I suddenly decided I could not wait until Monday to contact Brunswick—when someone else might approach them with the same idea. I did not know the name of the Brunswick president, but I finally got in touch with a member of the White Plains office of our organization and asked him to open the office for me so I could obtain Brunswick's financial manuals.

I called all over Chicago that afternoon and finally tracked down Edward Bensinger, the president of Brunswick, at his club. He knew only too well who I was, as he had just learned of our purchase of Chris-Craft the day before.

Before calling him I had telephoned the Owens brothers and obtained their authority to deal with Brunswick. When I told Bensinger of this possibility he was casual, but I knew he was seriously interested. A few days later he came to Baltimore with his associates to meet the Owens brothers, whose father had founded the company in a Chesapeake Bay backwater. The negotiations were completed in less than a week, and Brunswick acquired Owens for $16,000,000.

We had made a real double play. My Sunday efforts were most timely; on Monday, a St. Louis firm tried to obtain an option from the Owens brothers, stating that they were confident they could quickly sell the company. I learned later that their prospective buyer was Brunswick. This fortunate Sunday urge once again bore out what I have experienced so many times: if you are blessed with an idea, capitalize on it immediately; otherwise there will be a dozen reasons for delay. Enthusiasm may then evaporate or some enterprising competitor will make your deal.

Our relationship with Chris-Craft has been an extremely pleasant one. Because boats are involved it is all the more enjoyable for me. I was delighted that I could persuade the company to enter the sailboat field with a 35-foot fiber glass motor sailer. As power boat manufacturers this seemed a logical move for a first sailboat. We engaged Sparkman & Stephens to design her, and she was an immediate success. A keel center-board 30-foot cutter, also by Sparkman & Stephens, has just been introduced. She, too, was received very well. They are now programming a 20-, 24- and 27-footer, all fiber glass.

Youngsters all have dreams of heroic achievement. I vividly recall many of mine. I would, in some magical way, make a great deal of money and buy my mother a beautiful automobile. I wanted a sailboat that I could race. I pictured myself becoming another Charlie Barr, legendary skipper of the America's Cup yacht *Reliance*. Another, of less importance of course, was when I made my first slingshot: one Sunday during a long sermon I imagined myself shooting down every bit of bric-a-brac in the church—I never missed. When I grew older and learned to play football, tackling intrigued me more than any other part of the game; again in church I became the hero who made beautiful flying tackles and brought down a group of robbers who were attempting to escape up the aisle after stealing the proceeds of the collection plates.

Fanciful dreams carry over, and grown-ups, too, express their wishes through this wonderful mysterious medium where everything we desire materializes. Sometimes they really come true; one of mine did.

For many years I have observed the great problem involved when series are conducted and it is necessary to borrow one-design boats for the contestants to race in. The committee must persuade owners of class boats to loan their boats, and owners are reluctant to do so for obvious reasons. Then contestants are unhappy because seldom are the boats evenly matched. Of greatest importance, sails are not equal on all boats. Some boats are generally run down. In other words, important series have had to be conducted on lop-sided bases. It was forcefully brought home to me in all our series for the North American Sailing Championship and the Mallory Cup.

I have gone somewhat astray in reciting the foregoing, but it does have some relationship to my dreams. What a wonderful thing it would be, I thought, if a class of completely one-design boats were presented to the Yacht Racing Association (YRA) to be used for the various important series that are run in the Long Island Sound. The Hipkins Trophy and its qualifying series; the Mallory series when it came to the Sound; the SYCE Cup for the Women's Championship on the Sound; the Adams Cup for the National Women's Championship when it came to the Sound, and the Sears Cup for the National Junior Championship. Well, this was a sizable dream because of the cost of the type of boat that would be appropriate for these important events. People just can't make gifts of this magnitude, and I couldn't see how it could be done.

Then, in 1961, we were being blessed with a wonderful year in our business, which placed me in the position of being able to make a gift. But the YRA didn't qualify as a recipient. Why couldn't I make a gift to a university or a school and ask them to consider building a fleet of one-

The author's Shields Class *Do Do*.

The new 35-foot Cris-Craft
fiber glass motor sailer, by
Sparkman & Stephens.

design boats, and when they were not using them in the summer to loan or charter them to the YRA? I approached a number of institutions and obtained disappointing reactions. Time was running out by late November as I had to make my gift before the year's end. I went in other directions with no promising results. I will always remember a call I made on the subject (it was getting to the point where there wasn't time to wait for replies to my letters) to a professional member of the Olympics Committee. He was actually rather annoyed and said he would call back when he found time to give further consideration to the proposed gift. I never heard from him.

I was really becoming discouraged. I have always taken pride in being able to sell my ideas, whether it was the sale of securities, industrial companies, etc., and here I was unable to convince an institution that it should accept a considerable gift. In a talk with Drake Sparkman about my problem, he asked if I had considered the U.S. Merchant Marine Academy at Kings Point, Long Island, and the New York State Maritime College at Fort Schuyler. Here were two logical candidates right in our front yard. It was exactly the same reaction I used to have in the firm when we were trying to sell a difficult deal and I unexpectedly found two possible purchasers.

I couldn't wait to formally write them; I telephoned Captain Tyson at Kings Point and Admiral Moore at Fort Schuyler. They exploded with enthusiasm. In fact they couldn't believe it was true. I think I was even more excited than they after some of the receptions I had received. The idea of the boats being made available to the YRA was entirely agreeable to them, as the cadets were away a big part of the summr on cruises and vacations. The final arrangements with each academy were completed a week or ten days before New Year's, so it was indeed a happy ending for us all. One of the nicest parts was to come some months later when I met the cadets. Their enthusiasm and appreciation was most inspiring to me. They immediately named the boats the Shields Class and suggested the sail insignia be a shield with the letter S on it.

"My dream" pictured a boat of about 30 feet overall, with a nice, long, straight, countered stern and a dainty little transom, and with the bow a straight raked stem. I had always loved sheer, so of course this was embodied in my fanciful boat. As a token of appreciation for Drake Sparkman's many favors to me, I wanted Sparkman & Stephens to do the designing. Olin Stephens made her come true in beautiful fashion. He shaped an underbody whose sections are ideal. She is extremely lively in light weather, and very stiff and able in a hard breeze—an unusual combination indeed. Cape Cod Shipbuilding Company was selected as the builder because of that company's long experience with fiber glass. They delivered a magnificent job of construction.

The winter of 1963 was a very sad one for me as that was the year my brother Paul died. His loss was a frightful shock to me and continues to be difficult to actually realize. He had always looked out for me, and wanted me at his side in everything he did. He was most interested in my plans to give ten of the Shields boats to the New York State Maritime College and the U. S. Merchant Marine Academy. I know he would be very pleased that the Paul V. Shields Foundation, which he created, contributed five of these boats to the U. S. Naval Academy and two to the Naval War College at Newport.

I ordered a boat for myself and have enjoyed it immensely.

As in any new boat there is the fun of rearranging small details, and perhaps the most fun of all—the enjoyment of thinking of her; and of course there is the delight of sailing her. This sounds like the introduction of senility, but if so I must say it is a pleasant state. I recommend it. Only another boat lover can understand, and I know I can count on his sympathy and wholehearted support. Golfers, who normally would not go down the block to buy a newspaper, delight in walking five miles every time they play eighteen holes. Horsemen enjoy the smell of a stable. Hunters risk being shot at by their friends in the woods, duck hunters lie in cold wet blinds in freezing weather—and so on in all sports. But isn't it wonderful to have an interest to lean on that permits us to forget the troubles that come to everyone?

Whatever other boats I may sail on nowadays, there's one in particular I return to with special pleasure. Her name is *Patience*. She's a sponge boat, 12 feet long. I've owned her for thirty-three years.

To tell the story of *Patience*, I have to backtrack a bit. I first saw her the year frostbiting began, 1932. At the time, she belonged to a wonderful fellow named Slade Dale, who owns a large yacht yard in New Jersey. Slade had purchased her in Tarpon Springs, Florida, from some Greek sponge fishermen. She was a workboat on one of the schooners. She's a heavy little boat, 400 or 450 pounds, with carvel planking and unique,

The author in his sponge boat, *Patience*, off Larchmont, New York.

saucy lines: a lovely sheer, a graceful stern and beautiful bow, and the prettiest forefoot I've ever seen on a boat.

I was completely taken by *Patience* the first time I laid eyes on her. Every weekend, during the frostbite races, I used to admire her while talking to Slade Dale. One day he said to me: "You know, you love this boat so much, I'd like you to have her."

I told him I'd welcome a chance to buy the boat. His reply was typically generous. He said I didn't need to buy her—when the Frostbiting was over, he would lend her to me, and I could rerig her and fix her up any way I liked, and sail her during the summer.

We lived on the water at that time, between Larchmont and New Rochelle; there was an anchorage right off the beach where I later kept *Aileen*. I took *Patience* home, and I had a centerboard put in her. She had a lateen sail and gunter rig; I replaced this with a pole spar and a dinghy mainsail—the same rig she has today. She was painted white with yellow and black trim—I understand many boats built by Greeks have that combination—and I repainted her my favorite shade of light green. At the end of that summer, Slade did me a second great kindness and again showed his generosity: he sold *Patience* to me for exactly what she had cost him, $85.

I love *Patience* more every year; every year, she gives me more pleasure and satisfaction. To see her jumping at her mooring, exposing that lovely forefoot, is an endless source of delight. Corny and I do most of the maintenance work on her, with an assist from Toby Brekne, the captain at the Larchmont Yacht Club. She's nailed, which is unfortunate, for the nails have a tendency to rust. Whenever Corny or Toby or I find a nail that has rusted, Toby pulls it out and replaces it with a brass screw.

Sailing *Patience* is sheer joy. She has the most wonderful motion in a sea you can imagine. She's dry and doesn't throw any water. She has great personality—more than any boat I've ever known—and she's a little tender, so you have to watch her. I take her out on race days, or any other day, and sail around, going out alone on the Sound, sometimes sailing to another harbor to see what's going on there. *Patience* has countless admirers: wherever I go, people hail me and tell me how pretty she is.

Every morning, before setting off for the city or wherever else, I drop down to the harbor to take a look at *Patience, Aileen* and *Do Do* and the other boats and to see and smell the water. If for any reason I'm feeling a bit down, I find I get great solace and comfort from these visits. If I'm cheerful—as I generally am—the half-hour at the harbor makes me even more so. The pleasure I get out of looking at the boats and feeling the breeze is great no matter what the weather—but it's greatest when the wind is from the northeast, producing that wonderful air, giving the water that special sparkle.

People have asked me why I don't get something bigger—a motor sailer, for example, for cruising. I just don't think I'd get as much fun out of an elaborate, demanding boat as I get out of *Patience*. She offers the kind of sailing that suits me best nowadays. It may seem strange: perhaps it's odd to enjoy that simple little boat as much as I do. All I can say is that the facts are the facts: I don't want a bigger boat; I love every minute aboard *Patience;* and I always regret the sail being over.

Part Two

7. Choosing a Racing Boat

I envy the man who is about to buy his first racing boat. It is an experience that can happen only once in a lifetime, and no matter how many boats he buys after that, it is never quite the same.

All boats, of course, are beautiful, but they can be beautiful in different ways. A boat can be beautiful in her lines, in the way she carries out her function, in her speed, or she can be beautiful in your eyes because of the attachment you have for her. Don't let the beauty of one aspect or another blind you to the complete picture; when buying a boat, as in getting married, it pays to make your choice carefully. Don't judge a boat hastily. As with many people their nicest virtues and characteristics are not always immediately disclosed.

First, you must consider the purpose for which she will be used. If your family does not plan to participate in your boating activities—and I certainly hope that this is not the case—then your choice will depend only on your own preferences. You can pick any design that appeals to you. Be sure, however, that there are other boats of the same design available to race against. The best way to do this is to spend time around the yacht clubs in your area. Make inquiries to find out just what classes are popular in local waters. Make an informal survey to find out how many boats are in the various fleets, and if there is a proper feeling of spirited competition. The larger the fleet, the more skippers you will have to match skills against. In any event, a good class organization is vital. If the fleet is small, you will soon lose interest after beating, or being beaten, by the same competitors over and over again. Armed with a sound knowledge of the local racing picture, you will be in a good position to choose the right class and boat.

Merits of the Dinghy

For the beginner, an unlimited amount of sailing know-how can be acquired from the small centerboard one-design dinghy. In these tender, fast little craft, you can learn all the complications of sailboat racing with a minimum of expenditure and a maximum of fun in competition. Everything happens at a tremendously accelerated pace, whether it's rules, tactics, or the sailing demands of the boat itself.

A larger, heavier boat has considerable momentum to keep her moving even if occasionally poorly sailed. But in a poorly sailed dinghy, mistakes are magnified. If you have not trimmed her properly, or if you are sailing her too high, it will be immediately reflected in her speed. Her reaction in this regard will be much quicker than that of a boat of larger displacement, which will carry her way longer and help to overcome your errors. Conversely, everything that you do to improve the trim and handling of a dinghy will pay off in an increase of speed that you can feel immediately.

Another thing to consider is that on a single day of dinghy competition, you can have as many as eight races with 24 triangular course marks to round, as against one race and only three marks in the bigger boats. In other words, you will sail 21 more courses and meet many more tactical situations in a day of dinghy sailing than in a day of big-boat racing. In terms of a season's competition, the gain in intensive experience is obvious. With this kind of practice and racing drill, both you and your boat cannot help but improve.

I began sailing in my brother Paul's 27 footer; there were no dinghy classes in those years. Since then, I have regularly raced dinghies, and I have gained more racing knowledge from dinghies than from any other class of boat I've ever sailed. I learned an enormous amount about tactics, construction, racing rules, helmsmanship, sails, and boat handling from these exciting little craft.

There is another advantage to beginning in dinghies; the learning can be naturally transferred to a bigger boat. Anyone who can sail a small boat well can step up to a larger one, whereas it is seldom that the man who learned in a bigger boat can take over a small one and get the most out of it. Many of the fine 12-meter sailors who defended the famed America's

Cup against the British challenge of 1958 were men who had been first trained in dinghies.

Since the price of a racing dinghy is well within the reach of persons of moderate income, there are a lot of these dinghies. This makes for good competition. There will always be someone with less skill whom you can beat, and there will be first-rate skippers you can strive against. If you live in northern climates where the larger boats are hauled for the winter, you can take advantage of frostbiting. The catchy label is actually a misnomer, for—as I said earlier—you don't feel cold while sailing a dinghy, however low the thermometer. Even a mid-January capsize isn't as harrowing as you might imagine, and I speak from three such experiences. But the possibility of capsize will keep you on the alert and you will think faster, develop split-second reflexes, and therefore become a better skipper.

If the idea of winter sailing does not appeal to you, then wait for summer, but start racing in a dinghy anyway. You will have the pleasure of keen competition and you will receive a basic training in sailboat racing that will be of priceless value for the rest of your life, no matter what boat you sail. Incidentally, one of the greatest pleasures of cruising is to have a sailing dinghy. Don't miss this opportunity.

WHAT TO LOOK FOR IN A DINGHY

I would like to be able to recommend a particular class of dinghy, but there are many of them that are excellent. There are, however, certain qualities that I would look for in any class. Liveliness under sail is always the first thing that interests me. A boat that plows along sluggishly— pushing a wall of water before her, a boat that refuses to tack smartly, or is cranky and trialsome, will soon dampen the joy of sailing. Look for a smart sailer that handles excitingly and has pretty lines. Remember a boat is to be looked at and admired as well as sailed—an aesthetic bonus granted the sailor.

The dinghy you choose should be in reasonably good condition, requiring only minor painting and refurbishing to put her into racing shape. The novice who hopes to buy a boat cheaply, in advanced stages of deterioration, and fix her up, more often than not is deluding himself. As with an old home or automobile, too often the "bargain" turns out to be an expensive one requiring more investment of time and money than had been anticipated. Extensive rebuilding can be a giant headache even for the experienced, well-equipped boatyards. Better to start with a craft in good condition and keep her that way.

Choosing a Racing Boat

Different classes seem to achieve popularity in different areas of the country. The famous Interclub dinghy one-design by Sparkman & Stevens, for instance, has had great success in eastern waters. On the West Coast, the El Toro has had a great many adherents. In some classes, however, there are considerable individual differences from boat to boat. For over 30 years I have maintained a vehement conviction that for proper racing, boats must be truly one-design in nature. Therefore, pick a class that has a reputation for rigidly maintaining class standards—you will enjoy better racing and become a better skipper. There are, of course, dozens of dinghy classes across the country. Some I've had experience with and that have appealed to me are the Beverly (Mass.) Yacht Club boats designed by Sidney Herreshoff and built by the Cape Cod Shipbuilding Company; the fiber glass Dyer 10-footer; and the Penguins, which are probably the largest class of all. The latter two were designed by the famous Phil Rhodes.

Racing and Family Fun

If racing will be only a part of your sailing activity, and you plan to take your family afloat when there are no races scheduled, a boat a little larger than a dinghy is called for. Something that will accommodate about three passengers besides the skipper will generally do very well. It's possible to select a good, fast, seaworthy racing one-design and still have a good family boat. Dual-purpose boats are available for both class racing and occasional family day-sailing, including the Sparkman & Stephens designed Chris-Craft 20- and 24-footers, and the Dolphin, and the Rhodes 18- and 19-footers.

In a family boat, look for good stability and ease of handling. The cockpit should be large enough to seat passengers comfortably, but this is usually no problem in a racing boat, since the cockpits of these boats are generally designed to accommodate racing crews.

There should be some kind of small cabin or shelter cuddy so your wife and children can get in out of the rain, and so youngsters, when tired, can nap out of the sun and wind. A good one-design racing boat has nothing in her nature that prevents her from being a seaworthy pleasure boat for family use as well. Planing boats, mentioned below, naturally would not qualify.

Advanced Racers

For the really agile and supple-backed, the wonderful Alcort Sailfish, Sunfish and Catfish Catamaran are great fun to sail and race. They have brought thousands of people into sailing and have taught them to sail more quickly than any other type of boat.

Olympic one-design planing sailboats also provide the thrill of fast sailing. The hulls of this type of boat skim across the top of the water with a minimum of wetted surface. Unlike displacement hulls, the live ballast of the crew provides the only stability to prevent capsizing. To facilitate proper balancing, the more sophisticated of these craft are equipped with extension tillers, trapezes that hang from the rigging, and hiking straps, so the crew can get as far outboard as possible in stiff breezes.

Although they are wonderful fun to sail, these boats represent a very specialized type of sailing craft, and because of their tenderness and large sail area in proportion to their size, they require experienced skippers to sail them. Typical of such classes are the 5.0.5., the International 14, the Flying Dutchman, and the Finns.

Aileen Shields Bryan racing a Sunfish in Bermuda. These wonderful Sunfish and Sailfish have introduced more people to sailing than any other class. There are now over 50,000 distributed around the world.

99

The advantage of these high-speed planing hulls lies in the large number of boats in the fleets. Competition is extremely keen, and sailing skills develop rapidly. Because of constant international competition, these craft are carefully kept to rigid one-design standards, which is the prime requisite for the best racing.

The Ocean Racer-Cruiser

There are two schools of thought on ocean boats. One school holds that the best and safest craft for long-distance cruising is the heavy scantling, heavy displacement, and heavily built ketch with a low rig, along the lines of the Colin Archer North Sea Lifeboats. The proponents of this type are traditionalists. They are stubbornly insistent about the superiority of their type, and of course they have the evidence of decades of successful round-the-world cruising. The other school is composed of men who sing the praises of the modern, fine-lined Bermuda-rigged ocean racer. These modernists are just as vociferous in the defense of their ideas. Both groups are usually constituted of very fine sailors, men of great courage and skill. Unfortunately there is practically no understanding between the two schools, and even less exchange of ideas and experience.

I think both groups have a lot to recommend them. As many of the older Herreshoff designs will show, we still have much that we can learn from the past. On the other hand, in the past decades we have made such strides in the art of design and the technology of sea-going materials that it is downright stubbornness not to profit from the present.

My feeling is that even if a man is buying his boat for cruising purposes, there's no reason why he shouldn't have a boat that is pleasant and lively to sail—therefore, a fast boat. All true sailors, after all, love nothing better than fast and able runs. A man will get a lot more enjoyment out of a lively boat than one that is sluggish, dull, uninteresting to sail, and won't move at all except in a hard breeze. It is just as easy to get comfort, stoutness, and everything that you could need for family cruising with a boat that is fast, as with one that will not get out of her own way. I think it's safe to say that there would be more permanency in an able boat than in one whose sailing is on the drab side, because interest is bound to dwindle in sailing a poor performer.

It might be argued that the big, heavy, beamy ketch is a safer, stauncher boat. I don't agree. Certainly such a boat is no safer than a well-designed modern ocean racer, which will out-perform the heavy ketch a hundred to

John Nicholas Brown's *Bolero* in the 1950 Newport-Bermuda Race.

one in sailing. You can get just as much seakindliness in a good performer as in a poor performer, you can get places quicker, and you can get out of trouble faster.

If the rig must be divided, I favor the yawl. It is very tiring to get anywhere to windward in a ketch. By nature of her design, she will not go to windward with the speed of a yawl and certainly not with the speed of a cutter. This holds true for the schooner rig also. If a boat doesn't sail up to expectations, I might tire of getting anywhere with her, and she would become more of a floating home than anything else. I believe that a boat ought to be a joy to sail as well as to live on.

Then there is the matter of scantlings in the modern ocean racer. Massive timbers alone do not guarantee strength in a boat's hull. Undoubtedly there are some poor boats built today, but I think that a well-designed ocean racer is undoubtedly a more staunchly built boat.

101

Most designers today comply with rules for the building of yachts laid down by Lloyds. You have only to read through these rules to realize that ideal standards for the modern yacht are extremely rigid with a more-than-adequate built-in safety factor. There will always be unscrupulous builders who will cut corners, but these individuals are soon discovered by serious yachtsmen, and they do not remain in business long. By hiring the services of a skilled yacht surveyor before buying, you can protect yourself from this kind of profiteering.

I don't think there's ever been a yacht built as staunchly and as thoroughly strong as John Nicholas Brown's *Bolero,* and I don't care what the scantlings are on the other boats. I think that if you were to thoroughly study the old-fashioned, gaff-rigged cruising boats that some people believe to be about the most rugged boats, you would find that these boats fail to measure up to the overall ruggedness of *Bolero* because of weakness in the rigs of these older designs.

The modern masthead rig is a marvel of engineering, with each element working toward the efficiency of the whole. It has evolved through many decades of trial and error, plus imaginative, creative thinking by designers and yachtsmen alike. If the object is maximum drive for a given weight-to-strength ratio, the Bermudian permanent-backstay rig is unsurpassed. Certainly for handicap racing under the Cruising Club of America Rules, the older rig is a serious drawback. I love the traditional "character" boats as much as the next man, but I love racing more.

8. Building a Winning Crew

To win races it is necessary to bring together an effective, first-rate crew and mold it into a working team. How well this crew functions will be the responsibility of the skipper. He is the most important man in that crew: there can and must be only one skipper. I know personally of some boat teams that make strategy decisions by consensus of opinion after calling what amounts to board-of-directors meetings. While opinions are being solicited, purposeful, well-commanded boats usually drive by to leave these budding democracies in their wakes. In boat racing, even more than in business, deciding and effectively carrying out policy must be the responsibility of one man. Remember that any third-class seaman can steer a ship but it takes two smart captains to wreck her.

A good skipper must have, or must develop in himself, a peculiar combination of talents and qualities if he is to be successful. Paradoxical as it sounds, I believe the ideal skipper should have a mixture of humility and egotism; he must also have an ability to quickly grasp over-all concepts, and he must have a computer-like memory for detail.

The most necessary of all the qualities for a winning skipper is an intense spirit of competition. A competitive instinct and a will to win are the first requirements for racing success. The man who avoids competition, for whatever reason, had better avoid racing yachts. But if you enjoy laying your talents, your skills, and your belief in yourself on the line to defend against all comers, the chances are you will become a good skipper. You must dislike being beaten, you must feel a sense of pleasure at being the best, and you must have an overwhelming drive to win.

A winning skipper also values his own judgment; he enjoys gambling on his educated opinion. Indecisiveness has to be ruthlessly eliminated from his personality, and after having evaluated a racing situation, he must make decisions as quickly, firmly, and casually as he breathes. The responsibility for the results of these decisions must also rest lightly upon him. Whether this choice results in a win or a loss, the responsibility is his alone, and the blame for a loss should never be divided up or shoved off on the crew—although the credit for a win may be.

Frankly, I do not select anyone for my crew in order to make use of his judgment; first because I want to race the race myself, and secondly because I do not want to race against one of my own crew members as well as 25 other skippers in the class. I have no objection to talking over the fine points after it is over, but I want no one to tell me how to sail the boat during a race. Thinking back, I've been very fortunate in that respect. I can only remember once when a crew member started to tell me how to sail the boat, and I will never forget him or when and how he offered his advice. I tried not to offend his feelings, but I told him I was in the habit of sailing the boat, that I didn't agree with his opinions, and that I didn't want any more interference. There was no quarreling or unpleasantness, but needless to say, that was his last sail with me.

Of course everyone experiences flashes of anxiety and momentary doubts, and it requires restraint not to solicit the opinions of others for reassurance. It is also painful to be curt toward your friends and bring them up sharply, but in this respect, you must be absolutely adamant. There can be no equivocation, no vacillating, and no back-talk aboard the boat if you are determined to win races. Every order has to be carried out quickly and willingly, and the man who will not do so must be promptly eliminated from your crew.

Whatever the pressures, a racing skipper has to train himself not to let tautness and excitement affect his decisions. It is forgivable if you get upset once or twice, but make sure it doesn't happen habitually. Even when someone has let go of the spinnaker halyard instead of the sheet, and you see your lead on the fleet evaporating, you must express your criticism only in calm tones. It requires monumental control, but it can be done. If you get mad, your anger colors your decisions, and you might as well leave the race and sail back to your mooring, for you have already lost. You have defeated yourself.

Try to develop a good head for detail. As a winning skipper, you must have instantly available a thousand points of information. You must carry a plan of campaign in your head, a timetable of tide and current changes, knowledge of standings in the fleet, and an awareness of wind and weather conditions for the day. To enter competition with a well-tuned boat, you will have to know about hundreds of maintenance needs. Besides this, you must remember race-committee instructions for the courses, and numerous flag and time signals that will be used aboard the committee boat. Much of this information can be written down; some of it cannot. Often it is the little things that determine whether or not a race is won, so try to train yourself to cope with this mass of detail.

I think so highly of patience as a quality that I named my favorite little sailing sponge boat *Patience*. It is an attribute that can be a great asset to the racing skipper. No one can attain perfection at the first try; if one could, the joy of attainment would soon disappear. If a crew member with promise doesn't do his job right the first few times, have patience with him, and you'll probably succeed by explaining again what you want. Have patience with yourself also if you don't reach your racing goals the first few seasons. No one who sails can ever learn everything. Each time I leave the mooring I can truthfully say that, without exception, I learn something new and fresh and wonderful. No matter how long you sail, this constant newness and reawakening of stimulation will remain. It is one of the great attractions of sailing as a lifetime sport.

Perseverance is an important quality in the racing sailor. You will not go far if you are easily discouraged. You will be competing with some of the most dedicated and accomplished men to be found in any sport—men who talk, eat, and breathe yacht racing. You have to meet them on their own terms and keep on striving despite defeats. A dogged determination must pay off eventually. Even champions make mistakes, and as your skill grows, you will be able to capitalize on these mistakes. In the end, the winner is usually the one who makes the fewest. In any field of endeavor, talent alone is not enough to win if it is not backed up with perseverance. The world is full of talented failures.

Self-assurance and confidence will come to you as you race. The easy casualness in competition that distinguishes champions is the result of years of training and doesn't come about overnight. Frequently it is a façade to disguise violent inner tension, maintained with difficulty. So don't worry about lack of confidence: it comes with achievement, the same as with any other endeavor. Always comfort yourself with the fact that your competitors have for certain the same taut nervousness from which you are trying to free yourself.

THE SPIRIT OF THE BOAT

I believe that there is an almost tangible atmosphere that surrounds each sailboat that might be called the "spirit" of the boat. Composed of a complex of many things, it can be a negative, gloomy cloud or a positive, happy aura of jauntiness.

A good-spirited boat is that way because she has efficiency, harmony, aggressiveness, and pride. There is no greater pleasure to me than to sail on such a fortunate craft. On the other hand, the unhappy ship will carry ineptness, dissension, half-heartedness, and humiliation as an unseen stowaway: she is an unpleasant thing indeed and a trial to be aboard.

Now no boat is born on the stocks with this spirit, good or bad, built into her—it requires the personality of man to animate her. So if you would always run a happy boat, make these your goals:

1. *Efficiency*—Every maneuver smart and sailor-like
2. *Harmony*—Every man a friend and a respecter of the other
3. *Aggressiveness*—Every race your finest effort
4. *Pride*—Every rival respectful of you as a competitor

CHOOSING THE CREW

When you put together what will eventually become a winning crew, you must have people who are not only compatible and agreeable, but also able. You want no one on your team who is not a serious and enthusiastic sailor. The social aspect of yachting becomes entirely secondary; you can have that ashore or in your pleasure sailing. When you're racing, you're out to win, and you want the strongest team that you can procure.

Observe a crew candidate closely before you ask him to join your boat. A casual discussion will give some indication of his potential. Then, for example, you might like the way he rows a dinghy, or be impressed with the way he handles himself on another boat. Your aim is to select men who are handy and perfectly at ease around the boat. By all means exclude the chatty type; nothing is more disturbing to the skipper than empty conversation during a race.

I have known wonderful fellows, pleasant and charming to be with, but cursed with the bad coordination and clumsiness of the accident-prone. If you have a friend like this, spend time with him pleasure sailing, but out of respect for his longevity and your nerves, don't, for heaven's sake, ask him to race with you.

Youngsters make wonderful shipmates, for they are agile and eager to learn. In addition, they are usually pleasant and free of problems, which makes them enjoyable companions. Throughout my racing, I have always tried to have one or two youngsters available as crew members. If they are interested in racing at all, they are the easiest persons to train, and you have the added advantage of their willingness to accept direction without question. You will also have the wonderful satisfaction of introducing a youth to a healthy and fascinating interest. I believe that the youngsters are the most important people in sailing, and I will express my reasons in a later chapter on junior sailing.

Don't wait until the last night before the race to pick your crew, and don't fall into the habit of picking up someone from the dock at the last minute. Try to aim for a well-organized crew that will be with you all season. Choose two or three substitutes that can fill in when members of your regular crew are unable to race. Take the alternates out and train them to your method of working. This kind of foresight is a lot of extra trouble, but if you are aiming at becoming a champion, it will pay off.

THE SECOND-IN-COMMAND

When you are sailing to windward, even a mediocre crew can trim the sails to suit you. But crew efficiency is a vital factor when you are sailing off the wind: it is here that the crew makes its most valuable contribution toward winning. This is especially so in spinnaker work.

Your second-in-command, or first mate, whatever you call him, must be chosen with a great deal of discretion. Usually the mate is also your spinnaker man. He has to be experienced and thoroughly schooled in foredeck work and every maneuver or sail change that may be required of him. He must know how to get the most out of a spinnaker and understand what delicate adjustments of trim can do to make your boat go faster. Perhaps he has skippered his own boat in another class or perhaps you may have promoted him from the cockpit crew of the previous season. Whatever his background, he should not have to be trained during a race. You must turn over to him the complete responsibility for running the foredeck and bossing spinnaker handling, so he has to be absolutely competent. If it is your misfortune to have a green spinnaker hand, take care to do your training before the race. Go through an exhaustive practice drill so you don't have upsets when rounding the mark or at a critical moment of the race when there is no margin for error.

9. Sails, Your Source of Power

Long ago I became convinced that sails are the most important single factor in successful sailboat racing. I think that 75 percent of the success of a racing boat is attributable to the quality of her sails. Racing sails have the same relative importance to a boat as an engine would to a racing car. Their function is the same, to drive you at the greatest speed.

I don't believe that a talented skipper can overcome the handicap of poor sails, for there is no touch on the helm magical enough to surmount this disadvantage. For this reason, you can't have fair and equal racing competition unless all sails are completely one-design. Other things being equal, if the hulls of two boats are identical and the skippers equally matched, the boat with the better sails will win every time.

Here is a case that dramatically proves the importance of sails. John Nicholas Brown's magnificent 72-foot ocean racer, *Bolero,* was commissioned in 1949 with a first suit of 18-ounce Egyptian duck sails. She performed extremely well, and Olin Stephens, her famous designer, again showed that he could always improve on his previous boats. In her third season, Ratsey and Lapthorne constructed a beautiful mainsail of 14-ounce duck to be used in light weather, but even in 4- to 5-knot breezes, *Bolero* failed to go as well to windward as she had with the previous sail. The great power of the boat and the very heavy boom stretched the sail seriously out of shape. It was ineffective except for running in very light breezes.

Had *Bolero* been commissioned with the 14-ounce sail—and that's not light canvas—in place of the 18-ounce, she might have been considered an unsuccessful boat. It could have been said that the designer was at fault or that her very able owner-skipper was not sailing her properly. When the 14-ounce main was replaced with another of 18-ounce canvas, *Bolero* resumed her highly successful racing career.

Early in my racing, I tried to learn everything I could about sails. Few of us can be fortunate enough to have a professional sailmaker in our crew to achieve perfection, but if you educate yourself thoroughly on the subject of sails, you can come close to this ideal. I suggest that the racing skipper get several books on sailmaking, and learn how sails are put together. If at all possible, I would spend time in a professional sailmaking loft, paying close attention to the workmen as they go about the complicated art of building a sail. Talk with the sailmaker and learn the many factors that distinguish a well-setting, efficient sail. If you are familiar with sailmaking, you will be able to talk intelligently about changes—to know what can and cannot be done. Sailmakers are more than merchants. They are individualistic craftsmen practicing an ancient and skilled art. If you are cooperative and aware of their problems, your relationship can be a warm, personal one, as mine has been.

SYNTHETIC SAILS

In 1953, the Long Island Sound fleet of Internationals decided to adopt one-design sails of dacron: it was probably the first class in the world to do so. We had been using one-design nylon spinnakers with great success since the inception of the class. Since dacron was a relatively new development, we had the firm of Ratsey and Lapthorn construct a suit of test sails. We sailed a dacron-equipped boat against one with Egyptian cotton sails; we changed boats, we changed crews, and no matter what we did, the dacron-equipped boat proved her superiority.

We worked closely with Ratsey until we had achieved what we considered a perfect sail, and then we ordered 22 identical suits. So they would be as nearly alike as human skill could make them, bolt rope was taken from the same coil, and panels were cut from the same run of cloth. The same cutters, sewers, ropers, and sailmakers were used on all the sails. When we received delivery, there was not one-quarter inch of variation in the whole 22 sets.

110

Harry Powell, skipper of #22, keeping his boat on her bottom in this 35-knot breeze, with the main slightly eased.

The adoption of one-design sails was the greatest stimulus conceivable for the already highly-successful Internationals, and the wisdom of the change was evident. Skippers formerly at the tail of the class, because of poor sail equipment, began to improve their standings markedly. The racing was leveled out, and the skill of the crew and skipper became the greatest factor in winning championships.

When we decided on uniform dacron sails, we agreed that for economy, no new ones would be purchased for three years. The dacron sails have stood the test of time, and in seven years we have had only two new suits—and these boats are raced hard from the first of May to the middle of October. New skippers were attracted to the class when they realized they would not have to build up expensive inventories, and everyone was relieved of the irksome necessity of deciding which suits of sails to use for different weather conditions.

Synthetic sailcloth, together with fiber glass construction, will, I believe, prove to be one of the greatest developments to come to yachting in this century. Synthetic sails unquestionably make a boat go faster. They are less porous than cotton and therefore utilize the wind power to greater advantage. Factory finishing techniques smooth the surface of synthetic cloth sails so they do not have surface fuzz such as cotton has. This reduces turbulence in the boundary layer of air passing over the sail. Synthetic sails have practically no stretch, and the small amount there is is fairly predictable. For this reason, wider panels may be used and the number of seams reduced. With fewer seams to disturb the laminar flow of air, the sail presents a better airfoil. Since synthetics shed water, you no longer have to worry about increased weight aloft in wet weather. In a heavy rain, duck sails will absorb enough water to easily double their weight. Even in a moist atmosphere without rain, duck will absorb dampness and consequently add weight aloft.

Mildew may grow on the surface of synthetics, but the mold does not penetrate into the fiber. Surface mold can be washed off with mild soap and water, and other than looking unsightly it does no harm. With cotton, on the contrary, mildew reaches into the fibers, and it is only a matter of time before rot begins.

Because of the stability of the synthetic fabrics, and the consequently small amounts of shrinkage or stretch in the direction of the warp and woof, the characteristics and shapes built into the sail by the sailmaker will remain essentially unchanged, even when the sails are trimmed hard in strong breezes. For this same reason—no stretch—they should be cut almost to their full size along the hoist and foot. In my opinion, a synthetic mainsail should have considerable draft when used with a conventional jib, but not as much when used with a genoa. The jib should have full draft, although relatively somewhat less than the mainsail. The draft in both sails can be flattened through sheet trim if the sail is well designed. When a genoa is used, the mainsail must be rather flat in the lower two-thirds where it is influenced by the jib's backdraft, and the area above the jib should be relatively fuller.

I prefer a flat genoa, even for moderate and light weather. I think the common fault of genoas is that they are too drafty. A flat genoa can be given more power, when necessary, through the easing of the sheet. In

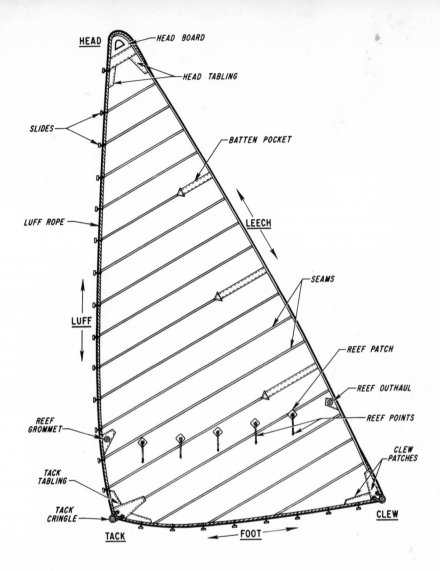

The mainsail and its parts.

synthetic sails, the draft (that is, the area of greatest concavity of camber) should be well forward, and it should be considerably greater than would be normal in cotton sail.

If a jib doesn't meet this requirement, it can usually be corrected by "pulling it up" on the wire luff. This is the equivalent of "tacking down" a mainsail. The seizings on the luff wire are cut, the jib luff is stretched out taut along the wire and reseized: it is amazing how this will throw the draft forward and revive an otherwise poor jib. A jib should have a nice flow from luff to leech; that is, the deep draft forward should gradually taper to a very flat leech. The upper 15 to 18 percent of the jib should be relatively flatter than the lower area so it will stand and not flutter or luff in moderate-to-heavy breezes. A well-designed jib should luff simultaneously along the entire hoist when your boat is headed gradually up into the wind. A genoa jib should be a very flat sail to provide the best performance in windward sailing. If necessary, it is easy to change the shape of a jenny and get more draft simply by changing the lead and trim tension of the sheet.

One of the great improvements in genoa jibs was made by Bill Luders in his rearrangement of the rigging and sail plans of the America's Cup winner, *Weatherly*, in 1962. He materially narrowed the spreaders so that the leech of the genoa would not have to be hollowed out for spreader clearance. This straight leech from head to clew added almost 100 feet of area. Probably of even more importance was the increased effectiveness of the slot between the mainsail and the jib.

The stretch luff genoa developed four or five years ago by Ted Hood has met with some success. The principal advantage is its adaptability to various strengths of wind. These jibs are made with both wire and rope luffs. The wire is used when the sail has no hanks, and those made with hanks have a rope luff. The jib with the wire luff rope can be hoisted harder to offset the lack of hanks. With the rope it is not necessary to hoist as hard, as the hanks prevent the luff of the sail from sagging away. The luff rope (or wire) is contained in a sleeve, and the sail itself is not attached to the luff rope (or wire) as in the case of conventional jibs, where it is seized to the wire luff rope closely spaced up the rope. The draft is regulated by the tension on the halyard; taut, to move the draft forward as the breeze increases, and slack to let the draft aft in lighter conditions. The original sails employed tack downhauls, but in recent years, because of the great power of the new Barient winches on the halyard, they have become unnecessary.

A Trick in Setting Synthetic Sails

Most racing men hoist their synthetic sails too taut and destroy the natural airfoil built-in by the sailmaker. I have seen this time and again and have been guilty of it myself. The tendency when setting a sail is to tail on the halyard with all your might, and even to crank the sail up a few extra inches with a winch.

This is the worst thing that you can do with synthetic sails. When a dacron sail is stretched too tightly, a hard roll of draft appears just aft of the mast, right up near the luff rope. You can also see this happen if you pull down on the tack with a downhaul. That bulge will come out only in a very hard breeze: in light and moderate winds the natural flow of air is disturbed, thrust is lost, and you're losing power.

Think of a synthetic sail as if it were made of light aluminum. Now the shape of that hypothetical sheet has already been determined by the press at the factory—the sailmaker is our press—and any violent tension on the halyard or outhaul is going to distort that sheet we've imagined. I would like to see dacron sails made right up to full measure along the luff. For instance, if the hoist were 37 feet, I'd make the luff of the sail about 36 feet, 6 inches, and then just haul the sail good and taut, but not enough to throw that awful wrinkle into the forward part. When we used the old cotton duck sails, we got into the habit of hoisting and downhauling mainsails to keep the draft forward. But with synthetics, this has the effect of distorting the sail. Try it yourself and you'll see a measurable difference in your boat's performance.

During the trials for the America's Cup in 1958, we would frequently receive a brand new mainsail from the sailmakers, run it up, and begin racing in hard breezes. We had to do this because time was at a premium, but I do not recommend the practice. It is true that a dacron sail needs little breaking-in compared to cotton sails, which require days of careful sailing in light breezes before the material sets, but some care is needed. A few hours of sailing on a good day with light-to-moderate winds will allow the ropes to set, the stitching to bed down, and the strain on the cloths to tauten the sail gradually. Then you can go ahead and race.

When you are sailing aboard your boat, it is difficult to get a full view of your sails. Even by going forward and looking back, you can see only a limited amount. A great deal more can be seen by turning the helm over to a friend and circling around in another boat. You will be able to study the sail plan thoroughly, and hard spots, wrinkles, or distortions of the natural airfoil will be obvious.

Pictures of your boat underway are also most revealing. Faults that sometimes escape detection become obvious in a photograph. For example, a hard leech is more pronounced in a picture than to the naked eye.

Although the basic shape of a sail is determined wholly by the characteristics that the sailmaker has built into it, some modifications can be effected by judicious adjustment. By means of the halyards, clew outhaul, downhaul, sheet leads, and boom vang, the shape can be altered considerably to suit downwind or windward sailing. The general rule is that sails should be fuller for reaching or running, and tauter for windward work. When running, however, be careful that you do not slack the mainsheet so much that the upper part of the leech sags off to leeward or chafes against the spreaders. This can be corrected by bowsing down the boom vang and trimming the mainsheet.

Much is being learned about the manufacture of dacron, which is constantly being improved. Ted Hood unquestionably led the field in material quality when he set up his own looms and made it for use in his wonderful Hood sails. Undoubtedly the fabric will be even more improved as the efforts of Hood and others are successful. I think of the great progress in the relatively few years that synthetics have been in use for sails, first as rayon, then nylon, orlon and now dacron. There is such rapid progress that perhaps the next decade will see an improved product of a totally different type.

The talented Ed Raymond of Hathaway, Reiser & Raymond, using his famous ketch *Chantey Man* as a test tube, has succeeded in simplifying sailmaking. For the last three years *Chantey Man* has been winning the majority of the races she entered, with no tabling on the leeches of her mainsail, mizzen and genoas. They are not only more economical to construct, but more important, distortion in the leech is eliminated. With no tabling in the luff the contour of the draft starts at the luff rope. This could be more important in smaller and lighter weight sails. I like the tabling elimination, especially for genoa leeches. It might well be a solution for the genoa's greatest problem, hard leeches.

When the tabling is not used the leech is sealed with a hot iron. This procedure can be repeated if necessary. Raymond, however, says his trial genoas have stood up for three years with no resealing.

Andrew Kostanecki pioneered the lamination of the cloths (no stitching) in sails up to five ounces in weight. At this writing he is not satisfied with the durability of the lamination. But this can undoubtedly be made so that it will eventually withstand the ravages of sunlight, salt water and stress in hard breezes. This principle appeals to me because of the elimination of the ridges caused in overlapping of the cloths. I am convinced that the *smoothness* of the sail's surface has great bearing on its efficiency. I predict that just as the tank has done so much to improve yacht design, the wind tunnel or its equivalent, will soon prove the importance of a smooth sail surface. If this thought is right, then a narrow cloth sail would not be as advantageous as one with wider panels.

I am sure, too, that we will soon learn the fundamentals of the "slot" between the mainsail and the genoa, an enigma that is far from solved today. We all seem to be endeavoring to mate these two sails on a hit and miss basis. Whenever we are right, it's usually for the wrong reason. In other words, my own belief is that a genoa should be moderately flat and that the most efficient sail will have a very flat, smooth leech in the entire after 40 percent. If the sail is drafty, it seems to me this type of leech condition cannot exist.

RECUTTING SAILS

If there is too much draft in a mainsail, the sailmaker can reduce it without disturbing the contour and size of the sail by trimming the round on the foot and the luff. Increasing the draft is more difficult, but it can be done to save an otherwise good sail. Have the sailmaker remove the bolt ropes from the luff and foot and sew on curved sections representing the depth of increased draft the sail requires. False seams can be stitched across these pieces to line up with the original seams for the sake of appearance. The tablings are replaced, new grommets for tack and reef

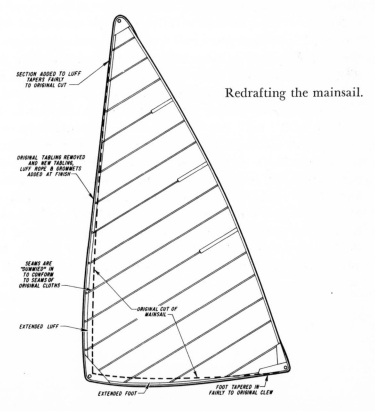

SECTION ADDED TO LUFF
TAPERS FAIRLY
TO ORIGINAL CUT

Redrafting the mainsail.

ORIGINAL TABLING REMOVED
AND NEW TABLING,
LUFF ROPE & GROMMETS
ADDED AT FINISH

SEAMS ARE
"DUMMIED" IN
TO CONFORM
TO SEAMS OF
ORIGINAL CLOTHS

ORIGINAL CUT OF
MAINSAIL

EXTENDED LUFF

FOOT TAPERED IN
FAIRLY TO ORIGINAL CLEW

EXTENDED FOOT

cringles worked, and the bolt ropes sewed back on. If you need more foot draft or fullness throughout the sail, don't be dissuaded from this reasonable, practical method of obtaining it. It will work. (*See* diagram.)

Caring for Sails

Nothing is so well made that carelessness and indifference cannot ruin it: this holds for synthetic sails. When storing your sails for the winter, keep them in a dry, well-ventilated place without extremes of heat and moisture. Don't leave them in the bag, but drape them out in loose folds so that air can circulate freely. An attic makes a good storage place; a cellar doesn't.

If you own a large cruising boat, it is impractical to remove sails from the spars after each use and stow them below. Sailcovers must be used. Don't lace up sailcovers tightly, but allow some air space for ventilation. Sailcovers should keep the rain and sunlight out, but not the air. When furling sails on the spars, flake them down loosely rather than rolling them into a tight, airless sausage. When bagging sails, fold them neatly instead of just stuffing them bodily into the open bag. Dacron sails have a smooth finish, and cramming them will crumple the surface, leaving minute cracks all over the sail. It is impossible to avoid them competely, but there's no use aggravating the condition.

Stencil all your sailbags with large, bright letters—#1 Mainsail, Small Storm Jib, etc.—and you won't waste time sorting through the foc'sle for the right bag when a change is needed. If it is not done at the sailmaker's, stencil the head, tack, and clew of all sails: you will save many precious minutes of swapping end-for-end when you get them up on deck.

Sails should be washed periodically. Small sails can be washed in the bathtub with a mild soap. I don't believe I would use strong detergents, because you can never be sure that the chemicals won't harm the fabric or threads. Anything you would use to wash your face is strong enough. Send larger sails to the sailmakers, for they need lots of room for washing and plenty of space to dry. A lawn is usually the only suitable place around a home, but grass stains, animals, and small children make the hazards too great. During the second season, when your boat is near a dock, a good hosing down will remove much of the salt. Do not permit your sails to be scrubbed with a brush. The stitching will be weakened or broken.

10. Spinnaker Handling

Spinnaker work represents a tremendously important part of yacht racing, and it is here that many skippers exhibit their greatest skills and their greatest weaknesses. I have tried to perfect techniques with this sail so that every detail of its setting is automatic, and to instill clockwork efficiency into my crews.

It is in light-to-moderate breezes that exacting spinnaker handling becomes critical—much more so than in heavy winds. When the wind is really blowing, your boat soon reaches its maximum hull speed. No matter what additional force is applied, no boat can exceed this optimum, which as you may know, is 1.34 times the square root of the waterline length. Under no circumstances, however, do I recommend the elimination of a spinnaker in hard breezes, except during ocean races in heavy seas. There are always lulls in the hardest of breezes in which the spinnaker can be advantageous. It's vital to realize that in hard winds the spinnaker must be sheeted very hard, making it as flat as possible, to prevent the boat from rolling to windward. When the breeze drops to gentle zephyrs, however, every additional ounce of thrust you can extract from that spinnaker will make the difference between winning and losing.

The downwind leg is where the spinnaker man really earns his keep, and if you have a first-rate man, you are fortunate indeed. This crew member must have the talent for intuitively anticipating the next cats-paw, he must have the patience needed for making endless minor sail adjustments, he must have a delicacy of touch that permits him to capture every little waft of breeze, and he must be an agile, experienced sailor. You must have complete confidence in him, for while you are at the helm concentrating on your sailing, it is impossible for you to supervise headsail work. In fact, you are intruding in the spinnaker man's domain if you habitually interfere in foredeck work. Once you are satisfied that you have picked a good man, turn the headsail work competely over to him. Don't try to be both skipper and first mate; it won't work. Voice your displeasure if something isn't being done to suit you, but then leave it to the spinnaker man to improve conditions on his own.

Training and Drill: The Key to Success

As soon as the committee signals your course, you should immediately run the compass course of each leeward leg and determine on which side the spinnaker will be carried and at what angle.

You must perfect the operations of setting the spinnaker, getting it down, and jibing it, and you must try to do these things in the least possible time. Now these things are rather elementary, but let's discuss each operation anyway, for nothing is as simple as it first sounds.

If your spinnaker is drawing a few seconds before your competitor's, you have gained just that much advantage over him. So you should aim for smoothness, speed, and accuracy in setting. The sail should be perfectly trimmed as it fills, and the jib lowered, in one smooth operation. The only way to do this is by practice—continual hard drilling. You must have mentally and physically prepared for setting the spinnaker long before you have approached the weather mark. Plan your tactics ahead of time, so when the order is given the operation will be performed smoothly.

The light or heavy spinnaker gear—whichever you have selected—and the pole will have been rigged before the start. The sheet should be gradually trimmed in as the sail is hoisted. Be sure you don't trim too quickly, or the spinnaker will fill prematurely and be difficult to hoist.

The goal of smartness and efficiency should also hold for lowering the spinnaker. It should come down quickly, without snags or hitches. Simultaneously, the jib should be hoisted and trimmed in one smooth continuous motion. The pole and spinnaker gear must be stowed if there are no further leeward legs to be sailed. Again, anticipate the actual

120

Columbia with her three-quarter ounce spinnaker nicely lifted.

maneuver when approaching the leeward mark, and have everything in readiness for the change of course, including yourself and the crew.

Spinnaker jibing is a powerful weapon in the arsenal of the racing man who can execute the maneuver quickly and properly. Jibing is simple in theory, but in yacht racing, the most hopeless foul-ups happen during this maneuver. You must constantly practice jibing by taking your boat out in different kinds of weather on a simulated racing course. Every man must know his job when going from jibe to jibe.

During the 1958 America's Cup races, *Columbia,* like the old sailing men-of-war, had a written station bill that ensured that every hand knew his position during each maneuver. If necessary, do the same for your boat so confusion doesn't reign. There is really no standard way that jibing techniques can be written down to the minutest detail. Each skipper must work out the procedure that best suits him and is within the capabilities of his crew.

Jibing from reach to reach is usually termed the "free-wheeling" jibe. It is the most difficult jibe of all, especially in a fresh breeze. Precision crewwork is most necessary. In this maneuver the sheet is eased, the spinnaker pole fitting removed from the tack, the pole dipped under the jibstay, and the fitting snapped onto the former clew, which has now become the new tack. For a brief moment during this procedure, the spinnaker is not attached to the pole, and the sail is in danger of collapsing or twisting upon itself unless, by careful helmsmanship, it is kept filled. The tiller must be put over at exactly the right moment. As the main boom swings over on the new tack, the sail should not break. It takes long practice by the crew to make the free-wheeling jib an effective part of your racing repertoire.

In your spinnaker practice sessions, be organized. Keep a critical eye open for methods that are cumbersome and require a lot of fumbling back and forth: simplify so there is no wasted time or motion. Keep a stopwatch from start to finish on the setting, lowering, and jibing, and seek constantly to shave seconds from your time. As I related earlier, during the 1961 International One-Design Class alumni race, when I had gotten together a crew of youngsters from the *Columbia,* including my son, I glanced over my shoulder to make sure we would clear the buoy mark for the downwind leg, and by the time I looked forward again there was the spinnaker up and drawing. The setting didn't take the boys over eight seconds: that's my idea of smart spinnaker work!

George O'Day, one of the finest small-boat sailors, has even gone so far as to get a friend to take movies of his boat in action. He then analyzed them, with the crew present, to see how performance could be improved. His record in small boats has proved the efficacy of this kind of attention to fine spinnaker handling.

THE TURTLE

The setting of spinnakers has been revolutionized since the "turtle" came into being. This ingenious device is a container that holds the spinnaker in a compact bundle on the forward deck where it can be instantly run up. It eliminates the need for tedious "stopping" with thread to prevent the wind from breaking it open and filling it prematurely. Originally the turtle was thought to be practical for smaller boats only, but during the America's Cup races in 1958, *Weatherly* housed her huge spinnakers in specially made three-pocket turtles with great success. The turtle is an improvement that I consider the greatest spinnaker-handling asset to come to the sport of yacht racing.

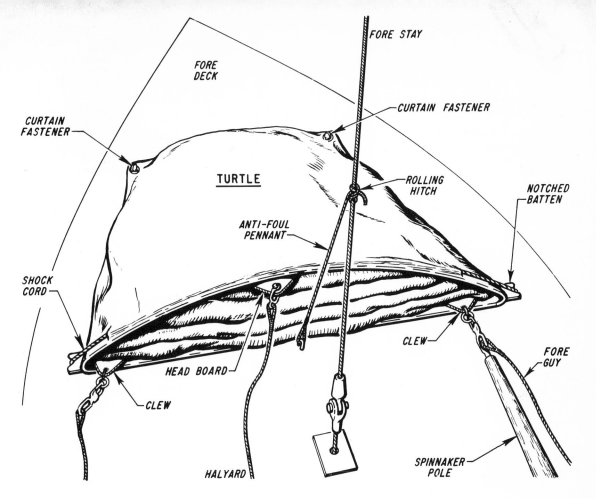

The spinnaker turtle.

The turtle was originated by Philip Benson of Marblehead and was introduced to Long Island Sound by my daughter Aileen. Many different versions of the turtle are in use. The one pictured here is made by Charles Ulmer of City Island; it consists of a dacron bag cut to fit the foredeck and held down by curtain fasteners. The size of the spinnaker determines the fullness of the upper part of the bag. A notched batten is inserted to hold the bottom flat against the deck: shock cord keeps the neck closed and holds the batten in place.

When the turtle is used, the spinnaker is folded with the two edges of the sail together and carefully stuffed into the bag; the tack, clew, and headboard protrude for attachment of the sheet, halyard, and guys. To prevent the spinnaker from fouling on the forestay as it is hoisted, a 12- or 15-inch lanyard is led from aft of the turtle up the headstay and secured with a rolling hitch. In larger boats, especially when the boat is rolling,

123

a spinnaker "net" or "web" is vital. Otherwise the spinnaker will turn around the headstay so tightly that it can take hours to clear it. A net is made of small line similar in size and shape to the working jib and is hoisted in the forward triangle.

Trimming the Spinnaker

There is a knack to trimming a spinnaker so that it pulls most efficiently. You want to get the sail up as high as you can, where it can catch the flow of the least-disturbed air possible. It should be set so that it lifts as high as possible with the wind; when the thrust is forward and up, the sail is developing its greatest pulling power.

The spinnaker man should not gad about the deck during a run, but should stay on the foredeck where he can watch the spinnaker's every ripple. In very light weather he must "play" the sheet with all the subtlety of a violinist, keeping it always full and drawing. He must watch the luff carefully, for it is here that ripples or a breaking of the spinnaker will show the first sign of wind change. The sheet of the spinnaker should be well flowed—eased out so the clew lifts as much as possible. Frequently, a smart yank on the spinnaker sheet will restore the contour of the sail if the airs are extremely light and it tends to collapse.

The spinnaker man should also glance constantly at the masthead fly, or permanent backstay tell tale, to make sure that the pole is always trimmed at right angles to the wind: the wind may back or veer a few points, and the trim must be adjusted accordingly. These flys are the surest indication of the apparent wind. Flys in the shrouds are of no use for gauging spinnaker trim, because stray air currents from the mainsail deflect them and they will not accurately indicate wind direction. These, however, should be used as indicators under reaching conditions.

When the breeze drops to vagrant puffs, the weight of snap shackles and heavy sheets will sometimes prevent the spinnaker from standing. A trick is to remove the heavy gear and tie a light but strong cord to the clew. Hold it in your hand, giving and taking with the varying strength of the breeze. You will be surprised how this will ghost you along when the puffs are hardly discernible.

To be properly set, the spinnaker pole should always form a right angle with the boat's mast. The exception to this is sailing on a close reach: here it is advisable to cock the pole so that the sheet can be flowed as much as possible. On a reach also, it is important to slack the spinnaker halyard slightly until the upper leech clears the jumper strut stays.

The foot of the spinnaker, from clew to tack, and the outboard end of the pole should form a straight line parallel to the horizon, no matter what the heeling angle of the boat. It is the horizon, not the deck of the boat, that should be the line of reference for the spinnaker foot, and adjustments should be made until this is so.

THE SPINNAKER IN HEAVY WEATHER

When sailing a spinnaker reach in heavy weather—the helmsman should sail below his normal course to avoid the unpleasant and some-times dangerous results of broaching. This can easily happen if the rudder rises clear of the water and loses its controlling force, or if the spinnaker suddenly breaks from the lurching of the hull in violent seas. Remember, with a spinnaker your boat is not always as responsive

Ray Hunt is designer and helmsman of *Chaje II* (#24), the 1963 5.5 meter World's Championship winner. His spinnaker is well lifted and perfectly trimmed. The spinnaker on the second boat is larger and not standing as well. It appears that if the sheet were eased considerably, the sail would lift and be more effective. The sheet on the third boat should also be freed. The main sheet could be eased further. The jib is bound to disturb the spinnaker and should be lowered. Even if the wind were on the beam, the jib would still bother the spinnaker.

A clear demonstration of what happens when the spinnaker sheet is eased too wide on a dead run.

and maneuverable as when under normal sail, and you must be psychologically prepared for all eventualities. This quality of alertness is one that yachting constantly demands.

In ocean racing during heavy weather, the genoa jib can frequently be set as a spinnaker. It is of much heavier material and will stand up where a nylon spinnaker of lighter material would break—if it could be set at all.

How to Stop Rolling to Windward

In very strong winds, a boat carrying a spinnaker, with the wind dead astern, will sometimes take violent rolls to windward, slatting and breaking her gear, and seriously concerning her crew. This unnatural leaning can be an unpleasant experience, for many sailors do not understand the forces at work. When the boat you are sailing is narrow beamed, this rolling to windward is accentuated and can be quite detrimental to her speed.

This sequence of photographs shows *Columbia* going through a jibe.

Now the reason for this rolling is that the spinnaker sheet has been flowed too far out and is causing the luff of the sail to cup inwards at the tack. The wind from aft drives into the center of the spinnaker, and because of its great force, is deflected around until it strikes the cup-shaped luff of the sail. Here, as can be seen from the diagram, the wind is concentrated with tremendous force and thrusts the vessel down on her beam ends to windward. The luff of the mainsail cupped against the mast adds further force to this windward heel.

As I have said, this is a disagreeable experience. The men of the ocean racing fleet who sailed to Bermuda in 1958 found this to be so to their dismay. The yachting magazines carried photographs of the many knockdowns at the start. By studying these photos carefully, one could see that each of these craft had been pulled over to windward by the luff of the spinnaker, just as if the wind had been blowing from the leeward side.

In my opinion it was not good judgment in the first place to have attempted to carry a spinnaker in those winds, which were of near gale force, because the advantage to be gained was not worth the risk, where gear must be preserved over a four- or five-day race. But once set, they could have been carried *if the spinnaker sheets had been trimmed as flat as possible.*

When the sheet is brought in, the spinnaker is flattened and the cup doesn't form at the luff. The wind cannot exert any thwartships pressure because there is nothing for it to get a grip on. A look at the second figure of the illustration will make this plain.

I realize it is hard to believe that so simple a thing can make such a great difference, but it does. I used to sail a 6-meter with an enormous spinnaker, and one day this very thing happened to me. I was sitting to leeward, when suddenly we rolled to windward in a heavy gust. The next thing I knew, I was up in the air and actually looking straight down at the water *to windward*. I was certain she would swamp as the water was coming in over the weather cockpit coaming. She righted herself, but the experience was the start of an important lesson for me. I finally realized that the problem was caused by incorrect trimming of the spinnaker sheet. After I learned that it should be trimmed hard in strong winds, this seldom happened.

If you sail 5:5's, 6-meters, Internationals, Lightnings, or narrow-beamed boats that carry abnormally large spinnakers, remember this heavy-weather technique with the sheet. It really works.

11. Tuning the Rigging

If your rigging is not well tuned, your boat cannot sail her best. There are many schools of thought on how rigging should be set up for racing. Most of them agree that a great deal of variation in the set of sails can be achieved by different adjustments to the rigging. I am convinced, however, that the most important requisite is that the mast be absolutely straight athwartships. This can be achieved by either slack or taut shrouds.

I prefer to start tautening the upper shrouds first and then the lower ones. I also like the uppers to be considerably tauter than the lowers, for they will carry the thrust of the major part of the rig. I set the lower shrouds much slacker than the uppers. Only by sighting up the mast with the eye at *deck level,* using the track of the mast slot as a guide, can you see the effect of tautening each adjustment.

The jumper stays counteract compression-strain to the headstay. Tauten them until there is a slight forward bow at the top of the mast. Next, set up the backstay until the mast is perfectly straight fore and aft. This is your zero or maximum forward position of the mast. Incidentally, it is a great convenience for adjustment purposes to have the stays lead to a position on the mast where they can be regulated from the deck. Diamond stays support the upper area of the mast, and in my opinion these stays should be set up as taut as physically possible before the mast is stepped.

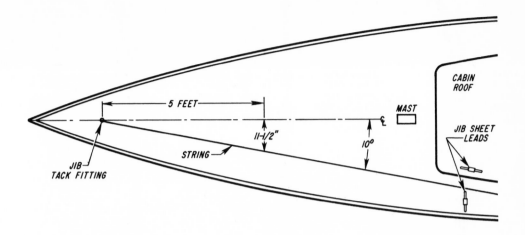

Determining the position of the jib leads.

After preliminary adjusting, take your boat for a sail and turn the helm over to a crew member. Sight up the mast from deck level to be sure it is straight when sailing on both tacks. There should be no inequality whatsoever.

Every time I sail my boat, I marvel at the ingenuity of Starling Burgess, who developed the permanent backstay rig, which I believe first came into being on his Atlantic Class boats in 1929. It is a triumph of modern engineering design, with each member a vital and interdependent part of the whole. With the exception of the upper shrouds, the whole intricate network is designed for one thing—to tauten the headstay so your boat will work to windward efficiently.

I think there is a lot of confusion regarding the functioning of the rig. If, in our imagination, we can follow the sequence of events that takes place when the permanent backstay is tightened, we can obtain a clear picture of the process. As the backstay tautens, the head of the mast comes aft, tightening the jumper stays. The jumpers in turn apply compression-loading to the jumper struts, which forces the upper part of the mast aft. This after movement of the mast then tautens the headstay.

Another case: as pressure fills the sails, the lower shrouds (which are secured to the mast opposite the jumper stays) and the jumper stays

133

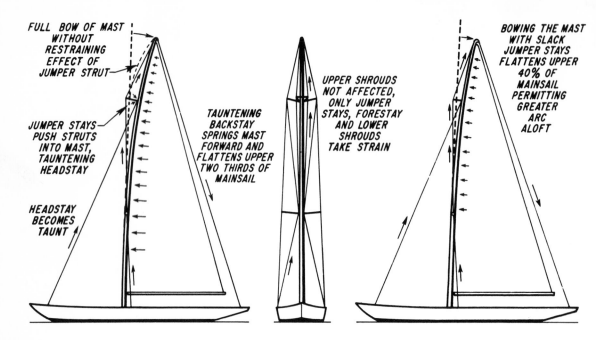

FULL BOW OF MAST WITHOUT RESTRAINING EFFECT OF JUMPER STRUT

JUMPER STAYS PUSH STRUTS INTO MAST, TAUNTENING HEADSTAY

HEADSTAY BECOMES TAUNT

TAUNTENING BACKSTAY SPRINGS MAST FORWARD AND FLATTENS UPPER TWO THIRDS OF MAINSAIL

UPPER SHROUDS NOT AFFECTED, ONLY JUMPER STAYS, FORESTAY AND LOWER SHROUDS TAKE STRAIN

BOWING THE MAST WITH SLACK JUMPER STAYS FLATTENS UPPER 40% OF MAINSAIL PERMITTING GREATER ARC ALOFT

Bowing the mast.

tauten. Again the mast is forced aft and the headstay must become more taut. The upper shrouds stiffen the mast so the full sail does not sag off to leeward. They are, however, completely unaffected by strains on the backstay jumpers and the headstay.

You must be careful not to overtauten stays. The word "tuning" makes some people think that shrouds and stays should be so taut that they "sing" like a violin string: this is not so, with the exception of the diamonds, as mentioned. Too much tightening puts an abnormal compression load on the struts and spreaders. When the sail fills, this stress further increases and may reach critical limits. I think a good rule of thumb is to tighten stays only hand taut (again with the exception of the diamonds), just taking up the slack.

The 12-meters use dynamometers to measure rigging and sheet strains. Simpler devices are available for use in small boats.

EFFECTS OF BOWING THE MAST

One of the great virtues of the permanent backstay is that changes can be made in the shape of the mainsail by judicious tightening and slackening of the backstay. When the backstay is tightened the center of the mast goes forward, thereby flattening the mainsail. You will decide the amount necessary by the strength of the wind. This adjustment is, of course, only made for windward work. The mast should be straight for reaching and running where maximum draft is required. Furthermore, tautening of the backstay in windward work makes the jib stand better because the headstay will be tauter. How much bow you will want in the mast depends on the amount of draft you want to remove from the mainsail at the head or along the entire luff. If in your opinion the mainsail is too drafty aloft, slack off your jumper-strut stays from their normal positions, thereby increasing the bow aloft, which will produce flatness in the upper area of the sail. Bear in mind that other compensating adjustments must therefore be made in the backstay and headstay, to arrive at a new zero mast position. A word of caution: *Do not bow your mast aft unless your upper spreaders can swing aft to conform to the new lead of the upper shrouds.*

When it becomes necessary to replace wire rigging, it is a good idea to make measurements with the turnbuckles opened about halfway. Wire will stretch along the direction of pull as it settles down and breaks in. After new wire has been installed, recheck the tuning frequently, and sight-in the mast again for straightness. Tighten turnbuckles as needed to take up the slack from stretching.

SHEET LEADS

The position of jib and mainsail fairleads affect the tuning and performance of your boat. The jib should be trimmed on a line about 10 degrees off the centerline of the boat measured from the jib-tack fitting. If your boat is beamy, you may need to place it along a 12-degree line.

To determine the 10-degree line, measure back 5 feet from the jib-tack pin and then 10½ inches outboard from the deck center line, and make a pencil mark. A string stretched through this point will represent the 10-degree line on which the jib sheet fairlead is to be placed. The lead on a genoa-equipped narrow boat such as a 6- or 12-meter would be reduced to 6 or 7 degrees.

I believe I place my working jib leads further forward than most racing men, for I find it makes the jib stand better and gives the foot of the sail a good airfoil shape. Don't worry if this looks strange—as if the clew were too far inboard; if you try it once, I think you'll be pleased at the way it improves your boat's performance. In harder breezes I move the leads a little aft and outboard. I am, of course, referring to conventional working jibs—not genoas.

135

The genoa mitre is a good guide for the lead. Normally, a continuation of the sheet should fall below the mitre line. In any event, make certain that the lead is not too far aft; if it is, the head of the sail will not stand.

Because I have found so much uncertainty about the proper trim of genoas, I suggest that the sail should never be trimmed beyond a point where the upper spreaders begin to interfere with the set of the sail.

I am a firm believer in the wisdom of using a wide traveler to carry the main sheet lead block if class rules permit. If the traveler extends across the whole width of the deck clear to the rail, you will have a more effective device for trimming the main than is possible with a single midships lead. By fixing the block to an adjustable slide, you will be able to position the sheet lead anywhere along the length of the traveler.

The advantages of using a wide traveler are several. On a reach it should be extended to its maximum; this will flatten the upper part of the sail, permit a wider trim and produce the same effect as a boom vang. For windward work the traveler should be amidships, thereby producing the greatest draft. As the breeze increases, the traveler should be moved out. This lead will tend to flatten the sail and trim the upper area more efficiently. A high-cut mainsail should be trimmed more amidships than a lower-cut sail. Except for reaching, I have found the traveler to be rather treacherous, and again I caution you to limit your adjustments in windward work to normal movements.

Once you have tuned your boat as well as you can at the mooring, take her out against a favorite competitor. Keep experimenting with the things that you have heard, learned, or suspected about tuning a boat's rigging. When you are convinced you have achieved perfection, assist your competitor while he tunes his boat. I have profited in this way on many occasions by sailing tuning trials with William S. Cox, an excellent helmsman in any size boat, and especially adept in trimming his boats well.

Use a Boom Vang

There is hardly a sailboat that cannot be improved by fitting of a boom vang, or "boom jack," as it is sometimes called. The refinements of sail trim that you can get by using it are many, and it is especially valuable off the wind. If your boat is not already fitted with one, and the class rules do not prohibit it, I would certainly urge you to try one of these effective devices. The accompanying diagram shows in detail how a vang is made and fitted.

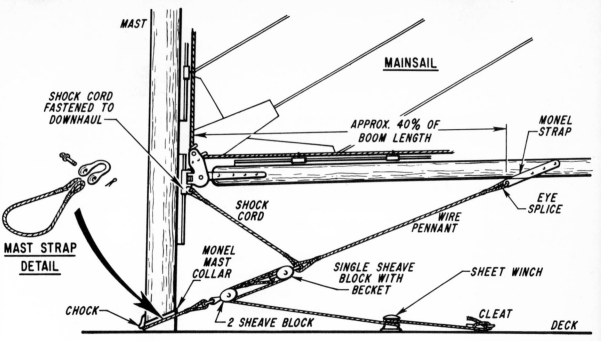

The boom vang.

The vang keeps the boom from lifting when the mainsail is suddenly filled by a gust of wind or the boat lurches from a violent seaway. It allows the sail to swing in only one plane like a door: all the power that would otherwise be wasted is captured to drive your boat ahead. The sheet can be eased much further without luffing if a vang is used. A mainsail always luffs aloft first, and must be trimmed to remedy this condition. The upper and lower areas of the sail will luff simultaneously if a vang is used, and this is a decided advantage. In light airs you need as much draft as you can get, so do not set the boom vang, for it flattens the sail too much.

Because a boom vang exerts enormous strain on the boom, and because all fittings must have a large built-in safety factor, I would use oversize hardware and through-bolt the gooseneck track and mast. The bolts should be of small diameter and widely spaced so the mast is not weakened by excessive drilling.

Arthur Knapp, Jr., skipper of *Weatherly* in the 1958 America's Cup trials, a man who habitually gets the most out of a boat in light weather, has capitalized on the use of the boom vang more than any competitor I have ever raced against.

RUNNING RIGGING

With the advent of synthetic rope, keeping the running rigging in shape is a pleasure. Nylon and dacron will not rot or mildew and have an excellent diameter-to-breaking-strength ratio. We can now use smaller lines than formerly, when only manila and linen were available as rope materials.

I prefer conventional three-strand dacron line for sheets, guys and halyards. I find that braided line kinks and, furthermore, can produce more severe hand burns. Three-strand nylon can be used anywhere that elesticity in a rope is desirable. It makes superior anchor rope and docking lines, as the elasticity cushions shock well.

Since synthetic lines do not swell, it is possible to buy lines that exactly fit the sheave groove of blocks; no extra clearance is needed. Where rope-to-wire splices are common, as in halyards, be sure to inspect the point of joining frequently. This is a vulnerable area, and it is fairly certain that dacron reacts to stainless steel unpredictably because of incompatible chemical characteristics.

Chafe is the greatest enemy of running rigging, so watch for it and try to prevent it. Split pieces of polyethylene tubing can be taped around shrouds to provide a roller bearing surface wherever sheets contact them. Turnbuckles and sharp metals should be wound with tape to prolong the life of rope and fabric.

Keep lots of small maintenance materials aboard your boat for emergency repairs and jury rigging. A roll of stainless steel annealed wire is the bosun's best friend for any number of seizing jobs.

Learn the sailmaker's whipping. Don't be guilty of leaving running rigging unserved. It marks the landlubber, or even worse—a slovenly sailor.

12. Maintaining Your Boat

About half the pleasure of sailing for me has been maintaining the boat. When I was a boy, I could never sail until I had cleaned her up and polished all the brass. It would take me close to an hour to polish all the cleats and winches, and after a half-hour's sail the salt spray made the brass just as dull as ever. I didn't consider that work futile, because I had the satisfaction of seeing the fittings shiny and sparkling in the sun.

To my eyes there is something beautiful about boats, and I love to spend hours just looking at them. I am very demanding in my standards of maintenance, and I can't tolerate seeing a boat in a run-down condition. I think that even minor neglect reflects on the character of the owner. In my opinion, he doesn't deserve the joy of owning a boat if he will not properly maintain her.

PAINTWORK

Caring for paintwork is a fussy, time-consuming chore, but fortunately it is the kind of work that the owner can do well himself. Shipyard costs come high these days, so after the yard has applied the initial fitting-out painting, the owner should do routine touching-up and varnishing.

I wonder if there will ever be a foolproof paint for use on boats. When wood is exposed to water, many actions and reactions occur. Paints that are successful in one place under certain conditions sometimes fail when used in another location under different conditions. When I present the shipyard with the annual work list, I generally specify the brand of paint I want used and do not leave the choice to the yard's discretion. I don't know exactly why, but a brand that works well in one part of the country is sometimes unsuitable in another. Probably the chemical composition of the local atmosphere and waters have a great deal to do with this variation.

When you discover a boat in your area with a beautiful finish that you admire, ask the owner what brand he is using. Also ask how well it stands up, for a coating that looks good only during the first week after leaving the yard can be an expensive disappointment.

Topsides

Nothing looks so beautiful as smooth, gleaming topsides, which show the natural lines and curves of the freeboard to good advantage. The secret of smart-looking topsides is time and care spent in preparing the surface before painting. The seams must be smooth, and any nicks and gouges should be carefully filled with a hard-curing trowel cement.

There is a knack to applying trowel cement. It should be put on with a very flexible, wide-bladed putty knife. Best results are obtained by applying several thin layers rather than one thick one. Allow the cement to dry thoroughly between each coat, and brush lightly with a fine open-coat garnet paper. Try to get your topsides to look as if they were molded of one piece rather than made up of many strakes of planking. By rubbing your fingers over the hull, you can feel bumps and unfairnesses that might not be apparent to the eye before the hull is painted, but that would show after painting.

For topsides, I prefer a glossy paint rather than a semi-gloss paint, even though greater care is required to get a smooth finish with glossy paint. It is true that semi-gloss doesn't show laps as much as gloss, and that hull irregularities are more easily hidden, but I think that the greater beauty of the glossy finish is worth the extra labor involved.

The Underbody

If your boat is to win races for you, it must have the smoothest underbody obtainable. One of the factors that slows a sailboat is skin friction of the water flowing past the bottom surface. Any bumps or irregularities increase this friction: the smoother you can get the bottom, the faster your boat will go. It is interesting to note that tank tests have shown that wax does not improve the surface of the bottom. Certain detergents, however, are effective in this regard, although they, of course, are soon washed off. Both *Columbia* and *Sceptre* used detergents in this way during the 1958 America's Cup races.

William E. John, chairman of the International class, contacted scientists at the Stevens Institute, hoping for a definitive answer to the question of what exactly is the fastest bottom finish. He was told that the speed variation between bottom finishes in the modern racing boat was less than one-half of one percent, or hardly enough to be significant. In addition to its physical effects, keeping the boat's bottom clean and free of unfairness will help keep you psychologically at ease, and this is important in winning races also. I have recently learned that new bottom paint tests are about to be conducted with the Stevens Institute tank, and the results should be interesting.

A bottom finish must also be antifouling if you race in salt water. Any hard finish, such as epoxy, serves well for a racing dinghy or any boat that is dry sailed. But if your boat stays in the water any length of time, or if your class rules limit the number of times you may haul during the season, then you will want your bottom finish to have anti-fouling properties. Since different local waters have different marine organisms that foul the bottom, it is best to find out what finish the racing men in your club have discovered to be most successful.

Even after only a comparatively short time at the mooring, a coating of slimy algae can accumulate on the bottom of your boat. At least once a week I swim under the hull and wipe the bottom with a towel to remove this growth; it is surprising how much drag algae can create—especially after the middle of the summer. Since aqualungs have come into general use, many of the International skippers have bought them for this specific purpose.

DECKS

On my boat I prefer to keep a glossy deck without anti-skid compound mixed in the paint. Bleached teak decks, of course, are very beautiful, but when decks are canvas covered, I like to see them shine. I even go so far as to lace my deck paint with varnish to build up a mirror-like finish. Many racing men think that decks should be coated with an antiskid agent to help prevent crew members from falling overboard. Personally, I don't like this treatment of the deck, since it is so difficult to keep clean. "Topsiders" or even wet socks will make for surefootedness even on the glossiest decks.

When antiskid compound is added to deck paint, it is well nigh impossible to keep decks looking really smart. Dirt and harbor-film lodge in the little valleys formed by the added particles, and no matter how diligent you are with your washing down, the surface always looks dingy. If pumice is used as an antiskid agent in the paint, decks become like a huge sheet of sandpaper: clothes will wear out and knuckles are skinned with regularity. If ground-up rubber particles are added, the paint coating wears off the tops of the little bumps first; your deck soon has a "salt-and-pepper" look and must be repainted.

Try your best to maintain the water-tight integrity of your decks. Fresh water from rain or snow promotes the growth of mold and rot fungi quicker than anything else. Where shrouds or stays run through holes in the deck, put rubber stoppers in the holes when you leave the boat at the mooring. White rubber sink stoppers from the hardware store can be cut with holes of slightly smaller diameters than the shrouds or the stays. The stoppers can then be trimmed to fit and shoved into the deck holes, and the shrouds or stays can be threaded through the stoppers. This will keep a lot of water from seeping below.

Interior

Keep the interior of your boat's cabin as dry, fresh-smelling and clean as possible. There is no reason for the interior to become fetid or musty-smelling and therefore unpleasant. To avoid this, keep the cabin well ventilated and the bilges scrupulously clean. When sailboats are left at the mooring, they are generally wind-rode, that is, they lie with the bow facing into the breeze. This, in effect, creates a forced draft that can be utilized to ventilate the cabin.

A patent cowl ventilator, which permits air to enter but excludes water should be fitted as far forward as possible. For racing, a deckplate can be installed in the deck with a screw cover, permitting removal of the ventilator to keep the deck clear. The companionway slide can be made with louvered vents and covered with a plastic screen to let air through but no insects. The breeze will enter the forward ventilator and exhaust through the louvered slide, providing a constant flow of fresh air. When you leave the boat for any length of time, open locker doors and drawers slightly to permit fresh air to enter freely.

Don't allow rope, wiping rags, or other gear to accumulate into sodden piles at the backs of lockers. Fit hooks and shelves to hang life preservers and rope neatly where air can circulate through them. Make sure that all nonstructural bulkheads and partitions that divide the cabin into restricted areas have patterns of ventilating holes bored into them. Proper ventilation is extremely important if you would keep your boat's cabin pleasant and livable.

Most of the International class members prefer a lustrous white or slightly off-white paint in the cabin. It brightens up the interior. Don't use a dark color. Not much light penetrates into a small boat cabin, and darker colors have little cheeriness.

Sometimes, despite adequate ventilation, mildew will grow on cabin surfaces. A fungicide added to the paint will prevent mildew from forming. Most of the major paint manufacturers produce effective fungicide additives under different brand names. Incidentally, check all hidden spots—such as underneath the deck, or behind clamps, knees, etc.— for fungi.

BILGES

Be sure that the cabin sole floorboards are fitted so they can be easily removed for inspection and cleaning. If your hull is ever holed, you want to be able to get down into those bilges quickly to ascertain the damage and stop the leak. I have been aboard boats where all the cabin furniture was securely screwed to the floorboards, and others where the boards were either swollen so tight or fastened down with so many screws that it would have taken a day to pry them loose.

Cleaning the bilges regularly must be a part of routine maintenance. It is inevitable that dust and dirt will drop down to lodge there. A weekly cleaning with a good detergent followed by a rinse with fresh water, which is then pumped overboard, will prevent foul bilgewater odors and help insure a long life for your boat. A long-handled bathroom brush is ideal for scrubbing out the bays between the frames.

In most boats, the limber holes are not large enough. Sooner or later they clog up with debris and fail to drain bilgewater to the pump intake. Take a rat-tail file or wood rasp and enlarge the openings to a generous size. While you are down in the bilge, use a small oil can to squirt Cuprinol into the limber holes and the ends of the frames, for this is a favoraite place for dry rot to start.

If your boat does not already have one, rig a limber chain through the holes to clear them. A limber chain is merely a brass chain of small diameter that is threaded through the limber holes fore-and-aft and attached by one end to a spring. When the chain is tugged the holes are cleared of debris and drain freely.

PLANKING

Inspect your planking frequently for unfairness and breaks in the paint. Paint that is cracked in a long fore-and-aft line usually indicates a check that has opened in the wood. Unfairness is an indication that fastenings have either pulled out or wrung off in drying. Pulled-out fastenings are usually the first sign that ribs have developed dry rot in the way of the screw. Hairline checks can be filled with trowel cement and repainted. Small seam openings can be recaulked with some of the new synthetic Thiokol-base compounds, such as Alroy's 707 or Woolsey's "Caw King." These compounds expand and contract as the planking dries during storage ashore and require no specialized skills to use.

FRAMES AND FASTENERS

Frames should be inspected at the turn of the bilge, as improper shoring-up during storage will sometimes cause transverse cracks. Dry rot seems to affect oak ribs more frequently than it affects other structural members, so include them in a regular inspection program. A good preventive measure is to paint ribs with Cuprinol or one of the other copper-naphthenate preservative-fungicides. If ribs are badly damaged, sister frames can be installed alongside the defective ones. Unless you have near-professional skills, however, this is a job for the shipyard.

Occasionally, in an iron-fastened boat, rusting of a fastener head will cause the wooden plug over the fastener to obtrude. This can be cured by removing the plug, chipping off the rust, daubing the head with several coats of red lead or Rustoleum, and putting in a new plug with waterproof glue. If many plugs are raised, something is wrong with the fastening method, and a thorough inspection should be made to determine the cause. If large numbers of the fastenings are bad, refastening of the complete hull may be necessary; this too is a major repair job and should be done by a yard.

TIE RODS, KNEES, AND BRACES

Sometimes when a racing boat is built with too light scantlings, the designer finds it necessary to support the mast partners, the shelf and clamp in the way of the mast partners, and parts of the hull with bracing, strapping, and tie rods. Quite often these members will be made of galvanized wrought iron. Now wherever iron passes through wooden timbers, especially if they are oak, a rust problem arises. It is essential that ferrous-metal components be maintained carefully to prevent failure under stress. Keep iron well painted and use an oil can to drop a light fish-oil rust preventive wherever iron contacts wood and cannot be painted. Whenever feasible, iron members should be replaced with bronze or monel, if replacement does not involve tearing the hull to pieces. Sometimes insulating the iron part from faying surfaces with a rubber or tarred-felt gasket will stop excessive rusting, but this too generally requires major carpentry.

HARDWARE

When installing hardware, be sure that you place padding blocks under the deck and on the inside of planking to help distribute the strain upon the fastenings. The blocks should be smeared with a luting compound on the faying surfaces. Especially, never install seacocks or scuppers through the planking without padding blocks.

If it is necessary to change the locations of cleats, fairleads, or other hardware, make certain that you plug the old fastener holes. Do not use common dowel sticks, but use the same kind of wood as that to be plugged: dip the plug in waterproof glue before driving, and it will never fall out.

MAST

The racing yachtsman must pay great attention to the proper maintenance of his mast. Any failure will surely cost him not only a race, but a loss in overall fleet standing as well. The International class boats have Sitka spruce masts, and Sitka spruce has a tendency to splinter when it is not protected from the effects of weathering. Be certain that you get some paint or varnish into the mast groove where the bolt rope of the sail slides. Some skippers use neither paint nor varnish in the groove, but wax it so the sail slides up and down easily. If you use wax, be sure that the surface of the interior of the groove is well covered with wax, and keep waxing the bolt rope and the sail stitching at the luff throughout the season.

If your boat uses sail track instead of a mast groove, the track must be securely fastened to the mast to withstand the twisting strain of the gooseneck. Since Sitka spruce is soft, the track should not be fastened directly to the mast, but to a hardwood batten that is glued and screwed to the mast. Several through-bolts should be driven through the bottom of the track, at the region of the gooseneck fitting and at the top of the mast. Do not use bolts of overlarge diameter, however, or you will seriously weaken the mast.

Where spreaders, jumper-strut pads, or tangs are secured to the mast, be sure that a bedding compound is used beneath the metal parts. Moisture has a habit of collecting in these locations, and they are ideal places for rot to start. Always use a bedding compound that will maintain its elasticity and not dry out with time. While you are working on the upper mast, it does no harm to brush Cuprinol beneath the hardware.

One section of the mast that frequently causes trouble is the base. Unless precautions are taken, dampness here promotes dry rot. Every hollow mast and the mast step itself has drain holes to allow condensation and accumulated water to escape. These drain holes must be kept open and cleared of obstructions. Use a long, stiff wire to clear the mast and mast-step drain holes before the mast is stepped at the beginning of the season. While you are at it, take this opportunity to apply Cuprinol to the base of the mast and the mast step. It is a good idea at this time, also, to fit a metal collar around the base of the mast to protect the butt when lowering and stepping the mast. This collar should ride on bronze or stainless steel straps secured to the mast step.

Boom

It is seldom that a boom not fitted with a boom vang causes trouble. However, when a boom vang is used, tremendous strains are exerted as the vang is bowsed down. We had a great deal of trouble with broken booms in the International class until we found and remedied the cause. The vangs formerly consisted of a wire that led through a hole in the boom near its center. The concentration of strain at this hole was causing the booms to break. Now we use long monel straps to distribute the strain, and broken booms have become a rarity. It is most important that your gooseneck track be thoroughly reinforced on the mast. The thrust of the boom when the vang is set is enormous.

Incidentally, do not let the boom bang across in a hard breeze when the vang is set, since the boom can be broken.

Rigging

Rigging failure is the greatest cause of racing-sailboat breakdown. Despite this well-known fact, the rigging is usually the last item to receive attention. I would no more think of entering a series without a thorough rigging inspection than I would of entering without sails; frequently it amounts to the same thing.

Wire rigging is usually 1 x 19 stainless steel wire rope. Though stainless steel withstands loading and weathering well, it reacts poorly to vibration. With constant vibration, stainless steel fatigues; the metal crystallizes and the strands break. For this reason you must keep a constant check on your rigging for broken strands. By running your hand down the full length of a shroud of stay, you can immediately feel a broken strand. Stainless steel, incidentally, is not completely stainless; it will rust somewhat. It is necessary, therefore, to lubricate wire rigging with light machine oil from time to time.

Patent fittings, which have all but replaced eye splices, often cause rigging failures. There are any number of them on the market; most of them utilize the principle of swaging under pressure. This operation is usually done at the factory and requires specialized machinery. If a fitting is improperly swaged, damage to the fitting sometimes results. All fittings should be carefully inspected under a magnifying glass for imperfections or hairline cracks, and if any are found, the shroud should be removed and sent to a professional rigger for installation of a new fitting. If these patent devices are made of stainless steel, they too are subject to failure from metal fatigue. Patent fittings are usually designed with a large built-in safety factor, but this is no reason to neglect them.

Patent fittings should be sealed with a rubber sealant where the wire rope enters the fitting. This should be done before the rigging is put into use; if the sealant is run in after use, it only traps moisture already present, and rust will develop. If the rigging has been used, do not employ a sealant, but occasionally run oil into the fitting to prevent rust. Wherever

147

rigging wire terminates in sockets, clevises, or toggles, pay close attention to maintenance; these often cause trouble.

It is best to avoid the use of turnbuckles aloft, because they are difficult to service. If a turnbuckle aloft is necessary, use silicon bronze rather than stainless steel; it is less subject to vibration fatigue.

13. Piloting and Navigation
for the Racing Skipper

Next to wind and water, I think that the Lord's greatest gift to the seafarer is the mariner's compass. This simple device is responsible for more of man's triumphs than would be possible to record in a good-sized library. Though the most important feature of the compass is its ability to point the way, for the racing man it has other functions as well.

Besides getting you home in a fog, the compass can show the favored end of the starting line; it can locate an elusive buoy; it can reveal hidden currents; and it can help to show whether you are sailing well. Therefore, I consider it one of the most important pieces of racing equipment in the boat. It should be constantly used in sailing to windward to determine if you have been headed or lifted.

Like most man-made things, the compass is subject to errors. These errors are magnified with a cheaply made instrument; for this reason, try to purchase the best compass you can afford. The features to look for in a mariner's compass are as follows:

It should have a large card that is easy to read; it should be sensitive; and it should have good damping action, so the card does not swing crazily with motion of the boat. There are many good compasses on the market, and choice is largely a matter of preference. For the larger boats, I like a spherical-domed compass such as the Kelvin and White "Constellation," because the plastic dome magnifies the card and makes it easier to read. This model also has a built-in set of variable compensating magnets so it can be adjusted without placing external magnets.

I also prefer a compass that is graduated in both points and degrees. I was brought up with the point system, at a time when the degree-graduated compass was referred to as a "steamboatman's compass"—not without a note of derision. Yacht sailing is the last residing place of many venerable traditions, a heritage from the days when a rugged breed of men carried the world's cargoes and fought the nation's battles in wind-driven ships. Perhaps I will be thought overly romantic or nostalgic, but I think that the sailboat man should keep some of that tradition alive if it is not to become dead past—but not to the point of eliminating gear that adds to your racing competence or sailing pleasure.

Besides the historical implications, there is a practical value to a compass card graduated in points. Since they are larger, points are much easier to see. It is consequently simpler to keep the lubber's line of the compass lined up and a lot of sawing back and forth with the tiller is eliminated.

If you are a newcomer to sailing, be sure that you are thoroughly acquainted with the use of the mariner's compass and the meaning of and difference between the terms "deviation" and "variation." Any good elementary book on piloting, such as Chapman's *Piloting, Seamanship and Small Boat Handling*,* or a course at the United States Power Squadrons or the Coast Guard Auxiliary, will teach the essentials of basic compass work. Be sure you thoroughly understand this subject, for it is absolutely indispensable to successful racing and cruising.

PLACING THE COMPASS

Whenever possible the compass should be placed on the centerline of the boat in a manner that makes it visible from both port and starboard steering positions. When this is impossible, it should be placed on a fore-and-aft line parallel to the centerline. Care must be taken that the lubber line represents the true direction of the keel, or serious errors will result.

I like to mount my compass forward in the cockpit, and high enough that it is within the natural line of vision when sailing the boat. I don't

* Charles F. Chapman, *Piloting, Seamanship and Small Boat Handling*, New York: Motor Boating.

believe it wise to take your eyes from the progress of the race more than is absolutely necessary, and if the instrument is below the line of sight, you must lower your glance constantly to check the course. For night sailing it is good practice to install a rheostat on the compass light, so the intensity can be varied to suit conditions and the preference of the helmsman.

Movable iron should not be stored within 7 feet of the compass or it will aberrate the magnetic field of the needle. Permanent iron is less critical, since it can be compensated for by adjustment. Unless you have had previous experience and thoroughly understand the technique, I would leave annual compass adjustment to a professional. Their fees are moderate and you can be sure that the job will be properly done. After the adjustment, run a series of courses, say four in each quadrant of the compass, using prominent landmarks that will not likely be subject to change. Record the readings on your chart, in a log book, or on a card, and file it away for safe keeping. Each year when your boat is recommissioned, and at other intervals, run the courses again and note whether there have been changes in the compass readings. If none appear, the instrument has not developed errors and can safely be used another season; if there is significant difference, the compass must be readjusted.

A compass, like any other precision instrument, must be carefully handled and properly maintained if it is to remain accurate. To protect the plastic dome from the sun's rays, a canvas cover should be kept over the compass and binnacle when the compass is not in use. A domed compass is made with a chamber to allow for expansion and contraction of the fluid under different temperatures. The appearance of an air bubble means that the expansion chamber diaphragm or the gasket has sprung a leak. Do not attempt to repair this yourself, and do not add fluid to eliminate the bubble. Return the compass to the manufacturer for a complete overhaul and accuracy check. When the compass is stored for an extended period of time, turn it upside down to remove friction from the jeweled pivot.

THE COMPASS AS A RACING AID

The first thing the compass can do to help win your race is establish the best spot to cross the starting line. In theory, the race committee will try to lay out the starting line perfectly square to the direction of the wind. In practice, however, this is not always done. Usually the line is not at true right angles to the wind, and one end or the other will be the "favored" place to cross. Now your major concern will be to find out which end of that line is the favored end.

One simple and quick way is to place your boat with the head into the wind right on the starting line. Whichever end of the line her bow falls off toward is the favored end. A better and more accurate method is to establish the favored end by compass bearing.

To do this, bring the boat exactly head-to-wind; the compass reading at this time shows the true wind direction. Next, sail along the starting line on the starboard tack with your jibstay on the white flag on the committee boat and your backstay on the buoy flag at the other end of the line. At the moment when the fore-and-aft centerline of your boat is identical with the line from the buoy to the committee boat flag, take your compass bearing. Be sure that you are truly lined up with the white starting flag and not merely the bow or stern of the committee boat, because your start is observed from this angle only.

If too many competitors are in the area and the starting line is jammed, sail out beyond the buoy, line up the buoy flag with the committee boat white flag and while sailing directly on this line take your compass bearing.

Now, whichever end of the line is closest to the direction of the wind will be the advantageous place to cross.

For example: Using a hypothetical wind direction of north, if the bearing obtained when the flags were lined up was west, then it is obvious that the starting line is square to the direction of the wind. In this case, it is possible to cross anywhere on the line without losing advantage, since the distance to the weather mark is the same everywhere on the line.

Again with a wind direction of north, let us suppose that the bearing is west-by-north—or its reciprocal, east-by-south. In this case, we can see by consulting the diagram that the westerly end of the line is favored. Conversely, if the bearing was west-by-south—the reciprocal is east-by-north—then the favored place to cross would be the eastern end of the starting line.

If you have gotten out of practice, it is an excellent idea to go through simulated compass work at home. Use a compass rose with a pencil laid over it to represent the boat, and a cut-out cardboard arrow to represent the wind. Keep changing the direction of the imaginary starting line and work diligently until you can immediately call off the reciprocal of any compass bearing without hesitation.

There are other important ways that the compass can help you to sail a better race. For example, before the race starts, put your boat on the same heading as the second leg of the course and see if you will be able to carry a spinnaker and how well it will stand. This will save time and costly mistakes when you reach the weather mark. Similarly, for the third leg, which will probably be a run, use your compass to sail on the heading and see on which side you will carry your spinnaker. With this information you can rig spinnaker gear in advance and save many boat lengths over competitors who have arrived late or who have neglected this important preparation.

Your compass can also be a valuable tool for ascertaining whether you are getting the most out of the available wind. Frequently, when sailing on a large body of water with few landmarks, when there is light haze, or when the legs of the course are so long that the marks fall below the horizon, you must rely wholly on compass courses to raise the next mark. This is an ideal opportunity to use the compass to develop your "wind sense." Regularly check your heading; it is possible to tell whether you are being "headed" by the breeze, or if, perhaps, you might be getting the advantage of a momentary "lift." Playing the puffs this way can save you a tack and sometimes gain yards that might otherwise have been lost.

CHARTS

You should not fail to carry a local chart aboard even if you are racing in an area where you were born and brought up. It is rarely feasible to chart courses during a small boat race—they must be prepared beforehand —but nonetheless the chart should be aboard. After the race is over, you can mark on it places where you picked up a certain land breeze, or where you hit a dead spot. By doing this over the course of a season, you can compile a kind of wind pattern chart for your local waters related to objects inland and contours of the shore.

It is a job for an octopus to lay out a course on a large-scale chart while a small racing boat is heaving in a sea. The skipper usually doesn't need the chart except under unusual circumstances, in which case the first mate can find the reference for him. There is seldom a flat surface large enough to spread the chart out fully. To lay an accurate course is most difficult. A much better idea is to compile an indexed book listing every possible course for the waters where you habitually race.

I would like to pass on the system I have evolved over the years, and which has proved invaluable to me. Except for regattas away from home, our International races are usually held in Long Island Sound. We race in an area that can be contained within a rectangle roughly 10 miles wide by 30 miles long. In my spare time at home, I have laid compass courses to, from, and between every buoy, every lighthouse, every prominent landmark within this area. I then entered the courses in a loose-leaf book, cataloged by area and listed alphabetically.

This involves laying hundreds of courses, and although it seems like a complicated and cumbersome device, it isn't; it is just a matter of good indexing and careful preparation. For example, if I want the Guggenheim tower or the Glen Cove breakwater, these courses are cataloged from my Larchmont home buoy; I list them the other way around and cross-index them, too—from Guggenheim and Glen Cove breakwater to Parsonage Point buoy, Larchmont, etc.

I constantly thank my stars that I evolved this method, because it has constantly helped me in my racing. Here is a hypothetical example. You start a race sailing a course of east-by-south, but you find that because a competitor luffed you way out, or because you altered your course to pick up a new wind, you are steering a totally different course heading. If you cannot see the next mark, if a light haze or a low-lying fog makes up, you have no departure. You started off east-by-south, but now you are way above that course and you must determine how far up you are and what new course to set to reach that mark.

If there is any object that is marked on the chart—a flagpole, a water tower, visible on the shoreline, or a buoy, you can take your departure from that. You flip to the proper page of your book and select a new course that will bring you to the mark. If the mark you are searching for is not directly on the line of your new course, you can make a quick mental adjustment of a fraction of a point, but at least you will have a fairly accurate idea of where to head.

It is a blessing to have these courses laid out beforehand and not have to go through the throes of frantically plotting an emergency heading in the middle of a demanding race. This is just another one of those hundred little things that can mean the difference between becoming a champion or remaining an also-ran.

TIDES AND CURRENTS

It is important for the racing man to have a knowledge of the action of the tides. Not because the tides themselves are so important, but because tidal action bears an important relationship to currents. The currents we are primarily interested in are those called "tidal currents," because they are caused by the ebbing and flooding of the tide. Other currents exist, such as the ocean currents of the world, a result of the earth's rotation. These are of extreme importance to the ocean racer and many of them have fascinating histories and peculiarities. The Gulf Stream is an example of an important ocean current that is not caused by tidal action; it is a large factor in successfully competing in the classic Bermuda race.

The actions of tidal currents are of primary interest to the small boat racer; and unfortunately many small boat sailors are profoundly ignorant of this importance. I would venture to say that half the skippers at the starting line of any race have no idea what the current will be doing at every hour throughout that race. And yet current can make or ruin your start: it can win or lose the finish.

For the beginner in racing sail, I would again recommend thorough study of Chapman's *Piloting, Seamanship and Small Boat Handling,* to provide a basic understanding of piloting problems and techniques—including corrections for current. The book is a classic and should form part of the library of every sailor. Courses given by the United States Power Squadrons are invaluable, and they are given free of charge.

The chief techniques and factors that you should know about are: how to construct a vector diagram to allow setting of a compass course that allows for current; the rhythm of rise and fall of the tide and how it affects current velocity; the meaning of the terms *set* and *drift;* the difference between speed over the bottom as opposed to speed through the water; and the effect of leeway in making good a desired course. Let us now discuss the aspects of current that are of particular significance in sailboat racing.

Before you sail out to the starting line, you should have learned the times of current change (which are not the same as the times of low and high tides). From this information and the U.S. Coast and Geodetic Survey current tables you can figure the times of the tide change. If the C. & G.S. publishes a set of tidal-current charts for your area, you should certainly invest in them. With the aid of these tables and charts, make a small card that lists the current conditions at every half-hour throughout the length of time you might be racing. Don't overlook the possibilities that starts can be delayed, and that the wind can fall light, and that you may be out on the water past the time the race is scheduled to end.

In addition to the velocity of the current, be sure you have its direction firmly in mind. Remember that direction does not always merely reverse itself by 180 degrees from, say, flood to ebb, but often makes considerable deviations at half and maximum flood or ebb conditions. It is for this reason that the current charts are particularly valuable, as they graphically show the true direction of the current at any time. In any case, try to have a complete and accurate picture in your mind for each sailing leg of the course, including whether the current will be with you, against you, or at an oblique angle to your course.

The first occasion you will have to use tide calculations is at the start. You can always use a head tide as a "brake" or retarding force to gain time before the starting gun fires. On the other hand, you must take care that a fair tide does not set you over the line prematurely, or cause you to foul the committee boat. A fair tide can also set you in a position where you will become the burdened boat, and you will be without rights over boats that are to windward of you. So in every maneuver that you make at the start, be aware of the effects that tidal currents will have on your strategy.

We are all aware of current in light weather because it is so evident. As you go by a buoy, the committee boat, or any object that is anchored, you can see the current streaming by and it makes an impression on your consciousness. When the breeze is hard, even many good skippers will discount tidal currents, under the assumption that because the boat is moving fast, current is largely overcome by speed. This is a decided mistake. Current is just as much a factor to be reckoned with in heavy weather as in light.

With a little reflection it is easy to visualize the reason for this. Consider the current as a river, and think of your boat as sailing within a huge basin of water that is floating in this river. Now, no matter how fast your boat is sailing within this basin, the basin, boat and all, is being carried along by the flow of the river. This displacement, as it were, is constant for the velocity of the current and unaffected by the speed of the boat. Therefore, be sure you do not neglect to figure the effect of current even in hard sailing breezes.

When you are running out your time at the start, be sure that you have allowed minutes—either subtracted from or added to your running time—for the effects of adverse or favorable tide. No one can figure this margin by mathematics alone; there are too many factors involved. The best procedure is to make several practice runs and time the exact requirements of each leg with a stopwatch.

Here is an important suggestion. If the tide is favorable—that is, if it is setting you across the starting line, jibe back to the line after your run instead of tacking. By jibing, you will be able to cross at the precise spot that you had previously selected. If you tack instead, you will obviously be set to windward and unable to run the same course on your return.

CURRENT AND THE WEATHER MARK

Your tactic, naturally, should always be to arrive at the weather mark as quickly as you can, and it is important to arrive there on the starboard tack. Tidal current as you approach the weather mark can make or break your race. It is unforgivably bad seamanship to overstand the weather mark because you have failed to allow for current. If you overstand, you will have donated hard-earned distance to your competitors and you can consider yourself lucky if there is a single boat in the fleet that you are able to beat. Tide or current must be a constant consideration both to windward and off the wind.

LEE-BOWING THE CURRENT

It will often be found advantageous to understand the weather mark. This can be done when the tide or current is flowing at an oblique angle to your desired course. Since the tide under the lee bow will move your boat to windward, it is possible to understand the mark, as the current will set you to windward. By playing the currents in this way you can gain immeasurable advantage over your less-knowledgeable competitors. It is simply a matter of obtaining a good knowledge of tidal-current action over the course throughout the racing day. Incidentally, when you are sailing an invitational race or regatta away from home, be certain that you invest enough time in study and that you understand tidal current conditions over the strange race course. If you do not, the local skippers will have a decided advantage.

LEEWAY

Every sailboat will have a certain amount of leeway when sailing upwind. That is, the boat will be displaced in a downwind direction. This caution is superfluous for veteran sailors, but do not fail to consider the effects of leeway when planning a smart arrival at the weather mark. The only way to measure leeway is by experience: no two sailboats are the same. The amount of leeway depends upon the underwater configuration of the hull and, of course, upon the manner in which she is sailed. The greater the area of lateral resistance, the lesser will be the amount of leeway. In actual practice, allowance for leeway becomes instinctive.

PILOTING AND NAVIGATION FOR THE OCEAN RACER

Navigational procedures in ocean racing become, in some respects, more simple than inshore racing, and in some respects much more complex. Celestial navigation, which is of no concern in day racing, is extremely important in ocean racing. However, the ocean racer carries a trained navigator, thereby relieving the skipper of this responsibility. I will discuss the matter of ocean-racing navigation in the next chapter.

14. Some Thoughts on Ocean Racing

I have had my greatest successes in triangular-course day racing, but I have been no less interested in the subject of ocean racing. It is a wonderful experience to prolong the intensity and excitement of the 10-mile triangle to a 4- or 5-day race. It is a precious gift, unique to the yachtsman, to relive in some measure the same experience and emotions felt by those who sailed the great tea clippers, who for economic reasons were compelled to make fast passage. An ocean race will be a long-remembered event in any man's life.

I have sailed many Bermuda Races, and I have by great fortune campaigned on two of the finest ocean racers afloat, *Good News* and *Bolero*. Reflecting on my experiences in this kind of racing, I have come to one overwhelming conclusion. I think the reason more ocean racing skippers do not do better is because they do not continuously race: in most cases, after the first six or eight hours, the race deteriorates into an off-shore cruise.

Now, this may seem like a harsh judgment, but believe me, I have seen it time and again and I know that I am right. It is only human to let down after an extended period of intense effort; we all know that. When the ocean racer is out of sight of the rest of the fleet for days at a time without the constant spurring of the sight of competitors, it is the natural order of things for efficiency to slip.

But if he is to be successful at ocean racing, the skipper must prevent this loss of efficiency at all costs. The great ocean-racing skippers like Olin and Roderick Stephens, Carleton Mitchell, Richard Nye and Hugh Long have learned this, and from all reports I have heard from men who have crewed for them, the concern for never letting down is constant and foremost in their consciousness. These men are champions, thanks to that philosophy. Carleton Mitchell, especially, has proven it by the feat, unequalled in yachting history, of winning the Bermuda Race three times in succession.

Here is an example that will prove my point. In 1946 I took the *Good News* to Bermuda; after five days of sailing, we crossed the finish line at Saint David's Head only minutes behind the winner. Without the slightest doubt, we could have won that race had we not lost many, many minutes each day because of slack helmsmanship. Understand, the helmsmanship was of a high order, but sometimes we lost minutes because it was not the best we could possibly do.

And so it goes: minutes are lost in a watch, an hour is lost in the day, and the lost hours lose the race. How does one go about remedying this human failing?

A Philosophy for the Race

I think there is a simple, but perhaps not easy way to cope with the common problem of the let-down in ocean racing. The solution I offer is this—*treat every watch as though it were one leg of a triangular-course day race and sail it with supreme concentration.*

By maintaining an attitude of this sort, a certain effect is achieved, and here is why this solution is not easy. In a day race the distances are short; every board of a windward leg must be fought tooth-and-nail. The best man at making that boat go to windward is the windward helmsman. The same holds true for the reach and run—the finest hand available is the one that must coax everything possible out of the boat; the tautness is maintained until the end. It should be the same with every watch of an ocean race.

Again by way of illustration: in one Bermuda Race, we had passed through the Gulf Stream and it was one of those beautiful sunny days you so often get in those tropical latitudes. We had gone through some bad wet weather and were drying out. The wind had fallen very light, and the minute I came on deck I had the impression that purposiveness had somehow inexplicably vanished and that the whole ship had the atmosphere of a cruise. Sure enough, when I looked aft, who was steering but the junior crew member, and he was simply murdering that boat!

Now he was one of the most able youngsters on deck, but he was not a racing helmsman. What he was doing to that boat was so heart-rending that I couldn't stand it. It was unpleasant to do, but I had to take him off the wheel immediately, because the speed of the boat meant much more to me than his personal feelings. I hated to think of the precious time that inexperience had cost us. I hope to heaven that as long as I live I never again hear the words, "Would you like to take a stab at steering for awhile?" aboard a boat actively engaged in racing. No one should touch the helm who has not been chosen for his skill and appointed to the task.

THE WATCHES

No matter how you set up the watches, whether four-hours-on-and-four-off, or any other system, this principle should guide you: each watch should have a watch captain in whom you have complete confidence. He should have equal, or greater abilities than yours, and he should be a first-rate helmsman. If, because of heavy weather and a limit of physical endurance, a relief helmsman is necessary during the watch, the relief should be the next best man in the watch; and he should be supervised by the watch captain.

It is in the nature of things that one must go below occasionally for a cup of coffee or whatnot, but the watch captain must never absent himself for more than a few minutes, if at all. He should never leave the deck until he is certain that the helmsman is doing well. I also believe that a boat should not sail shorthanded in an ocean race, because every member of each watch should be available on deck during his whole tour of duty. In this way men are available for necessary chores and the helmsmen can pay strict attention to the steering.

It is vital to place your best helmsmen in the night watches. Sailing in the darkness requires a good hand and steady nerves, especially in heavy weather. It is in the long night watches that the poorest sailing is done. And now, of course, the inevitable question arises: "How do I know who the best helmsmen are when this is the first time I have sailed with them?"

The answer to that question is that you must sail with them before the race. The best of men need a period of time to settle down to a routine, to learn the ways of a strange boat, to know what is expected of them. And the first few days of an ocean race is not the time to begin this process of breaking in; by then it is already too late; the race has started and everything must be improvised by trial and error.

The Shakedown

If you are serious in your desire to win, you must somehow find time to spend three or four days in a shakedown sail. When I was asked to campaign the *Good News* in 1946, I wanted to do everything in my power to win, and yet I was faced with the prospect of a grueling 700-mile ocean race on a strange boat with men who, although most had sailed with me before, had yet to learn their duties. I, too, had to learn about ocean racing, for although I had my own ways of doing things, I needed the practical experience aboard the boat to test them and to apply them to the *Good News*.

It seemed to me the best way to obtain this experience was by actually going to sea for three days and simulating a real race. In effect, this would be more than racing, because in racing, you can sometimes stay on one tack for days on end. But we did everything that I thought would be necessary during a race, and some things that I hoped would not be necessary, like man-overboard drill and damage-control practice. We reefed and shortened sail, shook out the reefs, tacked, set and doused spinnakers, jibed spinnakers, changed from working jib to genoa jib, and made so many sail changes during those three days that I began to fear the boys would have no enthusiasm for the actual race.

We stood regular watches, we cooked and served hot meals, and since we were way offshore we had plenty of opportunity to test our navigation. It was early June and there was plenty of heavy weather to deal with, to try men and gear, and we learned an awful lot in those three days. By the time we crossed the starting line at Newport, bound for Bermuda, we were a pretty rugged, seasoned bunch aboard that yawl. Most important, the shakedown gave me a chance to observe the hands in action, and I now knew where both our strengths and our weaknesses lay. The experience was extremely valuable. It is astonishing to me that this is not regular practice in offshore racing.

I have often thought that the greatest ability one can have is the ability to recognize ability in others, and this is certainly true of the ocean-racing skipper in the selection of his crew. This kind of training session, with the hands learning to know and work the boat, affords an occasion to evaluate the crew's potential and to form the men into the most efficient watches.

162

As I stated before, the two or three best helmsmen should be chosen captains of the port, starboard, and middle watches. The three next best should be ticketed as relief helmsmen, one to each watch. The balance of the crew is best assigned so that there is a good seaman-sail trimmer for each watch.

During the shakedown racing, you must make judgments, not only as to ability, but as to character. You must eliminate from your ship any man who is ill-tempered or quarrelsome. Five days or a week cooped up in a racing sailboat with an antisocial personality of this type can be very disturbing; morale will sink and with it your chances of success. Try to pair off men in the same watch who get along well or whose personalities complement each other.

If it is at all possible, two men should stand no regular watches—the navigator and the cook. The navigator, if he does his job well, will be up and down at all hours during the night searching for star sights to obtain a line of position. During dirty weather when the sky is overcast, he may have to wait for hours to grab a quick sextant altitude through the scud. He also needs a certain amount of time to work up his sights and maintain his records. During the day and in clear weather, he can be called upon for assistance if necessary, but his job is to get you to your destination accurately, with no interference.

As for the cook, if you have a man who can reef, hand, and steer, who is immune to seasickness, and who can turn out good hot meals in a wet, lurching cabin that's dripping damp and laden with the assorted smells of a small boat battened down in a blow—and still remain cheerful—then hang on to him for dear life. Treat him royally, for every skipper in the ocean-racing fleet will be after him when the word passes around. It is really a difficult job to turn out three meals and innumerable snacks a day under ocean-racing conditions for a crew of ravenous men. So, like the navigator, the cook should be relieved of the added chore of standing regular watches. He deserves it.

The Indispensable Man: the Navigator

Aside from the skipper himself, the navigator is the most important man aboard an ocean racer. Upon the skill of this vital crew member will depend the success or failure of your ocean-racing campaign.

It is for this reason that the choice of navigator is even more important than the choice of the crew. A good crew will avail you nothing if the boat cannot be accurately pinpointed each day and if you are unable to lay a course that will, at noon of each day, put you in the most advantageous position for the next day's run.

You should know the potential navigator, and though it is possible to pick one by reputation, it is better if you have sailed with him. He must be a man who understands the subtleties of ocean racing; a man who can just lay a "steamboat course" is not sufficient. There is the windward ability of the boat, and the effects of leeway, currents, and many other things to consider. Again, he must be a chap who will be a compatible member of the organization. No matter how great his talents, be sure he meets this requirement, because he will be under pressure night and day. Five days at sea can seem an eternity if he is not compatible with the other crewmen.

After you have picked your navigator, for heaven's sake leave him alone and let him do his job. Once you have committed yourself and given the man the berth, remember that he is head of his division, and accept his decisions without reservation. Don't be the type of skipper who is constantly popping topsides armed with a sextant and a stopwatch to work sights of his own and who then proceeds to interrogate the navigator. He might assume that you do not fully trust his ability, and this tends to make navigators unhappy.

Naturally, you will want to understand the navigator's thinking on certain matters. In the case of the Gulf Stream, for instance, you might want to know what the navigator had allowed for drift. If he allowed 30 miles, the skipper might not agree because of some special knowledge about the boat's performance—for example, the knowledge that the wind is from a quarter that would not knock your yacht unusually far off course. This is a rare example of when a skipper may interfere in the navigator's work.

If you have no confidence in his ability, it is better to relieve him of his duties completely. But the rule should be that the navigator's decisions are final, because if you don't have confidence in him, you might as well leave your boat at the mooring.

We have spoken about the skipper's "choosing" of the navigator. In effect, however, this is not often the way it works. You will find that the best navigators usually pick their own boats. The reputations of successful navigators keep them in constant demand. They will only ship aboard yachts where they find the skipper and crew congenial, where they will unqualifiedly head their divisions, and where there will be no attempt to interfere with their decisions. The skipper of an ocean racer has enough work running the boat and sailing her fast without trying to do the navigating as well.

PASSING ON THE RECKONING

When I began ocean racing, I developed a custom that I think is a practical one. The watch is required to record the boat's speed by the log every fifteen minutes. The speed of a hull can vary a great deal during the course of an hour, and I do not believe that reporting the speed once an hour, as is customary, is often enough. There are plenty of unpredictables in ocean racing as it is, without introducing any unnecessary ones. A record of speed for fifteen-minute intervals will give the navigator a basis for calculation that is bound to be more accurate than an hourly record.

Navigators are a breed of men in themselves, and like skippers they have their temperaments. I suspect that the navigator considers his daily work a creative act—and it is, too. All creative people should be allowed a few idiosyncrasies, so if your navigator should turn into a bleary-eyed, mumbling monomaniac because Venus has been perverse enough to stay hidden behind a layer of cloud throughout a whole night, you must, above all, be discreet and softly whisper your condolences. After all, it is a kind of desperate, unrequited love, this star-crossed profession.

15. Match Racing

The following situations have been set up in an endeavor to demonstrate some of the possible maneuvers that can occur in match race starting. With these as a base, many more less fundamental maneuvers may be developed as the attack and defense continues.

In match racing, the start is all important. Your competitor must be controlled through various techniques so that your boat will be in the advantageous position when the line is crossed; and *when* is not important as long as your sole competitor is behind you. In fleet racing it is desirable to be on the line at the starting gun and also in the favored position. In match racing you can start as late as you desire, but you must have the other boat covered.

Practically all of the many maneuvers in match-race starting are controlled by the Golden Rule—and forcefully supported by North American Yacht Racing Union Rule #2, Appeal #63.

In the match race start you must be the aggressor. Don't let your competitor have this opportunity. You must be the one to get on his stern, a psychologically strong position to be in. He is upset, surprised and maybe even unnerved when you attack. Your technique and tactics in this tailing operation must of necessity be precision perfect. Even a touch on the wheel or an improperly trimmed mainsail or jib can cost precious position. As in all racing, you must know the rules perfectly and how to use them to your advantage on a second's notice. You must constantly anticipate the possible movements and positions of the other boat. Your decision must be instantaneous and, of course, correct.

This is all fine, so long as you are the aggressor and in control. The important question, however, is "How do you get your boat there?" Difficult as are fleet starts with some 30 or more boats, timing the start in match racing is, in my opinion, even harder. In the former, no one is trying to prevent you from starting (with the exception of a barging situation at the windward end of the line). In match starts, each boat is endeavoring to control the other.

Because it is a more intricate operation than regular starting, management, thought, and endless practice is more necessary. It is important, of course, to understand techniques and maneuvers, but it becomes entirely different when you attempt to execute them in actuality. This, of course, is no different from any other activity.

Those who love golf, for example, in looking at pictures or experts in actual play, think they can take many strokes off their own game until the heartbreak comes when they try to put into practice what they thought they had learned. To practice properly you should have a friend who is a sharp helmsman, knows the rules, and has a good understanding of match starting. These are severe requirements, because very few realize the demands for this type of starting. Nevertheless, endeavor to find a skipper that wants to learn, if an experienced man is not available. Study the fundamentals, then go out in two one-design boats for your actual practice.

You will find, as my son Corny and I did, that it can be the most interesting and thrilling department of all the wonderful phases of racing, perhaps even as advanced as chess is to checkers when compared with fleet starts. However, before entering into actual practice, you must familiarize yourself with certain fundamentals that are most necessary in "tailing" maneuvers.

One of the rudiments in match starts, and even more valuable than in fleet starts, is the ability to judge the sailing time for various distances and at various speeds. The importance of this cannot be overemphasized. Practice this continually. Know your tacking and jibing times, especially reach-to-reach. Regularly test your judgment for time on approaching buoys, anchored boats, boats dead in the water, and driftwood. Always use the stem in judging times and in assimilating actual starts. Learn how to slow her down if you are early, either through violent course variations or easing the jib, which can usually be more easily controlled than the mainsail. On a big boat, always know your exact speed on the speedometer, a very important factor in your judgment of time and distance. Be aware of what your loss in speed is in a jibe or tack. Learn how long it takes to regain full speed.

It is necessary to practice incessantly to learn when your stem is on the line. In large boats it is especially difficult to be accurate in this regard. When the helmsman is 50 or 70 feet aft of the stem, he will find the angle surprisingly difficult to measure. For large boats, I recommend having a man on the stem to assist in starts. He should be a helmsman himself with the ability to judge speed and distance. A good man in this spot is invaluable to the skipper. In the tailing operation, he can also be most helpful in determining overlaps and the boat's ability to swing clear. He should also have the knack of using psychology on an opponent. For example, he should call the overlap with great emphasis. He must loudly and repeatedly caution the opposing skipper not to bear off after you have obtained an overlap. Furthermore, you or your navigator should immediately call out your course, loudly and clearly, as soon as the overlap is established. This, too, is extremely important psychologically, and could be useful in the event of a protest.

In endeavoring to get on the stern of your competitor, meet him on an opposite course, widely separated to permit you to start your turn early, well before you are abeam. This would be when he is approximately 45 degrees on your bow. The distance between the two courses should be three to four boat lengths, permitting you to maintain speed on a gradual slow jibe or tack. Should you be fortunate and have timed your turn well, you will be approximately a boat length astern. A course slightly to leeward of your opponent's will permit you to control him. If he luffs, you should do likewise and prevent him from tacking. If he bears off, you will gain an overlap and not allow him to jibe. Then, maintain this controlling position until you are certain you can jibe or tack for the line, with your competitor in an unfavorable position. Remember, *when* you start is of no consequence as long as you do so in a controlling position. If in control, don't start until you are satisfied that you can maintain this advantage at the start.

If you are unable to gain the controlling position and more than a boat length separates the boats, your competitor will of course attempt to

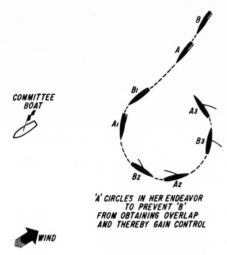

A, endeavoring to prevent B from obtaining an overlap and control, enters into a circle.

COMMITTEE BOAT

'A' CIRCLES IN HER ENDEAVOR
TO PREVENT 'B'
FROM OBTAINING OVERLAP
AND THEREBY GAIN CONTROL

WIND

BUOY

escape your efforts to control. He will luff and tack, or bear off and jibe, continuing this circular course in an endeavor to prevent you from getting an overlap. You must follow, trying for this key to your control. In this situation you must have previously determined the time required for a full circle—in both light and fresh breezes. At the start of a circling maneuver, make certain you or your navigator know the exact time and check off each full circle. You must decide as each circle ends whether the time calls for another circle before the start or whether you could leave your competitor and permit him to be on your stern, with your getting to the line without being early for the gun, thus having exactly the position you have been striving for. Naturally, you must also judge, when the circling starts, the time required to get to the line—so you will not be early.

The circling maneuver is extremely confusing and requires the utmost concentration. It is not an exaggeration to say that it can be as bewildering as a small boy spinning with his eyes closed, wherein it is impossible to maintain equilibrium or direction when ended. Because you are in such a state of concentration on your own boat and your competitor's, on occasion you will not know where the line is, let alone where its two ends are. For this reason, you must have assistance from either the navigator or a member of the afterguard who is concentrating solely on time and position.

You will, of course, have determined the favored end of the line, if any. Needless to say, you should attempt to start in that area when you have the choice.

After the start, the match race becomes like any other race, with certain important exceptions. Following are some pointers for racing.

Always cover your opponent. If he double tacks, you must do the same. However, if he triple tacks in an effort to get clear I believe it better not to follow, because you will have an opportunity to gain two to three boat lengths as a result of his almost complete loss of way. If you are the leeward boat and covered, you will, of course, reach off a little in your endeavor to get clear. Under the present rule he cannot bear off to prevent your doing so. There are no other boats to worry about, so tack as often as possible. Try to tire his crew out, or hope for a bad tack on his part.

Incidentally, in your tacks, free up your mainsail and jib to aid you in gaining speed. If you are covered and decide to sail wide, make certain your boom vang is set taut. It will be of enormous importance in quickly building and maintaining speed. Adjust its set to the strength of the wind. Be wary of tacking under his lee bow, especially in a bigger boat. You should be able gradually to gain a position to backdraft him. But if you don't and he is sufficiently clear of you to windward, you are really locked. If on the starboard tack, I believe you are better off to cross him and tack on his weather quarter, clear of his disturbed air. If on the port tack and you would be forced about, go under your opponent's stern and tack on his weather quarter, and as aforementioned; clear of his backdraft. In both cases you are then in control.

In a tacking duel watch for false tacks. If he falls back on his tack, do likewise. However, make certain that you maintain maximum way on your boat. Your tacks should be slower than normal, but after getting head to wind, fill her away quickly, because after this point you are gaining nothing to windward.

When you are weather boat immediately after being filled away on your new course, read the compass heading. This will permit you to disclaim any charge of your bearing off. Your navigator should constantly take bearings on the other boat to help you decide on the need for sail adjustments, and to consider whether you should sail her finer or wider through the seas.

If you are ahead when you get to the lay line for the windward mark, under no circumstances overstand. It only brings your competitor closer, and you have given away the precious distance earned to windward. Say you both go by the lay line: your opponent, when you tack for the mark, reaches in your wake with his wind clear, whereas he would have been in your backdraft had you tacked on the lay line. If he continues on his course he will have to reach off for the mark, thus sacrificing valuable distance. This may be elemental, but it is surprising how many experienced skippers will continue to cover their opponent after reaching the lay line. The skipper of the leeward boat is hoping for such a situation when he goes by the lay line.

Before the start you will presumably have run the courses of the reaching and running legs to determine the jibe for the run and the possibility of a spinnaker on the reach. If you plan to carry the spinnaker on the reach, then as you proceed on the windward leg, you and your navigator must watch for any change in the wind direction that would affect your spinnaker decision for the leeward legs. Study wind direction by observing the compass while you are head-to-wind in tacking, by looking at the water over the compass at other times, or by knowing how close to the wind your boat can sail in points or degrees. The latter is especially accurate after you and your navigator have previously determined how many degrees off the wind she will sail in various strengths of winds.

There may be opportunities for special maneuvering at the weather mark. For example, say the boats are overlapped and not laying the mark which must be left to port. The leeward boat is maintaining her position because of having her wind clear. The weather boat skipper, although he is ahead, is not in the lead because of his requirement to give room as they tack and reach the mark. He therefore decides that if he goes by the lay line, he will be in a better position to break the overlap as he tacks and reaches back to the mark. The leeward boat must be adroit in tacking simultaneously to maintain a relative position. In fact, when endeavoring to obtain this advantage she should gradually luff to bring the boats as closely together as possible before both tack for the mark.

When the boats are overlapped on the starboard tack, and very comfortably laying the weather mark to be left to starboard, the helmsman of the lee boat—with luffing rights—may see an opportunity to reverse the positions and gain an overlap at the mark. He luffs his opponent to weather of the mark, continues a sufficient distance to permit himself room to jibe, and return to the mark with an overlap. Probably his greatest advantage is that he has done the unexpected, causing great turmoil on the weather boat. It is likely that the skipper of this boat, in his surprise and confusion, may become "frozen to the handle bars" and continue on course until he has lost his only opportunity to maintain his former advantageous position. In this circumstance he should, as soon as he sees he will be taken to windward of the mark if the bow of the leeward boat overlaps the mark, tack and jibe without letting the jib sheet go. This will bring the boat around quicker, and the jib will be filled and ready for easing on his short reach to the mark. The leeward boat's position requires most accurate timing and judgment in this maneuver. For this reason both conditions should be prepared for in previous practice. These maneuvers are not far-fetched and should be expected to occur regularly in match racing. If such situations do develop and advantages are not fought for, the helmsman is being too casual in his effort to win.

Remember again there are no other boats to be concerned with, and a fierce competitor will go to any length within the rules to win. Extreme as this situation may appear it is one with which you may well have to contend. You may well find an opportunity to employ it yourself.

If the next leg is a reach, few opportunities for trading positions will occur, because both boats are likely to be of equal speed in most match races. However, if the leeward boat is being overtaken she should luff as long and as far as possible. Her one hope is to get far enough to windward to jibe, set her spinnaker and obtain the overlap at the second mark. Presuming the boats are of equal speeds, the entire leeward legs must be sailed to gain the overlap. This is especially true on the spinnaker runs, the dead runs of windward-leeward courses in particular.

On the leeward legs, especially the runs, there is more room and opportunity for maneuver. You will start your run on the jibe that you have previously determined to be correct. The following boat will attempt to get on the wind of the leader by steering a course exactly for her masthead fly. If the leader is being bothered, he will sail higher to get free wind. Both boats, therefore, quickly get well above course and plans must be made to jibe. This should be anticipated first by the following boat, so she can make an opportunity to cover the leader after the jibe.

As they run their distance and approach the proper angle for the new course, the following boat should bear off, hoping to do this so gradually that the purpose will go unnoticed. The leader, of course, must eventually jibe. If the following boat has been able to get over far enough, she will be in a better position to cover when both jibe. The leader will repeatedly jibe in her struggle to get clear. This is exactly what the following boat should endeavor to induce, as the maneuver is all in her favor. The leader can make a poor jibe and have the further disadvantage of her adversary coming down with new breeze. Furthermore, she is being attacked, which, in itself, can be disturbing psychologically.

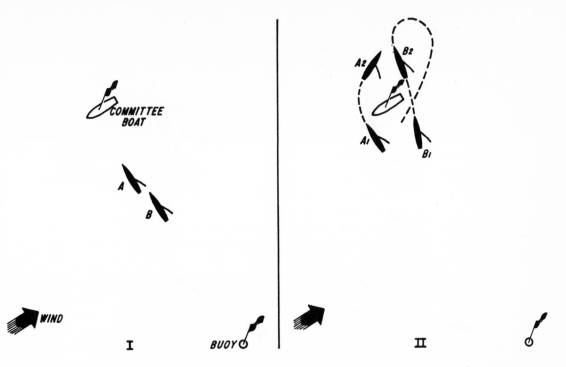

Both boats are early. A plans to absorb the time differential by jibing around the committee boat. B prevents this by bearing off to leeward of the committee boat.

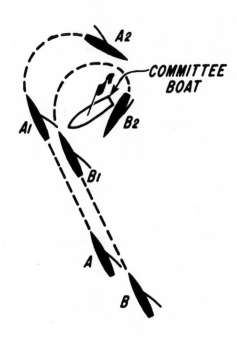

B, in control, prevents A from dipping the line to make his start, forcing A to windward of the committee boat, then jibes himself, which A must follow.

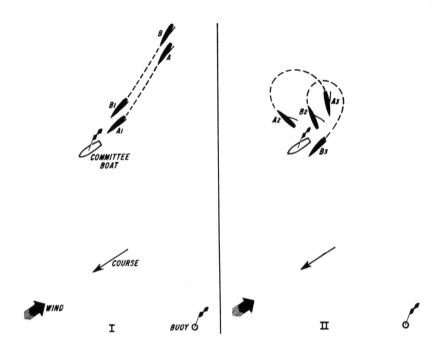

I. The hazard of "running time" in a match race start. "Sitting duck" B, running time, observing that he will be attacked by A, returns a minute early to upset A's plans and allow himself maneuvering time. Having obtained his desired position under B's lee bow and realizing that B's premature return will make him early, A, in his confusion, sets out to luff B to windward of the committee boat.

II. Because B has returned early, there is a minute extra to be absorbed. Judging poorly, A has elected to luff B to windward of the committee boat. This decision places A in an awkward position to reach the starting line favorably in relation to B. B should now tack and jibe, employing the remaining time, and approach the line with the right of way.

When A tacked under B's lee bow he was in control. He could kill the extra time and maintain control through better maneuvers than luffing B to windward of the committee boat. They are:

1. Realizing that both were early, A could luff B almost head to wind to pass the necessary time.
2. A could take several luffs to break the overlap, cross the line, then tack and jibe around the committee boat.
3. A could sharply luff and bear off, making certain he gets no further to leeward than a point which would permit him to approach the committee boat with right of way under the anti-barging rule.
4. A could jibe and tack as he reaches the line to leeward of the committee boat.
5. A could run down the line regulating his speed so B will remain overlapped to windward and as close aboard as possible. As both sharpen for the start, A can then lee bow and back draft B. In this circumstance A cannot put B across the line. If he did, B could then tack and dip the line. A could only follow or jibe and tack; in both cases he would be in B's wake.

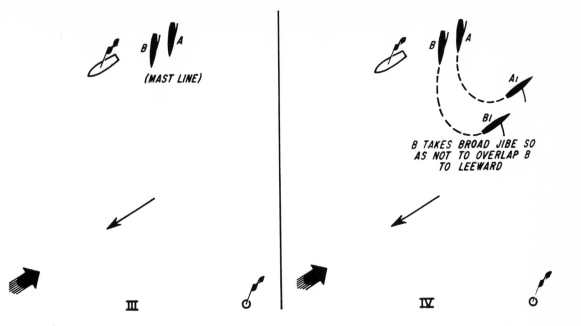

(MAST LINE)

B TAKES BROAD JIBE SO
AS NOT TO OVERLAP B
TO LEEWARD

III.   A in his endeavor to place his boat under B's lee bow has misjudged his timing and B has obtained "mast line" on A.

IV.   As A jibes to escape the mast line position, B takes a broader jibe in order not to overlap A to leeward and be locked. B is now in control of A and will win the advantageous starting position.

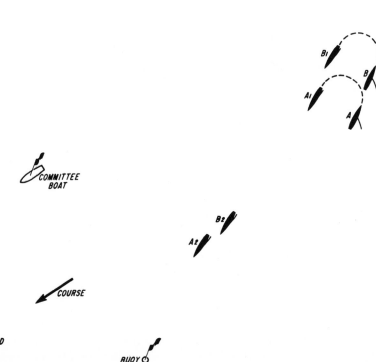

A is in control, and tacks for the line a little early for the distance involved, placing B in control. However, A overcomes this by regulating the speed of his boat to the distance involved, keeping B in his wake.

COMMITTEE BOAT

COURSE

WIND

BUOY

OBSTRUCTION BOAT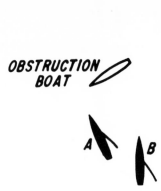

A   B

COMMITTEE BOAT

COURSE

WIND

BUOY

Endeavoring to get free of B's controlling position, A plans to jibe around an obstruction boat which is not under way. To prevent this, B bears off to pass under the stern of the obstruction.

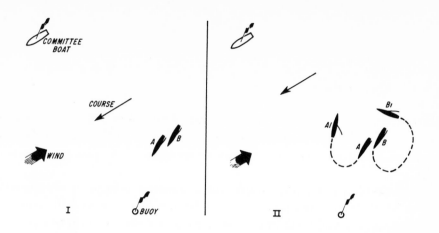

Mast line situation.

I. Both boats are early, A with controlling mast line position. B jibes to get free.

II. A must be cautious of tacking because B, coming out of his jibe, with right of way, could put A across the starting line prematurely. The alternative could be for A to take a wide jibe and place himself on B's weather beam. Naturally, these maneuvers must be judged in accordance with the time remaining to the start.

If the following boat is successful and does become close, careful plans must be made. In the event that another windward leg is to be sailed, she must program everything around obtaining an overlap at the leeward mark. The leader will naturally make every effort to prevent this. The one situation the following boat must avoid is getting in an overlapped position where she can be luffed, permitting the leader to jibe and be in command. Here the attacking boat, as she draws close to getting an overlap to windward, may jibe instead, again introducing the unexpected. She is then free to maneuver and is on the right side for the overlap. If the leader jibes, she will presumably be covered. She must therefore, continue her course and jibe later, but she will then be on the outside at the turn. Such an opportunity to do the unexpected must never be missed.

The leader must be prepared to luff his opponent to weather of the line, and then to jibe and return.

In the foregoing situations and in the following starting maneuvers, it is suggested that the reader set up matchstick models for purposes of clarification.

Various Maneuvers in Match-Racing Starts

B in control. A, in spite of an effort to slow his boat, approaches the committee boat and is early. He plans to leave the committee boat to starboard and jibe around it, expecting B to follow. B should stay to leeward of the committee boat to prevent A's jibe. B should then jibe for the line, or—if it is still early—stay to leeward of A, jibing when time dictates.

A obviously cannot jibe around the committee boat until permitted to do so by B. If he attempted to do so, he would risk disqualification for barging, as A would meet him on starboard tack after completing his jibe. A is in an unfavorable position either if he eventually jibes astern of B or—worse—if he tacks.

In such a situation where both boats are to windward of the line, B must keep A in this position of line until he (B) can jibe around the committee boat. A must follow and, in consequence, be in B's backdraft as the windward leg commences.

B must exercise proper caution and not bear off for the line, thereby permitting A to do likewise, dip over the line and be in the favored position at the start.

When both boats are to windward of the line, which presumably is square to the wind, and both become free (neither in control) to run off for the line, a reaching course should be faster rather than a dead run. Furthermore, greater speed can be maintained for sharpening up on the wind. If there is a favored end of the line, you should naturally start in that area to be in the advantageous position. Remember the time of your start is completely unimportant. It is *where* you are in relation to your adversary.

When your competitor is running time for his start, he becomes a "sitting duck" for attack. Running time is therefore not advisable.

Defense for a "Sitting Duck" Position

A plans to force B to windward of the committee boat.

B should foresee his problem. He should return to the line very early, expecting to make A early also. B can control the time of his start by regulating the speed of his boat.

In this situation B should permit A to luff him to windward of the committee boat until he (B) has reached a point where he can tack and jibe for the line and not be early for the gun. Delicate timing is required on the part of B; otherwise A can bear off and start. (Barging rule.)

Adroit maneuvering is necessary on the part of A when he places his boat under the lee bow of B. B is probably at full speed if he is running

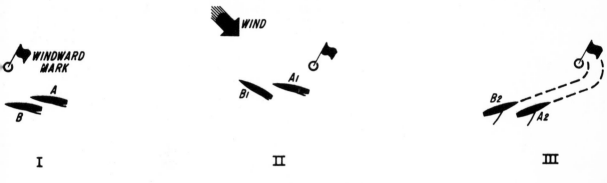

Carrying your competitor by the mark to leeward.

Carrying your competitor by the mark to windward.

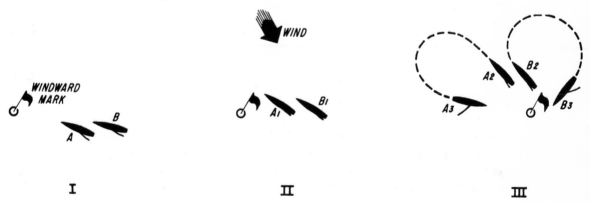

time and might well go on by A and obtain "mast line." He would thereby defeat A's plan to force him above the committee boat. A would probably jibe in an attempt to get free, because he could not run off with B on his wind at the start. So when A jibes, B would follow suit, become the "tailor" and be in control *(see diagram)*.

It is risky for B to tack, as he might meet A coming out of his jibe with luffing rights.

If your opponent, in his strenuous efforts to get on your tail, has a possibility of doing so, if the time is only two to three minutes until the start, and if there is sufficient distance from the line, an interesting opportunity may occur—either by design or accident—on which you could

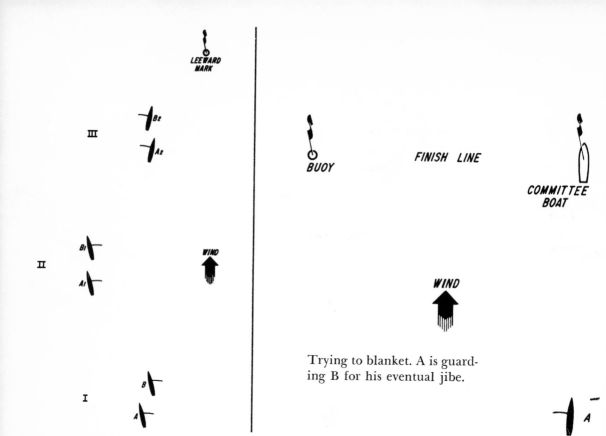

Trying to blanket. A is guarding B for his eventual jibe.

A is first. B is second. In a surprise jibe, B prevents A from obtaining a controlling position.

capitalize. Your eager opponent could well fall into a trap in which you permit him to become the "tailor." If you do this, you must be in a position of freedom from which you can get to either end of the starting line. Obviously, if you were headed away from the line, you would be completely controlled. In this situation, however, in spite of the fact that you are the "tailed," you are in control—provided, of course, you are far enough away from the line to control your speed and decide when you want to reach it. If he rides up to windward, you can luff. If in other words, to leeward, you can control him through the mast line rule. With only several minutes to the start, and after various courses in which neither boat has been successful in obtaining control, A permits B to become "tailor," thereby putting himself (A) into position to reverse the control, through regulation of his speed and freedom of maneuver, and gain the favorable position at the start.

Some skippers, in their efforts to avoid being tailed, have evolved a plan that has worked out to a degree, but that is in my opinion quite risky for both boats. Here the skipper delays breaking out his genoa until just before the start. If his opponent had set his jib, the opponent is not in a position to tail because of the greater speed of his boat. If both boats remained jibless, the control of each is materially reduced and fouls are more likely to occur. For this reason I consider it a rather hazardous procedure in the circling and other maneuvers attempting to gain control. Furthermore, I believe that a skipper should not take the defensive, but should become the forceful aggressor at approximately seven minutes (in large boats such as twelves) before the start.

To avoid being tailed, keep your boat moving at the greatest speed that wind will allow. On opposite courses, pass as close to your competitor as possible to deny him tacking or jibing room to get on your stern. If you are in control and your opponent plans to jibe around the committee boat or another of moderate size (not underway), prevent him from doing so by going to leeward of the boat he intends to go around. You can then keep your control. Some reduction of your speed may be necessary, as he may start his jibe and thereby reduce speed. If you don't slow down, you are likely to become overlapped after you pass the obstruction boat. A's defense would be to tack after B has overlapped the obstruction boat.

Aside from circling (a defensive move) the skipper of a controlled boat may luff head-to-wind very sharply in an effort to kill way and make the controlling boat shoot by or become abeam as the controlled boat loses way. To kill your speed under this circumstance, secure the spinnaker halyard in the grommet for the brail tacking line in the center of the jib foot. The forward part of the jib will then brake your speed as the halyard is hoisted. He can then go on one tack only and must not fill away on the other at the risk of disqualification. If the maneuver works out as planned, the controlling position could then be reversed. The same situation could prevail if the "tailee" *bears off* sharply and is overridden by the "tailor." In this case, make every effort to be on starboard jibe.

Nothing is lost in this effort by the "tailee," as he may at least be permitted to go into a defensive circle. This may give him an opportunity to go for the line when he elects, whereas previously he was controlled and was prevented from freedom of maneuver.

If by fortune you find yourself with "mast line" while you are reaching for the start, the courses may be such that your opponent cannot get up to the line (*see diagram*). His only defense is to jibe immediately and save as much time as possible for further maneuvering. He then might be clear on the start, and, if sufficient time remains, he might even be in a position to put your boat over the line (*diagram*) should you tack simultaneously with his jibing.

181

16. The Well-Found Boat

The racing boat must be "well found"—that is, it must have everything necessary for safe and efficient operation according to the best practices. To this end, I think it is foolish to leave the main anchor ashore to save a few pounds of weight, and it is foolish to load down a day sailer with fifty pounds of lunch, a beer cooler, and other unnecessary gear. When you are in competition, you are out there to sail a taut race: you should have the tools of the trade—good ones—and nothing more.

It is important not to load the racing sailboat with superfluous gear, for weight slows a boat, especially the light-displacement type. A great deal of thought and effort is expended in shaving ounces from the fittings of boats even as large as the 12-meters. And yet racing men often let unnecessary and seldom-used gear accumulate in their boats over the season until hundreds of extra pounds are added to their weights.

BINOCULARS

One of the tools you will need is a good pair of binoculars. They are most handy, and you will have occasion to use them many times in the course of a race. You will use them to find the mark when visibility is poor or the range is greater than the range of the naked eye, you will use them

182

to spot the numbers on the sails of competitors and to read committee-boat signals, and you will use them to look for the little cat's paws in the distance—the first indications of a breeze.

I suggest you buy a good pair, for they will last you all your life, provided they are well cared for. I use a wonderful pair of 7 x 50's; they are precision made, very rugged, and have a marvelous light-gathering power. Even at night under the most abominable lighting conditions, you can pick up objects clearly.

Do not purchase yachting binoculars any larger than 7 x 50's; they will be unsatisfactory for your purposes. Glasses that magnify more than seven times are too powerful for use on a boat; it is difficult to keep a target centered when you use them. Everything will appear to jiggle, making it impossible to define sharp outlines. On the other hand, glasses with less than seven-times magnification are not powerful enough to reach out and pull in horizonal navigation markers with the performance a sailor must have.

If you hang binoculars around your neck by the strap while you are racing, you won't have them long. Sooner or later they will smash, or snag on something and go hurtling overboard. Build a small wooden box to fit, and glue a lining of chamois on the inside to protect the glasses when you slide them in and out. Fasten the box to a bulkhead with wingnuts or other stout-but-removable fasteners: the glasses will always be handy, protected, and where they belong.

Although one shouldn't carry binoculars around the neck while racing, to guard against loss of an expensive favorite pair of binoculars, make it a rule aboard your boat that *for the time they are in use* the strap must always be placed around the neck. People are more butter-fingered than we think.

YACHT TIMERS

The accuracy of your starts will depend, to a large extent, on the accuracy of your yacht timers or stopwatches. An instrument that does not keep track of the time steadily, with a constant rate of gain, will find you early or late at gunfire. I am a fanatic about my watches for this reason. I run three of them on every start.

I keep one timer with a two-inch dial in a wonderful little watertight case at the forward end of the cockpit. Another, also with a two-inch dial, is visible in a sheltered spot under the port deck. I use the customary pocket-watch-sized timer for practice runs. All of these timers are regularly serviced and rated; I treat them carefully like the precious instruments they are.

The use and placement of watches is largely an individual matter. Some racing skippers hang the timer on a lanyard around the neck. I never cared for this idea because, again, it requires looking down occasionally. During a close start I don't like to lower my glance for even an instant; too much can happen in that fraction of a second in a close start. That is why I prefer a large-dialed, readable watch placed next to the compass at the forward end of the cockpit. Both instruments are in the natural line of forward vision and you needn't take your eye from the race to check them.

ANCHORS

Many skippers make the mistake of leaving shore with only one small anchor aboard. I think that two anchors, a light drifting anchor for racing and a large main anchor, are an obsolute minimum. A good anchor, preferably of the Northill, Danforth or plough design, with five or six feet of chain, should be stowed where it is readily accessible and rigged for immediate use in an emergency. Even in day of racing, so many unexpected things can happen that it is foolishness to neglect this precaution merely to save a few pounds of weight.

If a particularly vile blow makes up, or if you are dismasted, that anchor can keep your boat from going ashore or drifting into a foul area that might hole the bottom. I'm afraid that most skippers are not prepared in this manner, and either carry no storm anchors or else bury them under mounds of gear in the remote ends of their boats where it takes forever to extricate them. Also, have anchor drill occasionally so your crew becomes accustomed to the procedure. I would like to see even the little racing dinghies carry at least a small anchor on a light nylon line, for you never know when the anchor will be needed.

You cannot win a sailboat race by going backwards in a head tide. For this reason I carry a light "drifting" anchor with about 15 fathoms of very light nylon rope; it is kept with the line carefully made up to run quickly without fouling.

When the breeze becomes very light, and the tide is a head one, I have the anchor silently passed out, lowered over the side, and secured to the shroud on the side where it cannot be seen by competitors. I make no noise to give away the secret. The cabin of a small boat acts as a sounding board; the slightest clink or jingle resounds over the still water, so you must be very careful about this.

The maneuver has proved very profitable for me. Sometimes you appear to be sailing ahead while the other boats are going backwards. It is frequently possible to gain many lengths before the rest of the fleet realizes that the reason you are not losing distance is *because you are anchored*. All of which brings to mind a cardinal principle of racing—always try to conceal your next move from your competitors.

CLOTHING

Be sure that you and the other crew members wear proper clothing for racing, because it is hard to be efficient if you are uncomfortable. Even in the springtime it can become chilly on the water after the sun goes down, so be sure there is a sweater or woolen Navy shirt aboard for each crew member—as well as oilskins. In the winter, you will not need as many layers of clothing while racing as you think. The excitement and constant movement keep you quite warm.

Winter dinghy sailors have found that clothing need not be bulky or heavy to provide adequate warmth for frostbiting. Knitted thermal underwear insulates natural body heat so that only a light quilted nylon-dacron outer jacket is needed.

It is always a problem to keep the feet warm and dry in winter sailing. The best solution I have found is to wear soleless rubber slippers under heavy pullover socks.

BOSUN'S STORES

Even the smallest boat can keep a good supply of bosun's stores aboard. One need only select carefully and stow everything in a small waterproof plastic bag. The medium-sized racer can and should carry spares adequate for most emergencies.

Some things that come in handy are: plenty of marline and small-stuff for seizings; a sailmaker's palm, waxed thread, and different sized needles for whippings and emergency sewing; extra shackles and turn-buckles in graduated sizes, and jars of extra cotter pins and turn-buckle pins. A 6- to 10-inch length of quarter-inch chain, and wire rope clamps to fit the standing rigging, should be included. If a shroud or stay lets go, the broken end can be run through the chain, doubled back upon the standing part, and secured with the wire clamps. The short piece of chain will lengthen the shroud enough to reach the turnbuckle, which is then tightened. This jury rig is easily made and stout enough to allow you to finish the race and sail home, thereby saving at least part of your over-all fleet standing. Without the foresight to carry this simple emergency gear, a withdrawal is the only alternative.

The bosun's locker should also contain plenty of chafing gear, for chafe is the major cause of wear and failure aboard a sailboat. Wide sailmaker's adhesive tape is unsurpassed for quickly mending tears in spinnakers and other sails. A strip applied to either side of the sail over the rent will hold the wind and prevent further ripping. "Chafe-Guard" tape, sold at most chandler's and marine supply stores, is excellent for wrapping around shrouds, turnbuckles, and anchor rope where it bears on the bow chock. A spool of soft copper wire and one of annealed stainless steel wire will come in handy for safetying shackles and anchor keys and will have countless other uses aboard the boat.

For making repairs you will want to carry an assortment of wood screws and various sized bolts. Try to standardize on three or four sizes to save space. The best way to stow them is in a compartmented plastic box. Another good idea is to attach the lids of small mason jars underneath a seat or locker. When the jars are screwed into the lids, their contents are visible, and the jars are easy to get to, secured against breakage, and watertight.

For Safety's Sake

What to carry aboard your boat and how to stow it is mostly a matter of common sense and experience. You will pick up many hints by visiting the other boats in your fleet.

Whether or not you have a motor or a cooking stove aboard, you should have a fire extinguisher. If you will never need it yourself, you might some day render aid to another yachtsman. The same holds true for a first-aid kit: you should have one aboard and know how to use it. Thanks to the boom in pleasure boating, one unpleasantness has been removed from first-aid kits—many companies now make the kits of plastic so they do not rust away to nothing after one season. Especially, be sure a resuscitube is packed with the kit, and learn the most efficient methods of giving artificial respiration.

The Coast Guard regulation requiring an approved life preserver for every person aboard the boat applies to racing yachts as well as other boats. Do not neglect this rule of the sea. Carry one or two children's life preservers, because the adult size is useless for little fellows. Make certain you *always* have light-weight life preservers readily accessible for immediate use.

17. The Lore of Weather

As a racing sailor, you will have a vital interest in weather phenomena; you must change your thinking from that of the landsman who can make do with a look out the window or the sketchy forecast sandwiched in between the evening's television news. The needs of the sailor are more sophisticated, the necessary information more detailed than that required by the average person.

There is probably no need for a complete knowledge of meteorology, for this is a complicated and exacting science; but the sailor must work, at the least, on becoming "weatherwise." You must learn as much as you can out of self-defense, for if you are unable to read obvious weather signs, your better-informed competitors will have a decided advantage.

The study of weather, like the study of the other faces of nature, has always fascinated me, and I have spent many hours training myself to notice the skies and to understand the "why's" of change. Beyond a doubt, it has been invaluable in helping me in my racing. Ask yourself these questions, and see of you can really answer them:

Why is it cold in January? What is different between January and February weather? Why is it different? What conditions cause June to be fine and fair and January to be drear and unpleasant? What is rain? Where does the wind blow from? I wonder how many of us are really competent to answer these seemingly infantile questions.

The difference between the average man and the creative scientist is precisely the intellectual curiosity with which questions as simple as these are pursued. A child asks, "Daddy, why is the sky blue?" And we are embarrassed because we must answer with an oversimplification that is a half-truth. So it is with these other simple questions, for when something simple is explored to the end, it generally no longer remains simple.

We are interested in general weather patterns because they will be the largest influence upon our local conditions. Because of the work of the gifted Norwegian meteorologist, Bjerkenes, we now think in terms of large "packages" of air that are the "factories" that produce weather. The characteristics of a mass of air thousands of miles away will interest us, for sooner or later its effects will be felt in our own area. Though we are primarily concerned with local conditions for the day of our race, we will also find it to our advantage to become acquainted with over-all weather patterns throughout the world.

Some of the things that we must explore are the characteristics of high- and low-pressure areas, the meanings of warm and cold fronts, the names and significances of cloud formations, the all-important use of the barometer, and familiarity with the weather map. In this chapter I want mainly to discuss weather as it applies to yacht racing, since it would be impossible in the space available to cover the field of weather completely. I suggest that the beginning racer buy a good meteorology textbook to learn terms, principles, and methods of weather forecasting. One that is done in an entertaining manner, and that is complete but not overly technical, is *Eric Sloane's Weather Book.** Sloane is an artist who is also interested in meteorology, and his drawings are imaginative and illustrate the text clearly.

I would like to divide this discussion of weather into two parts, the first a discussion of conditions that prevail over the nation, and the second a discussion of purely local weather. When I talk about national weather, it will have application to racing men no matter where they live; when I speak of local conditions, I must, of necessity, refer to those that prevail mostly in the North Atlantic states, since this is where I have gained most of my experience. But the yachtsman must bear in mind that for every sign of the coming weather particular to my section of the country, there is a similar sign applicable to his.

* E. Sloane, *Eric Sloane's Weather Book,* (New York, Duell, Sloan, & Pearce).

In my talking about observations concerning Long Island Sound, the value will lie in illustrating the kind of weather portents one should be on the alert for. In my discussion of the characteristics of winds from different quadrants especially, the reader will have to bear in mind that they are meant for my own area. For example, a wind from the north will have different characteristics on the Gulf Coast from what a similar wind would have on the Middle Atlantic coast. The main thing to remember is that the wind from each separate quarter has its own individual identity and will bring conditions that are peculiar to it. This holds true no matter where you live.

For example, southeast wind of any duration on Long Island Sound is a poor weather sign and usually produces rain. Southeast wind on the east coast of Florida results in the best weather.

Westerly wind on the Sound predicts good weather, whereas on the east coast of Florida it is almost certain to bring rain the next day.

The Weather Map

We have mentioned that large masses of moving air will behave as gigantic "factories," building the varying conditions that we call weather. In general, because of the rotation of the earth, weather tends to move from west to east. The rate at which this weather moves depends upon the velocity of the air mass, as well as several other factors; but in general, it will advance at a rate that is roughly 500 miles per day in summer (750 in winter). So in all likelihood, we should expect that on Tuesday night, New York City will have the same weather that existed over Chicago on Monday. During advance planning of a weekend race, we must take cognizance of weather in the far west, because high- and low-pressure systems and cold and warm fronts there will eventually make their influence felt to the east.

Weather does not always move in a true easterly direction. Sometimes a high-pressure area will merge into a low-pressure area in another direction than east, or a front will dissolve, but in general, we can expect weather systems to follow this easterly course.

The daily weather map is a graphic representation of weather conditions that exist throughout the nation on a particular day. One thing you must remember is that the weather map you are reading in today's paper is really a picture of conditions as they were yesterday. Therefore, a weather map that pictures a cold front 500 miles to the west is already obsolete; by the time you read your paper, the front is overhead. Despite this lag, the weather map is the greatest aid we have for predicting the weather.

The passage of a front will be accompanied by rain and probably by strong- to violent-winds, depending on the season, nature of the front, and how close together the isobars are. I suggest you learn the characteristic clouds of both cold and warm fronts, because you must be able to recognize the approach of these weather systems when you are out on the water. As you look over the weather map, pay particular attention to the spacing of the isobars—isobars are lines connecting stations of equal pressure—for this is your surest indication of wind strengths within a pressure system. Also note the positions and directions of movement of high- and low-pressure systems. Remember that in the northern hemisphere, winds will blow clockwise out of high-pressure areas into low-pressure areas, where they will reverse direction and blow counterclockwise. The small arrows on the map show wind direction, and the feather barbs show the force in 5-knot increments.

Another aspect of large masses of air that concerns us, but that is not usually labeled on the weather map, is the nature of the air mass—that is, whether it is tropical maritime (mT), polar maritime (mP), continental polar (cP), or one of the five other types. Each type has distinctive properties, and except for minor modifications acquired as it moves will retain those properties. Thus winter cP air from Canada will be cold, dry, and of high density. When this strikes against warmer mP air already over an area, a well-defined cold front will be formed—with accompanying cloud formations, precipitation, and high winds.

So we see that the weather map is a picture that—if you can read it properly—will show you the general weather characteristics to come. Forewarned is forearmed, and the man who studies the weather is in a position to exploit what he learns.

On the morning of the race, we consult the weather map and move the positions of the highs and lows 500 miles to the east. Now we note which side of the high or low we will be on, what direction the wind can be expected from, what the strength will be, and how dependable it is likely to remain. If the high or low shows a good, well-defined pattern, we will be able to count on a steady wind. But if the isobars are far apart or, in other words, if the gradient is gradual, then the wind is likely to be uncertain and undependable.

191

The Lore of Weather

The Barometer

After the weather map, the barometer will be your next most important source of weather information. The barometer measures the weight of the atmosphere, and since a fairly good instrument is relatively inexpensive, it is a weather aid that you can have right in your home. The words *stormy, rain, changeable,* and *fair* that are printed on most barometers have no value or significance for the sailor or meteorologist. What we are interested in is not so much the pressure at a single reading, but the pressure tendency over a period of time, with the tendency during a three-hour period immediately preceding a radio weather report holding the most meaning. From this record we can ascertain whether the barometer is rising, falling, or holding steady.

If a man sees a high barometer, it is probably a 10 to 1 chance that there will be little wind of any strength that day; whereas a low barometer is an equally sure indication of vigorous winds. This is, of course, an oversimplification, but it is an oversimplification that will prove correct often enough to provide a good rule-of-thumb.

I think that a yachtsman who fails to consult his barometer at least twice a day doesn't deserve to win races. It is amazing the information that instrument is waiting to tell you if you only learn to interpret it. I would no more think of coming downstairs, morning or night, without noting the barometer and setting it, than I would of not saying my prayers; both habits are good.

On Clouds

It is wise to study cloud formations and spend time recognizing and naming them. Clouds are beautiful to look at, and they are weather indicators. The cold front, the warm front, the thunderstorm, and the squall all have their typical cloud formations. Get the *Manual of Cloud Forms, Circular "S,"* published by the U.S. Weather Bureau, and available for thirty-five cents from the Superintendent of Documents; it has excellent photographs of the major cloud forms. When you have learned to name clouds by referring first to their altitude and then to the ten genera of the formations themselves, you will be surprised how easy it will be to recognize and name those over your own area.

When utilizing clouds as an aid to weather forecasting, remember that it is not an isolated layer of clouds that is important so much as the kinds and number of formations that have preceded and will follow a particular time of observation.

ON THE WINDS

If sails are the engine of a sailboat, the winds are the fuel that moves it. As a racing skipper you must learn as much about the nature of the winds as is possible, and no one is ever able to completely master all there is to know. For the landsman, wind is just wind—something to do battle with for an umbrella or a hat. For the sailor, each wind is an individual, with an identity of its own, having a face and personality he can recognize. Like persons, too, winds from some quarters are inconstant and fickle; others are hard workers, steady and reliable.

In my area, when the wind blows from a particular quadrant, I know pretty well what to expect from it, both in the way of weather and sailing conditions. As I have said, the greater part of my experience has been on the Middle Atlantic seaboard, and I will have to confine my statements regarding winds to that area. I believe, however, that a listing of the characteristics of the winds that blow over Long Island Sound will have value to the general reader. This value lies in the example such a listing gives of the kinds of information that you should try to compile for your own area.

Because of the different rates of heating and cooling of the earth's surface, the nature of the winds will modify slightly during every month of the year. In practice, however, we can think of modification as occurring only four times a year—in spring, summer, fall, and winter. The typical behavior of wind from a given direction will vary in intensity, steadiness, and temperature with the changes of the seasons. Your list—or wind analysis, let us call it—should take this seasonal change into account.

ANALYSIS OF THE WINDS

The northwest wind is common in Long Island Sound and is character- ized by its dependability during the time it blows. In my opinion it is an unpleasant breeze to sail in, because despite its constancy, it will be spotty and full of holes, even in the hardest northwesters. In the winter the northwester will often result from a cold front and the winds will approach gale intensity; in the warmer months they are less severe.

Once it sets in, a northwest wind will blow steadily, depending upon the force with which it starts: the harder it is, the longer it will last. If you get a good hard northwester at 12 to 15 knots in the morning, it will last throughout the day, at least until sunset. If it sets in at 15 to 25 knots, it is almost a certainty that it will carry over into the next day and you will have two days of northwest winds. In northwest conditions on the Sound, I have found it best to plan my strategy so that I cross the Sound immediately to obtain the fresher puffs. As the northwester changes its characteristic, it most often hauls to the north.

The northerly, which usually follows the northwester, is a very undependable breeze. In both winter and summer, despite its morning promise, it is likely to die out in the afternoon. It can be a beautiful morning with the northerly blowing a spanking 15 or 18 knots, and you'll think, "What a wonderful wind for today's race." But by afternoon there will be no wind at all, for it will fade out or move to another quarter, probably east. The northerly, despite its flukey nature, is fun to race in because you never know what will happen. I have found in working to windward in a northerly that after getting halfway across the Sound it is an important advantage in favoring the east, because the tendency is for puffs to come approximately north by east. This produces sizable starboard tack lifts.

I imagine that everyone has his favorite breeze, and mine is decidedly a lively northeaster. It is the most delightful wind that we have in the Sound, and it is too bad that it is not our prevailing wind instead of the humid southwesters. I am often teased because of my enthusiasm for northeasters, but people are more susceptible to the influences of the weather than they realize. I can go to bed troubled, weighted down with cares and anxieties, and when I awaken—they are all blown away. I look out the window, and sure enough, there is that weather vane pointing northeast. The barometer is high, the air is light and dry and I can't help but feel exhilarated. The northeast breezes are true, not full of holes or spotty, and are perfect to sail in. They raise a good lump of a sea that is fun to contend with and that adds interest to sailing.

In normal good weather, when you are sailing in a northeaster, you must watch for any sign of the wind beginning to wane, for this is a sure indication that the wind will veer around to southwest. If you see a good 18-knot northeaster drop down to, say, 12, or a 12-knot breeze fall off to 6 or 8, you can be certain that the southwester is making up. Sometimes the southwester will advance across the water with the northeaster still blowing. It is important to watch for this condition, because it can get you into trouble with your racing strategy. We are often fooled by this sudden change of wind direction; it takes you completely by surprise. So in a waning northeaster, always watch for signs of the southwester. You can see these signs in other sailboats, in smoke rising from a fixed point, and most important, in the appearance of the wind itself on the water.

Also, it is imperative that you realize that a sailboat is not an automobile or a power boat; you cannot bear off and cut cross "lots" looking for the new breeze. You'll lose if you do. You will run out of the waning northeaster and wallow around in the doldrums while waiting for new wind to come to you. Meanwhile, the other skippers have stayed in the old breeze and kept their boats moving toward the new, and will almost surely obtain it first.

When racing in shifting winds, therefore, the idea is to stay with the existing breeze as long as you possibly can. In Long Island Sound, when we have this situation, with the northeaster about to change to southwest, we hold up in the northeaster till the last minute, even if it means we are being taken far above our course. The boat must be kept moving with what wind there is and in a position to pick up the southwester when it arrives. Again, keep in mind that you must *stay in the old condition as long as you can; keep your boat moving until you reach the new wind.*

We seldom have a true easterly wind, but we often have a southeaster; this is our most undependable breeze. We don't have them too often, and we all get fooled by them. They come in with a beautiful sparkly ripple, and then, after an hour or so, we are left becalmed, probably to slat around in the motorboat swell for hours. Even the southwester can't be depended on to come in in this weather condition.

A southerly—that is, a wind from due south—is very, very rare in the Sound. It is a nice breeze, solid and without holes in it. I have found that the best way to work a southerly is to move to the west and try to take advantage of starboard tack lifts.

The southwester is the wind that we have to contend with the most, and unfortunately it is not a good breeze except in the springtime. During this season, southwesters come across Long Island quickly, and they are solid and delightful to sail in. But as the weather warms, they don't come across the Island, though they are beautiful and sparkly on the ocean side of the Island's south shore. The southwester will, in May and June, blow steadily and true. But it will be spotty and full of holes. The warmer the weather gets, the more unreliable the southwester becomes.

Since the southwester can fool us regularly, it is always a problem in sailing across the Sound whether to go straight across to the south or to work to the west. I have evolved a formula that has been quite successful. If the southwester is strong and true, I will sail due south across the Sound, and thus capitalize on port tack lifts to the weather mark. If, on the other hand, I have any doubts about the reliability of the breeze, I work to the west. It is especially necessary to go to the west if the wind is a little west of southwest. If another class or other sailboats are ahead of you, watch in the west to see if they are obtaining starboard tack lifts; if they are, then it is safe for you to follow suit. Under these conditions, if you had gone straight across, you would have been lifted and would have rounded up under the whole fleet—needless to say, a most undesirable spot to be forced into.

Incidentally, on a flat calm day, we have a peculiar indication that the wind will go around to southwest. In certain atmospheric conditions, a kind of dark haze will develop in the southwest. It has a similarity to the look of the sky when a northwest squall is making up, although more grey than black, but it does not mean squall conditions. It does indicate that a southwest wind is in the area and if conditions are right, it will reach you.

I don't know what causes this black, cloudlike sign of wind. Perhaps it is smoke or pall being blown along in front of the new wind, but I do know that throughout my racing in Long Island Sound, it has meant the presence of a southwest wind. Whether or not it will come in is another matter. But it must be watched.

As I said at the beginning, only sailors who race in this particular area will be directly benefited by this discussion; but it can be of value to racing men no matter where they operate. If you live on the southern Atlantic Coast, the Gulf Coast, the Great Lakes, or the West Coast, you must try to build up a working knowledge of the behavior and peculiarities of your winds from each quadrant. When I leave my home grounds for national or international racing, I always make certain that I inform myself about the characteristics of the winds in the strange area. The skipper without this knowledge will find himself severely handicapped.

SOMETHING ABOUT SQUALLS

A squall, no matter where it comes from or where it is going, is a very violent, localized wind system, and it can be a fearsome thing indeed. I think that the man who dismisses squalls contemptuously is either a fool or has never been exposed to a fully developed line squall. When talking to the juniors, never be off-handed in your references to squalls, for they can be really serious; and the youngsters should never be taken unawares or unprepared. For that matter, they are serious for adults as well; not only can they destroy a race, but they can badly damage your boat.

When I was younger, I had the attitude, "Who's afraid of a squall? If you're going to swim, you're going to swim; and if you're going to sink, you're going to sink." But I know now that my attitude was the bravado of ignorance coming from my never having been caught out in a real squall. Since then, however, I have gone through many of them, and it is a downright unpleasant, even terrifying experience.

When the ominous black roll cloud that precedes a squall appears, make sure everything is secure. With your crew, review your plans for how you plan to weather it. A line squall in the northern hemisphere is a manifestation of a fully developed cyclone, so don't get into the habit of referring to a summer thunderstorm as a "squall."

The worst squalls on Long Island Sound are always those that come from the northwest. I have never seen a westerly, southerly, or easterly squall blow more than 30 knots, whereas a northwester can blow from 30 to 80. Sometimes they are very localized: I remember one that registered 50 to 80 knots in New Rochelle, and at Rye, a few miles away, there was not a breath of air.

Occasionally a northwest squall will break up before it reaches your area. Keep looking at the center of the blackest part of the squall cloud, and if there appears to be a slight lightening of the color toward the dull gray of a rain cloud—as compared with that awful blackness—it is breaking in half. In a matter of minutes, the blackness can dissipate; and in as little as three to five minutes the whole cloud can break up and disintegrate. This means that the intensity is waning and the storm center is moving off elsewhere. There is still the likelihood that you will get some vicious gusts and, of course, rain, but the immediate threat is gone for the present. However, it can re-form.

It has always been an awesome thing for me to watch this mountainous mass of air forming, re-forming, and collapsing with such tremendous speed. It is exciting to see and certainly reinforces the sailor's respect for the gigantic forces that nature can muster.

Weather Omens: Fact or Fiction?

Now if you are the kind of person who will accept knowledge only from the latest scientific sources, I suggest that you omit this section. But it will be too bad if you do, for you will not only miss some of the romance of tradition, but you will also skip some information that might just help you to win races.

There is a great deal of wisdom in the weather proverbs that have come to us through the centuries, and most of it is founded on practical experience.

"Red sky at night is a sailor's delight. Red sky at morning, sailor take warning!" This is how one proverb has come down to us today, and its truth is such that it is still included in texts for Naval officers. Much of this folklore can be easily explained by scientific theory, but some of it cannot and must be taken on faith.

In every section of the country there is some old-timer who will state, "we're in for a spell of bad weather." Skeptics laugh away this statement as pure mysticism, but most probably the prophet is merely more aware of tiny imperceptible signs than those of us who have had the faculty of of weather-awareness blunted by living in concrete cities. However, if you are racing sailboats, it is a wise idea to retrain this awareness back into your consciousness. Here are some of the weather signs that I have noticed in the East. There will be similar ones for your area as well.

When, on a summer's morning, there is dew on the grass and flat surfaces, it is almost a certainty that a southwest wind will come up some time during the day.

On a still day, when the light is right, you can sometimes catch sight of gossamer strands in the rigging. I don't know why or how they appear, but they do. They have the appearance of minute strands spun by a spider, although no spiders are involved, I am sure of that. In our area these gossamers are a sure sign of a coming southwest wind. In other areas they may predict something else.

Here is a passage from *The Sea and the Jungle** by the fine writer of the sea H. M. Tomlinson: "Gossamers in the rigging today led the captain to prophesy a storm before night." At the time, the *Capella*, Tomlinson's ship, was lying in the Amazon River.

The appearance of opening crocuses is unfailing in predicting northeast winds. The wind will come either on the day the flowers are first sighted, or the following day. Again, I don't know why this should be, whether it is the nature of the northeast air or what, but crocuses always mean northeast winds for me.

* H. M. Tomlinson, *The Sea and the Jungle* (New York: E. P. Dutton & Co.).

When seabirds cluster inland in large groups and are reluctant to fly, it is a sign of an approaching storm. The reason for this is obvious. The air is thinner within a low-pressure system; it is harder to fly in this air, and storms accompany low-pressure systems. So the birds stay close to the earth where the atmospheric pressure is highest. Birds are much more sensitive to pressure changes than human beings, and behavior like this is a sure indication of future foul weather.

Morning summer fog is always an indication of a beautiful day.

The appearance of porpoises on the eastern seaboard almost always foretells a northeast wind. Why, I don't know, unless, like me, they just love that sparkly northeast air. I have been teased about this belief of mine, but I have consistently gotten back my licks at the porpoise-scoffers.

During one Annapolis-Newport Race in John Nicholas Brown's *Bolero*, the wind was southwest, making the course down the coast a dead beat. We were on the starboard tack and headed off shore. It was my watch, and around nine o'clock that night my friends the porpoises suddenly appeared. We were beating off Montauk and taking a long board offshore because the wind would not allow us to lay the mark, the Chesapeake Light Ship.

I told the afterguard, "We're going to get a northeast wind, and we're foolish to depart from the rhumb line. I think we should go on the port tack to get closer to the course, so that when the northeaster arrives we can set our spinnaker and steer for the lightship." Well, we did just that, and within two hours, the northeaster came in strong. That was the year that we beat *Baruna,* our great competitor, by 24 seconds in the 350-mile race. From then on, the *Bolero* crew always believed what the porpoises told them.

While not strictly a weather sign, there is another phenomenon that I have observed. Very often at the turn of the tide, when it begins to flood, the wind will also pick up. When maximum flood is reached, the wind will slacken, and when the ebb starts, it will often die out.

When a wind shift is imminent, it often takes place when the tide is at the flood. In the summer, I've noticed that an easterly will shift to southwest at the very hour that the current tables tell you the tide will be at flood. I've talked about this ever since I have been racing, and I have never heard anyone else who has had the same thought; and I have never been able to find a completely satisfying answer myself. The best I have been able to do is assume that the rise and fall of that enormous body of water raises or lowers the atmospheric pressure enough to trigger the natural wind changes. No one has as yet refuted my theory.

Now, you might think that all the foregoing is a lot of superstitious nonsense. If you do, try keeping a weather log, as I have done. At the end of the year, when the gossamers and the porpoises have done their work, and when you begin to think of having a new mahogany breakfront built to hold your silverware, I will be happy to welcome you to the ranks of the Order of Mystical Weathermen.

One thing is certain; if a skipper dashes out of the house to his boat, glances quickly at a falling barometer, wets his sneakers in the dew on the lawn, brushes the gossamers in the rigging off his face, and then squints up at the sky and says, "I wonder what quarter the wind's going to come from today," he most definitely doesn't deserve to win.

18. Nautical Nuggets

Much of this chapter may be elemental and familiar to more experienced sailors, but there is so much for all of us to enjoy learning that everyone, when this is realized, becomes a beginner. In my own case I've sailed all my life, only to find out how actually little I know. The wonderful fascination of sailing is to realize that every time you go out, there is something new to learn.

The fly on your shrouds (black thread or wool, not ribbon) is the golden key to sailing your boat properly. Keep your eye on it constantly.

If your main halyard is not led inside your mast, use a light halyard in the harbor to protect your regular halyard from the weather.

Check your mooring line regularly for cuts or chafe. Also check swivels, shackles, and chain regularly.

Use cotter pins on upper barrels only of turnbuckles.

Tape all pins both aloft and below to protect your spinnaker.

Prior to the start of your season, lay off compass courses between all marks in your racing area.

Include any reference marks indicated on the chart—bridges, buildings, water towers, chimneys, etc. Bearings of this nature are invaluable in determining your course to an unseen mark in hazy weather. Cross index in a book for immediate availability.

Carry a government chart of your racing area and a pair of parallel rulers.

Carry rip-stop tape for spinnaker rips.

Helvetia will beautify your teak.

If you sail in salt water, wash your boat with fresh water after every sail to protect the paint and varnish.

A tiller strap of shock cord leading directly to the cockpit floor simplifies making the mooring when sailing alone and makes for more accessibility in the cockpit than a thwartship lanyard. The latter does not give the rudder freedom and causes wear on the key in the rudder post. Fiber-glass battens are the most durable and will permit the sail to take its natural shape, especially aloft.

Be constantly aware of what direction the tide or current is running. Even in your pleasure sailing, know how it is affecting you.

⚓ *Know the Racing Rules!*

Check halyard sheave pins in the spring and fall. Check swage fittings for cracks in the barrel regularly during the season, using a magnifying glass. Also examine shrouds for broken strands in the areas of fittings.

Do not permit sails to be scrubbed too hard when they are washed, as hard scrubbing is likely to break the stitching.

Should you upset a centerboarder, neither you nor any member of the crew should leave the boat.

Have an accurate compass. Check your new course after each tack to determine lifts and headers of that particular board.

Stow your anchor clear of the compass.

⚓ *Look at the fly.*

Make it a rule that no mediocre swimmers go off your boat when you are anchored in current unless you have aboard 30-40 feet of line streaming with a life preserver attached.

Practice man overboard procedures by throwing over a life preserver and attempting to recover it.

Exercise your powers of observation to the fullest degree. You will be astonished at the amount of knowledge you will acquire. Observe the tactics and the sail trim of your successful competitors. Observe the weather, the characteristics of the winds, the tidal and current flows.

Make certain the bottom of your boat is free of slime. The best of tuning, sails, and good helmsmanship cannot overcome this handicap.

To show no respect for a thunderstorm is a sure sign of inexperience. Don't try to pose as a hero in a treacherous squall.

Practice making your mooring in a seamanlike manner. A skipper can be judged by how he handles this department. Tide and sea are important factors to be considered.

Keep your boat immaculate and shipshape. You will enjoy her more.

⚓ *Know the racing rules!*

Look at your barometer morning and evening. It is very important in estimating the wind velocity and direction.

Unless you operate your boat on a very extravagant basis, a drifting genoa is an unnecessary inventory item. It is more practical and economical to put this amount of money in a light weather jib. Drifting genoas are good in theory but the actual distance gained over a regular light-weight jib is negligible. It must be taken off when the wind increases to two or three knots, and if there has been any advantage it will probably be lost, with added time consumed in changing to a heavier sail.

Theoretically a large spinnaker through the presentation of a larger area should be a faster sail than a small one. This, however, is not true except in fresh breezes of 18-20 knots and up. A big sail will not stand as well, especially in disturbed water, because it does not dispose of the wind as readily as the smaller spinnaker. A smaller spinnaker should not contain too much draft. We conclusively proved in the Twelves time after time that the small, relatively flat sail was faster in light to moderate breezes dead before the wind. On reaches, the larger sails are definitely faster but only when the apparent wind is 12-14 knots and up (see picture of *Nefertiti* and *Columbia*).

If necessary be sure and firmly demand your right of way when it exists.

Don't race or cruise offshore without a spinnaker net. When this sail turns around the headstay a textile machine couldn't wind it any tighter.

203

It can take hours to clear it. There are various types of net that are satisfactory. One is quite simple that can be quickly set. It involves a rope halyard set next to the jibstay with the device that is used in self-furling jibs secured to the foot and a swivel at the head. Four or five lines of ¼ inch nylon lines secured equidistant up the net halyard lead off to a foot line for setting. When the self-furling device is released the net rolls off like a curtain. The net has the profile of a conventional working jib. The foot or trimming line is placed where the clew of the jib would be.

A well-designed, staunchly built light-weight genoa is decidedly advantageous over a sail a few ounces heavier. The difference can actually be sensational. For example, in the Twelves, we learned that a five-ounce genoa could be carried in a breeze up to approximately 12 knots' strength of wind. Previous to this it was our practice to put on an eight-ounce sail in seven or eight knots. We proved that the lighter weight sail was very much faster until the wind reached the sail's upper limit of 12 knots. It is therefore recommended to skippers of open and cruising classes to put more emphasis on lighter weight jibs in their sail inventory.

Don't take chances at the start, crossing on the port tack, bearing off and tacking too close. Laxity in rule observance can only bring the same result as all other forms of carelessness. It is far better to be conservative in this regard, rather than to be disqualified in one race which could be most costly in your season championship standing.

In maneuvering for a downwind start in a centerboard or a keel centerboard boat, make certain your board is down. This will permit you to fully control your boat in close quarters.

After you have tested the starting line for the favored end, you and all crew members should constantly watch to make certain the Committee launch has not moved the flag end, or that the Committee has not rendered 40 or 50 feet more scope on the Committee boat causing a material change in the line. Too, see that the white flag of the starting line on the Committee Boat has not been changed.

Check course signals again at the time of the preparatory and enter it in your daily log. Don't trust to your memory.

Have a crew member assigned to the binoculars for a recall signal on the start. All crew members listen for your number. At the beginning of each leg, all the crew should call out the next mark.

⚓ *Don't overstand the weather mark.*

Constantly anticipate possible changes. If the spinnaker is set, be prepared to get it off and set the jib if the wind draws ahead. Be prepared to set the spinnaker if the wind draws aft. Boat lengths of profit can result if you are alert in this regard.

The same preparation must be made for changing to light and heavy sheets. It may not sound too important, but costly panic parties can occur when the crew is unprepared for these minor changes.

Don't carry your spinnaker too close to the leeward mark. The little you gain will be lost if you are unprepared to properly and quickly trim for the windward leg.

If you set your spinnaker and find the wind is too far ahead to carry it, get it off immediately. Don't fight your error.

Free up your jib and main in the lulls of breezes that vary in strength.

Move your jib lead out when the breeze is strong and the main luffs.

If necessary, change your sail trim on each tack for the different angle sea.

Don't fight for either end of the starting line. If you lose (especially the leeward end), it is much too costly. However, be sure to be on the line, and of course endeavor to have your wind free with full way. Select your starting point and plan your start accordingly. Don't flounder and hope to find a clear spot. Constantly keep your boat moving at good speed after the preparatory.

⚓ *Know the racing rules!*

Lower the main halyard a few inches on all light-to-moderate weather reaches and runs.

If you are leading, make certain you cover the second boat, and if possible the third. Under no circumstances get in a position where you are not between them and the weather mark.

Don't overstand and give away hard-earned distance to windward. Plan to approach the weather mark on the starboard tack.

Don't be harassed by power-boat swells. More harm to your boat's speed can come from the distraction than is lost by the swells. Let your competitors do the shrieking and complaining. If they do, you may well convert the problem to a gain.

No matter how secure your position may be in the race, permit no relaxation in your boat. Constantly expect the unexpected.

Don't cry about bad breaks. They come to all members of the fleet. If you moan about them, you can do yourself more harm psychologically than the bad breaks can do you. Dismiss them from your mind immediately and sail your boat.

⚓ *Minimize your tacks.*

Unless there is a good reason, such as ability to lay the windward mark, try to avoid tacking under a competitor's lee bow. If you do, you are locked (unless you are close enough to back-draft him) with no flexibility. Better to cross or go under and tack clear of his weather quarter. You are then in control.

In a large class, avoid luffing matches even if it costs you a place. At best you can win the battle but lose the war.

To prevent your boat from rolling to windward in a fresh breeze, dead before the wind, trim the spinnaker sheet as hard as possible.

⚓ *Don't overstand.*

In light weather, search for new wind constantly. Indications can be seen on other sailboats, fixed smoke, flags, and of course, in the appearance of wind on the water.

⚓ *Don't take your eye off the fly.*

A boom vang set up very hard will produce the same effect as a wide traveler, and will trim your sail aloft. It is recommended that you sail to windward in fresh breezes with the vang set very taut. If the vang is not set as you approach the weather mark, set it while the mainsail is trimmed. Be sure to ease your vang as wind strength diminishes. The boom or gooseneck fixture may break if caution is not exercised in hard breeze jibes.

Similar to the vang, the traveler, when positioned to a wide trim, flattens the upper part of the mainsail and permits the sail to be trimmed considerably wider, 12 to 15 degrees on a reach, thereby providing more power. Be sure you obtain this advantage, as with the vang, and slack the sheet to the maximum. In reaching, the problems associated with the traveler are not so difficult to deal with; but in windward work, the traveler presents many difficulties. Great delicacy is required for obtaining the correct positions for this point of sailing. Considerable judgment and patience are necessary in the skipper's experiments for the proper positions in various strengths of wind, for the shape of the mainsail is the most important factor. In light weather, for example, the sail should be trimmed from a midship position; as the breeze increases, a wider trim is required for trimming the upper part of the sail. A mainsail with a high clew should use little traveler, whereas a low-clew sail with moderate-to-full draft must be eased well over on the traveler to trim the upper area—even in light weather. The traveler is not an easy device to master, but it is a worthwhile one when properly employed.

⚓ *Don't permit a lee-bow current to cause you to overstand.*

Don't tack to leeward unless the wind is dead aft and light.

On the wind, allow your boat to have her head. Don't force her higher than she can sail. Let her sail herself. She can do it better than you. Merely guide and trim her properly. There is no mysto-magic touch of the helm that so many seem to think exists—especially some winners. It is a combination of various efforts that wins races. In a one-design class, it is the tuning, the bottom, and the helmsman's ability to select a good crew, to organize the boat, to start well, to be composed, to know how the sails should be trimmed in all conditions, to know where to go on the windward leg, to get out of trouble and not waste time crying about his bad breaks or gloating that the favorable breaks are his good judgment. Most important of all, unless sails are one-design and drawn by lot, are *sails*. The latter are, in my opinion, 75 percent of the factors that make a boat successful.

Don't trim your jib too flat, even in hard weather. This is a common failing about which you must be cautious. You deprive the jib of its power. It is a sign of tautness on the part of the skipper and crew. They believe this will make the boat point higher. The reverse can be true.

Make certain you call *mast line* when it is achieved.

Steer your boat from the windward side in moderate and hard breezes. It is more pleasant and comfortable, and you will see the breeze better. Also of great importance, you will have a better look at the seas and in consequence be able to work her through them more effectively. Of some consideration, too, your weight will be to windward. From this position, sail her by what you can see of the jib and, of course, the fly. Disregard the luffing of the mainsail in this strength of wind.

Feather her through the strong puffs. Keep her on her bottom. Never let the lee rail get in the water. Ease the main a few inches if necessary to prevent this.

The crew must concentrate 100 percent on sail trim during runs and reaches.

⚓ *Watch the fly.*

If you have a sufficient lead at the leeward mark, split the difference with the following boat—that is, hold a tack for one-half your lead, then tack to place your boat between the competitor and the weather mark.

At the leeward mark, start your turn away from the mark so you will lose no distance to windward in the turn.

⚓ *Complete concentration throughout the race is vital.*

Permit no undue excitement in your boat; yelling, scolding and tautness will immediately permeate the atmosphere aboard the boat, and performance is bound to suffer.

The head of your jib is not normally seen from the cockpit. If it is not standing, attempt a correction through moving your leads forward.

Persuade an experienced helmsman to come aboard and watch you steer your boat to windward. Ask him to comment on your ability to hold her high enough without being too fine—or perhaps he will find you are inclined to sail too wide. Also let him comment on how you work her through the seas. If possible, have him observe your tactics throughout an entire race from a power boat—or better yet, by sailing with you. Assistance of this kind from an interested friend is priceless guidance that could provide a shortcut to skills that otherwise might take years for you to acquire. Merely use the same procedure that the golf professional uses with the golfer, and the football, baseball, and tennis coaches use with aspirants in those sports.

Select a class to race in that has a large number of competitors. You will learn more, and faster.

Constantly study the racing rules. The appeals are most instructive. Robert N. Bavier's book, *Sailing to Win,* is excellent.

⚓ *Don't take your eye away from the fly.*

Constantly anticipate necessary changes and maneuvers.

Do not waste your time attempting to tell your friends and competitors why you did not win. No one is interested, and you will soon learn that you are talking to yourself. It is much better to ask questions of the more experienced, then *listen*—you will be surprised how much you can learn.

⚓ *Don't waiver in your concentration—*
   no matter what position you are in.

Do not be discouraged by serious blunders. Your competitors are making them, too. The one who makes the fewest usually wins. The greatest mistake you can make, however, is not to learn by your mistakes.

After you have gained a top position in your class standings, seek opportunities to enter open championship series in other boats. Do not give up your own class, but occasional broadening out will be instructive. You will learn to sail other types of boats and meet new competition. It is fine to be a big frog, but prove your ability in a larger pond. It may eventually be the means of getting you on an America's Cup boat.

To be successful in racing as in other sports, you must be intensely interested, anxious to learn, and constantly thinking, and you must fiercely want to win. As in practically any endeavor, you can accomplish almost anything that you really want to do.

⚓ *Don't take your eye off the fly.*

Have your anchor and line stowed in a convenient place for immediate use in an emergency.

In very light drifting weather, slack the jib halyard sufficiently to eliminate the draft curl at the luff.

Learn to pick up a tow in a seamanlike manner.

In light drifting weather, set the windward sheet slightly to produce better contour to the jib.

In the spring, before your season starts, sail your boat in severe weather to test your rig and gear. This is very important for you psychologically.

It will give you complete confidence to sail her hard when heavy weather is encountered during the season.

Check wooden spreaders at both ends for dry rot, keeping them protected with sufficient paint.

Racing in dinghies will teach both the beginner and the experienced sailor more in a shorter period of time than any other form of racing. Here he will learn that indefinable "feel" of his boat, develop concentration, acquire a knowledge of tactics, rules, starts, sails, etc. And if he isn't alert, he will also soon realize the importance of being able to swim.

Get to the starting area early. Abandon any crew member who keeps you waiting more than once.

Make certain you and your crew all know the course.

In any series always endeavor to obtain a good average position in each race. Don't take "long shots" to win. Stay in company with your closest competitors. You don't have to finish first in every race to win a series.

19. On Helmsmanship

The subject of helmsmanship embodies what is probably the most important single principle of successful sailboat racing. The sailor who grasps this principle will be well on the way to becoming a champion. It is this:

The helmsman does not assist the progress of the boat through the water; he impedes it.

Here is why I make this seemingly heretical statement. A boat is making her best progress when she is sailing herself. When the forces of lateral resistance in the keel or centerboard exactly balance the thrust of the wind in the sails, the hull is traveling at the greatest possible speed, considering the force of the wind and the potential of the hull.

When the helmsman corrects with the helm to make the boat follow a predetermined course, he is using the rudder as a brake to alter the natural direction of sailing. Therefore, it follows that the less a skipper uses the helm, the more efficiently he is sailing.

Now we all like to think that it is our magic touch on the helm that causes us to win boat races, but the reverse is true. The man who can balance his boat to sail a given course with the fewest possible helm adjustments is the better sailor. Naturally, during the race, he must put her in the proper places, and for this his good judgment merits credit.

Perhaps the most important element of helmsmanship is the ability to know when a hull is moving well. There are many devices that measure the speed of a boat, but there is none that is sensitive enough to register minute changes in a sailboat's speed. A fortuitous sail adjustment can sometimes affect speed by one-tenth of a knot, and this will not register on speed meters. It is a combination of experience with a given boat, and an intangible "feel" that permits the sailor to mentally sense the increase.

True, a certain amount of innate sensitivity is necessary to learn to steer a boat properly—I don't believe that someone with defective coordination or an inability to sense relative movements could ever become a champion helmsman—but performance can be improved by training.

I think that the best way to develop this "feel" is to sail with a companion boat for comparison, carrying an observer along. When open water is reached, the helmsman is blindfolded and forced to sail the boat without benefit of sight. The observer can guard against accidents and take over if a serious situation develops.

I suppose that a blind person at the helm for the first time would immediately do better than a person with sight. It is not that vision reduces efficiency, but the blind person will have trained himself to be aware of bodily sensations as an aid to orientation. We have gotten into the habit of relying on our sight and ignoring the nerve messages of our other senses. I think that with the proper training a skipper can make himself utilize more of these signs of the boat's performance.

An excellent way to attain feel is to sail at night. In the darkness you do not see swells and surges off the bow, and you must allow for them instinctively. A good nighttime helmsman is a good daytime helmsman.

I believe that talent at the helm of a boat is like any other talent—part of it is inherent. But talent without training and perseverance is of little value. As I have stated elsewhere in this book, the world is full of talented failures.

It is important to work on acquiring feel if you would become a successful racing skipper. When the boat is going properly, she feels "proper" and lively. Although she is pointing up high into the wind, she does not hesitate or stagger when she reaches the top of a crest. She carries her way through it gracefully even if she is hit by a lurcher.

The Two Major Faults

When the Sailboat Training Facility's programs were inaugurated by Herman Whiton to provide a kind of postgraduate training ground for sailors who wanted to become better skippers, I was privileged to act as observer and advisor. During the races I would watch the starts from the committee boat and then hop into an outboard runabout to tail the fleet throughout the whole race. It was an excellent opportunity to watch the skippers in action, and I learned a great many invaluable things. One of the striking facts that became apparent was that not one skipper in ten was sailing the proper heading for the existing conditions: supposedly experienced helmsmen were consistently sailing either too high or too low.

The most common of the two errors was sailing too high. Now the reason for this is easy to understand: in their excitement to beat competitors to the upwind mark, the skippers were sailing their boats too close to the wind and "starving" the sails. The pinching was not flagrant, and probably the loss of speed was barely perceptible, for an experienced skipper would be aware of any obvious luffing. But it was sufficient to prevent those boats from carrying maximum way for the given conditions of the sea. A simple glance indicated the boats were not moving properly.

This International is laying over so far that much of her rudder is out of water, causing her to broach. This can be avoided if in hard breezes a median course is steered slightly above the next mark. Your boat then may be held off in the hard puffs and brought back to course in the lulls.

When a good breeze causes chop to strike the weather bow, it is absolutely necessary to sail your boat wider than you would if there were no disturbance. You must "feel" for those seas, and work her through them. If there is any indication that they are slowing you down, then you must free her up: free up the jib, free up the main a few inches, and let her develop enough power to pull her through the seas. If you do not, you will not only be knocked imperceptibly to leeward, but you will also lose way. I find that many experienced sailers are unaware of this basic principle. They sail to windward in disturbed water with the jib and main strapped in much too hard.

Conversely, it is obvious that on the opposite board we sometimes sail too free. We have no resistance from the waves on the weather bow, but we are sailing with the jib and main trimmed the same as for the other board. Again, by way of illustration, with the wind from the same direction as before, we are now going to windward on the other tack. We are riding gently over the waves instead of slogging into them; we do not need as much power to drive her through them. Now we can strap her a little harder. The important principle to remember is that the two boards of a windward leg will be different and must be dealt with differently: one board or the other will always present more of a problem with the sea.

Another mistake that comes under the heading of sailing too wide is failure to take into account the course you must make good. To illustrate this point: I once sailed a Bermuda Race with a sophisticated helmsman who thought that "the course to Bermuda is 8 knots." We were sailing an exceptionally high-winded boat and could have made good a course much closer to the rhumb line than our actual course. As a result of this fallacious thinking, we must have sailed many miles longer than necessary. That skipper was lured by the idea of speed-through-the-water instead of course-made-good-over-the-bottom. The same error can occur in day-racing, too. Remember that the winning boat will be the one that gets first to the mark: do not sail too free merely for the sake of attaining hull speed.

On Tell-Tales and Wind Pennants

I can't stress too strongly how important it is to sail by the tell-tales on the shrouds and the backstay. Particularly in light airs, it is extremely difficult to gauge the wind direction without an indicator of this sort.

If you know some skipper who says he sails by the luff of the mainsail or jib and doesn't need tell-tales, look at his standing in the fleet before you emulate him—you might learn that he has more to learn than most of us. Perhaps the only reason my long-time rival and friend Arthur Knapp smokes that great chimney pot of a pipe is to find out what direction the wind is from.

Don't use ribbons for tell-tales; they flutter too much. And because of their heaviness, they are not sensitive enough to lift with light airs. I use black thread, since it can be easily seen against the sky. Put a tell-tale on the backstay for the runs; a tell-tale in the shrouds will be useless then, for it will be deflected by turbulent air blowing off the mainsail. Your masthead fly is also valuable on the runs.

Where to Sit

In light airs, and when carrying a genoa jib, it is preferable to seat the crew and to steer from the leeward position. Putting the weight on the leeward side when the breeze is not quite sufficient to heel the boat allows the sails to assume their proper set, and of course you can see the luff of the genoa better.

When the breeze is strong, it is preferable to steer from the windward side. It is a more pleasant sensation, you can observe the seas, and work her through them better. Even when carrying a genoa, I think it is a more comfortable and pleasant place to sit, although many skippers do not agree. Also there is some advantage in having your weight to windward in the smaller boats.

If you are working to windward, keep your crew low in the boat to lessen wind resistance. A few upright bodies present a lot of area to push to windward.

20. Passing on the Tradition

For me, youngsters and yachting are synonymous; many of the finest times I have passed on the water were spent introducing boys and girls to the water and sailboats. Frankly, I am always fascinated by the miracle of a child's growing awareness of the world around him, and it is like experiencing youth again to watch this unfolding of a new personality.

I learned so many things about my own children, Aileen and Corny, while we were sailing together. I could see them absorbing the sights and sounds of sailing, I could watch their curiosity driving them to try and understand what was taking place, and I could share their pleasure when something delighted them. I am certain I would have missed all these wonderful revelations of character if I had not spent so much time sailing with them.

I have no doubt that introducing a child to sailing at an early age makes becoming a champion easier for him. There is so much to be learned, if one is to become a racing sailor, that the youngster who starts early has a distinct advantage. Perhaps the most important asset gained from being around the water at an early age is that children develop a love of the atmosphere of boats and the sea that will stay with them always. Most boys and girls are entranced by the water, anyway, so it is not hard to channel this natural inclination.

Investing time and money in teaching youngsters about yachting is not a one-sided proposition for those interested in yachting, for youngsters bring an immense amount of talent and enthusiasm to yachting. If we who love yacht racing want to see it prosper, we simply have to take pains to interest young people in participation. Many of the sailboat-racing champions who now represent the United States in international competitions are products of organized junior sailing programs.

In some cases, yacht clubs can recover from financial difficulty and avert failure by simply starting junior sailing programs. During the bad years of the 1930's, it was the juniors that saved the Larchmont Yacht Club. Although the story isn't generally known, it is an interesting one that shows how the youngsters can strengthen a club. E. G. Anderson will everlastingly be thanked for his instruction of the first junior program on Long Island Sound at the Larchmont Yacht Club.

Back in the 1930's, as we all know, we were going through the worst economic distress the nation has ever known. Industrial firms, banks, clubs —in short, all types of enterprises—were either close to bankruptcy or had already gone under. Naturally, a yacht club is among the first hit because people economize on nonessentials first. I mentioned before that when I was newly married and just starting in business, I had to resign my Larchmont Yacht Club membership because I couldn't afford the dues.

So, during those depression years, the Larchmont membership had fallen to about 150 members. The annual dues were then about $150. I was a trustee of the club then, as I am now, and at one meeting we found it necessary to discuss the financial matters that threatened our survival. One of the officers suggested that we raise our dues to meet expenses, but I was very strongly opposed to any raise, since I felt sure that at such a time, when everyone was so hard-pressed, an additional expense would only reduce the membership further.

Some of the other trustees thought I was wrong at first when I was seeking a way to *lower* dues to attract more members. Luckily, just at that time I happened to look out the window and catch a glimpse of the club's beautiful swimming pool. "Why not," I proposed, "offer a swimming pool membership and charge only $60?"

Fortunately, the trustees approved the idea, and the results weren't long in coming. People flocked to take advantage of the swimming; the new members brought their wives and children, and it was the children who really got things moving.

At the time we had a rather meager program for juniors; but the youngsters in the swimming pool would watch their friends sailing the few boats we then had. When the parents saw how passionately and sincerely their children wanted to sail, many bought the $60 junior memberships and scrimped other places in their budgets. Soon we bought more boats for the program, and the junior club began to grow.

As the parents saw the facilities that the club offered besides the pool—the restaurant, the yachting, the social events—many of them became regular members and the families' summer recreation activities moved to the yacht club. I'll never forget how some fathers, fulfilling parental duty and full of righteousness for having given up the day's golf games, came down to watch their children's first races, wearing bored, patronizing looks. The following year these same fathers bought boats, their youngsters were crewing for them, and they were ardent racers. Within a few years, we had a fleet of fifty Lightning class boats at Larchmont alone, developed by A. R. O'Neal, Paul Forsnan, Richard Carr, Roy Amy and Alfred Amy. They were all owned by people who had been lured to the club by the enthusiasm of their children. Larchmont has been a financial success ever since, and we have one of the most active and healthy memberships of any yacht club in the country.

After the youngster has successfully completed the junior sailing program, he can best improve his ability as a sailor by crewing aboard a boat in one of the active one-design classes, rather than by skippering his own boat. By crewing for an able and experienced skipper, he will have an opportunity to apply what he has learned under the actual pressures of highly competitive racing. If he is alert, he will absorb an infinite amount of new knowledge that will further prepare him for the day when he becomes a skipper himself.

I think it is a serious mistake to buy a youngster a boat on his own after he has just finished a sailing program. It is a mistake for two reasons: first, because he may be too young to truly appreciate the boat and he may come to feel superior to his companions who are still struggling to get aboard boats as crew members; second, because children often get bored if things are made too easy for them—the boy or girl could easily lose interest in the boat and sailing as well. If you buy a boat for a child too soon, you run the risk of his losing interest in a sport that can be a priceless benefit and source of lifetime pleasure. So for the sake of the child, exercise judgment, and don't give him a boat of his own until he has evidenced a deep and serious interest in sailing.

In my opinion, things should not be made too easy for children. They should earn and merit what is given to them. Anyone who has seen the living-room floor of a modern home on Christmas Day, piled with expensive presents for the children, and also noted the lassitude with which the children receive them, will agree that there is a responsibility inherent in gift-giving that we sometimes ignore.

It is a dreadful thing to me to see some world-weary little tot of nine or ten who has been showered with so much that there seems to be no excitement or novelty left that can arouse him. I often wonder whether the adults are giving to please the children or only to satisfy themselves. I suspect that there is a kind of selfishness involved here, and that the sentiment, "I'd like to give them all the things that I never had!" might constitute an almost criminal lack of sensitivity and awareness on our parts. After all, a child's great charm lies partly in the way his imagination transforms the commonplace objects of his play. We should leave some room for the exercise of that imagination. I have probably belabored this point, but I feel strongly about it, so in anything as important as giving a child his first boat, be sure that the timing is right.

To fully develop his talents as a sailor, therefore, a youngster should, by all means, spend a period as a crew man aboard the boat of an older skipper. In my own boat, I have always made an effort to have one or two children available as crew members—either my own, when they were young, or else boys or girls from around the club who were eager and interested in learning to race. Quite a few of these young people have now become champions in their own right. I urge the skippers of the competitive one-design classes to draw on these children for their crews wherever possible.

You needn't worry about their lack of experience, for a child will astound you by the speed with which he learns even the most sophisticated racing principles. It is a mistake to patronize or talk down to children, because they have an unerring instinct for knowing when you are not being natural with them, and they understand more than we realize. I have learned a great deal about racing from the youngsters in my crew.

I will never forget, for instance, one International race where I was out to hold my position against the wonderfully able skipper, Bus Mosbacher. We had a typical southerly breeze and I was fortunate enough to have picked up a little lead on the reach toward the finish. Young Corny, who was only about six years old at the time, was aboard the boat, and he came across the cockpit toward me and said in a serious way, "I think you ought to watch that fellow over there."

I looked around and saw that Mosbacher had broken away from me and had gone out to windward. I went out after him and fortunately was able to maintain my lead. I couldn't believe that my son had that much understanding at that age, but he was right—I had gotten too confident about the lead I held. If he hadn't noticed the threat of that other boat, I would have lost that race. Here all the time I thought that the boy was just out there tying knots in my jibsheets and fooling around the boat!

One winter I was struggling with my racing dinghy; I couldn't, for the life of me, figure why that boat wasn't going the way she used to. It not only had me puzzled, it had me upset because I was losing races and not doing as well as I had in previous years. As I sailed dejectedly back to the dock from a race one day, my little daughter, Aileen, was waiting ashore where she had been watching the race. As I tied the boat up, she said to me, "You better do something about that mast."

Only half paying attention, I said, "What do you mean?"

"Well, it's got a funny big hook in it," she said.

A little impatient with what I thought was her lack of knowledge, and thinking she was mistaking the natural bowing of the mast for a defect, I grumbled, "Well, it happens I like to sail with a hook in it—it flattens the sail."

"No, not that," she replied. "It's almost 'V' shaped. I don't see how the boat goes with it." Then she walked away.

What she had said bothered me, and I looked the mast over carefully. The dinghies we were then sailing had two-piece masts that were made of aluminum and joined together with a sliding metal ferrule. I didn't think that the ferrule was long enough, so I had removed mine and replaced it with a wooden ferrule that was longer. I thought this would strengthen the mast and hold the two sections more rigid. Instead, what had happened was that the aluminum of the mast had chafed the softer wood as a result of the working of the mast. About an eighth of an inch of the wood had worn away, permitting the mast to sag toward the stern, distorting both the mast and the set of the sail. I replaced the wooden ferrule with a metal one and almost immediately began to win races again with that dinghy.

Since that lesson, I have never offhandedly dismissed the possibility of learning something about sailboat racing from children. They often can see the forest in spite of the trees.

21. How to Build a Junior Sailing Program

I certainly hope that my enthusiasm for introducing the youngsters to the sport of sailboat racing can be communicated and will somehow inspire the founding of junior sailing programs wherever there is a body of water large enough to sail on and there are children to learn. We adults who sail are fortunate that we can pass on the traditions and pleasure of boating to the young people; sailing is far more rewarding and positive than recreational programs that merely aim at keeping the child "occupied and out of trouble." The associations and memories formed in childhood last a whole lifetime, and what a wonderful opportunity it is to be able to give a gift of such enduring value to another person!

For those who might be interested in starting a junior sailing program, I have included this chapter. Some of the material is original, some is the result of our experiences at the Larchmont Yacht Club, and much of it I have learned from talks with many dedicated people who have helped in junior sailing administration.

Objectives

A sailing program for juniors should enroll the child from about age seven until fifteen or sixteen, and it should have the facilities to teach him everything necessary to become a competent boatman. By the time he has completed several seasons of training, the child should be perfectly at home on the water, and his parents need have no concern for his safety. The program should be a long-range one that will provide continuing development; the curriculum should be graduated in difficulty so there will always be new goals to keep the child's interest. Recently, more and more junior sailing programs have extended their facilities to girls and young women, and the ideal training program should, by all means, be coeducational. The officers of existing yacht clubs that at present do not have junior sailing programs should keep in mind that besides providing wholesome recreation and a good environment for children, it assures a continuing and growing membership recruited from these youngsters.

Organizations with Junior Programs

For advice concerning the practical problems of starting a junior sailing program, club officials may check with organizations that have had success with such courses. Among others, the Boy Scouts of America, Sea Scouts, Girl Scouts, Girl Mariners, Camp Fire Girls, American Red Cross, and the Y.W.C.A. and Y.M.C.A., in addition many progressive schools, have training programs in water safety and boat-handling. Many summer camps offer swimming and boating instruction; the United States Power Squadrons and the U.S. Coast Guard Auxiliary encourage juniors to attend their classes and they issue certificates of proficiency upon completion. The Knights of Columbus, the Lions and Rotary Clubs, the Elks, and the Optimists often sanction or sponsor boating programs or races.

As part of their regular activities, most yacht clubs train juniors. The parent club takes responsibility for maintaining affiliations with controlling organizations such as the North American Yacht Racing Union or an area organization such as the Junior Yacht Racing Association of Long Island Sound.

Planning and Staffing

A separate board of directors from that of the parent club should be chosen to supervise junior activities, so there will be no conflict of duties. One or two members should also be officers of the senior club to provide liaison, which will keep members informed of junior activities and needs, insure sufficient race-committee help, and avoid conflicts in scheduling the use of club facilities.

Unless finances are extremely limited, experience of the Larchmont Yacht Club indicates that it is preferable to hire outside instructors, instead of asking parents to volunteer for the teaching staff. The reason for this is that instructors between eighteen and twenty years of age have proven to be most successful with the children. Teachers in this age group are mature enough to handle responsibility well, they command the obedience of the children, and yet they are young enough to participate enthusiastically and to establish feelings of rapport. Older persons have the tendency to be too authoritative and austere, with the consequence that a child's natural exuberance and interest are sometimes lost.

Experiments at Larchmont indicate that children must be allowed to actually board boats as soon as it is reasonably possible or their interest will quickly wane. For this reason, classroom sessions should not be overlong; practical application of classroom work must be quickly forthcoming. If for the first few years of the program's existence, there are not enough boats to accommodate all the students, the enrollment should be limited so that each child has plenty of time afloat. As the children grow up, and after the junior sailing program has attained success, new instructors can be recruited from graduates; thus the program will be assured of a source of well-trained personnel.

How to Finance the Program

If your new sailing program is to be successful, it must eventually become self-sustaining. Few clubs can stand a constant drain upon the treasury to support a youth program of any size. Sound business principles should be used in all matters connected with the operation of the junior sailing program, and the enrollment fee charged for each child should be enough to cover, at least, the salaries of the instructors.

Members of the parent club can be asked to underwrite costs, and bonds can be issued that will mature in five, ten, or more years, depending upon the amount of money that will be needed. A fair rate of interest should accrue to the bondholders wherever possible.

In addition to these methods, the parent club can organize benefit dances, auctions, or other social activities to make up any deficits. A yearbook listing the results of the racing and containing advertising solicited from local merchants can be prepared. "Boosters" can be enrolled from local businesses to raise funds for the purchase or repair of equipment.

When a club is small, the do-it-yourself approach has been successful. Members contribute money to buy materials, and as a winter project they build a number of small pram-type boats. When purchasing sails, however, it is not a good idea to search for the cheapest possible bid; sails are an economical investment, since the new synthetics last many years. It is important that the sails be well cut and well made, and above all it is important that they be as nearly alike as human skill can make them. For this reason, it is wise to place the order with a sailmaker who has experience in making one-design sails.

THE COURSE OF STUDY

Proficiency in swimming must be required of the children before they start sailing; and it is best that they begin swimming prior to their enrollment in the course. To insure a continuity of development, the junior sailing program should cover a period of three to four years. The courses should be graduated in difficulty so that a great deal of theory is not presented in the early stages. Youngsters are more able to learn difficult material than most adults realize, but teachers have found that they do have limited concentration spans at the younger age levels. As I said earlier, by the time the series of courses is finished, the child should have been exposed to all the knowledge necessary to become a competent boatman.

The Junior Yacht Racing Association of Long Island Sound, for example, offers certificates for "Seaman," "Mate," and "Skipper."

To qualify as a Seaman, the candidate must have successfully learned the following subjects:

    a. Cordage: bowline, square knot, clove hitch, fisherman's bend, figure-eight knot, two half hitches, heaving a line, belaying a line, whipping, and coiling.

    b. Nautical terminology.

    c. Dinghy: rowing, proper landing, casting off, safety, hauling, dumping, and launching.

    d. Sails: bending and setting, reefing, furling, and care of sails.

    e. Casting off and picking up mooring, handling the anchor, towline handling.

224

f. Care of boat.

g. Care of personal equipment.

h. Knowing and observing all local rules governing conduct of junior members.

For the certificate as "Mate," applicants must know:

a. Cordage: eye splice, short splice, bowline on a bight, seizing, use of palm and needle.

b. Modern types of boats and rigs.

c. Spinnakers: stop, set, trim, jibe, and take in this sail.

d. Navigation: running lights, rules of the road and whistle signals, box and steer by compass, know buoyage and other aids to navigation.

e. Sailing and helmsmanship: trim sails on all points of sailing; know parts 29-32 of the yacht-racing rules of the Y.R.A.L.I.S., their spirit and purpose; land at a dock, a float, and alongside another boat when both are sailing.

f. Safety: how to provide for man overboard, capsizing, broken steering, squalls, and grounding.

To qualify as a "Skipper," applicants must know:

a. All rules of the Y.R.A.L.I.S.

b. General tactics: starting, windward work, reaching, running, rounding marks, finishing, and team-racing tactics.

c. Tuning up a yacht: standing rigging, running rigging, sails, care of bottom paint.

d. Etiquette: boarding and leaving, use of code flags, use of all flags.

e. Weather: use of barometer, use of weather map, predicting changes, familiarity with local weather conditions.

f. First Aid: resuscitation, open wounds, bleeding, burns (including sun burn), fainting.

This is a representative, comprehensive curriculum, and it can be varied to suit the nature of the boats in which the children are training.

Choosing the Boats

Many different types of small boats are successfully used in the training of juniors, and the selection of a craft depends a great deal upon local conditions. In general, however, the boats must be seaworthy and of good design, and they must handle well. Sluggish or cranky craft will soon dull the interests of the youngsters, and such boats are not representative of the pleasure of working with a lively, able vessel.

The boats must be well built, for they will receive hard usage at the hands of novices. Fiber glass is recommended for its durability and economy of upkeep. In sailing craft, great care must be taken that the class is truly one-design. As I've said already, sails should all be ordered from the same maker, and he should be given instructions that they be cut from the same bolt of cloth and roped by the same technicians wherever possible. They should be drawn for by lot, and boats should be rotated frequently so each child's skill will be the primary factor in his winning or losing.

22. We Sail a Race Together

While sailing out to the starting line, or before, the skipper should check the current tables so he knows the state of the tide at the start and during the race. It is as important to do this when there is a real sailing breeze as it is in light weather, which is when the majority is aware of the way the tide is running because it is more apparent then. The state of the tide must at all times be included in your calculations. A skipper who neglects it may find at the start that a fair tide will put him over the line before the gun or that a head tide will make him late in crossing. Also, if he doesn't figure tide or current in his windward work, he may overstand or under-stand when he tacks for the weather mark. On runs and reaches, consideration of the tide is no less important. If in doubt about the state of the tide, place a bottle or chip alongside the starting buoy or an anchored boat to obtain the direction and speed of tide or current.

No keen racing skipper would consider sailing without a compass, but many, especially on small boats, either do not carry one or fail to make full use of it. Yet a compass may be of inestimable value in determining the tactics at the starting line and during the race. For example, before the start you should sail the reaching leg on a compass course to decide if a spinnaker may be carried. The course for the run should also be tested to determine which jibe is preferable. A shift in the breeze may subsequently necessitate a change in your strategy, but nevertheless you should plan ahead.

Everyone on board should observe the signals on the committee boat, and the course to be sailed should be logged with the date so there is no possibility of confusion. Depending on memory alone is not enough. At the preparatory gun, every crew member should again look to see if the course has been changed.

THE START

The start can be the most important part of your entire race. It is most difficult to regain ground lost at the start. The starting line should be square to the wind, but it may not be, and the skipper must therefore determine which end of the line, or which spot, will be most favorable for a windward start. There are two methods for doing this.

The quickest and simplest method is to place your boat head to wind in the middle of the starting line. Her heading will be closer to the favorable end.

The more exact method is as follows:

1. Luff your boat head to wind, take the *exact* compass heading to obtain wind direction.

2. Sail on the starboard tack on the starting line. Line up the flag end with the white flag on the committee boat, through the headstay and permanent backstay. Read the *exact* compass bearing. If you are unable to get on the line due to the starting activity of other classes, line up the buoy end with the white flag on the committee boat from either end of the line—in other words, make an extension of the starting line. In this case there is only one bearing to be taken. Whichever end of the line is closest to the direction of the wind will naturally be the preferable end on which to start. For example, if the wind were due north and the bearing of the line were east by south (west by north) the easterly end would obviously be favored. If the reverse were true and the bearing of the line were east by north (west by south) the start would then be made at the other end to gain the advantage of the one-point differential. A little practice is required for those unaccustomed to using the compass regularly, but it soon becomes automatic.

If the committee has set the line square properly to the wind, you may start anywhere on the line without disadvantage. The position will be determined by where you have elected to go on the weather leg.

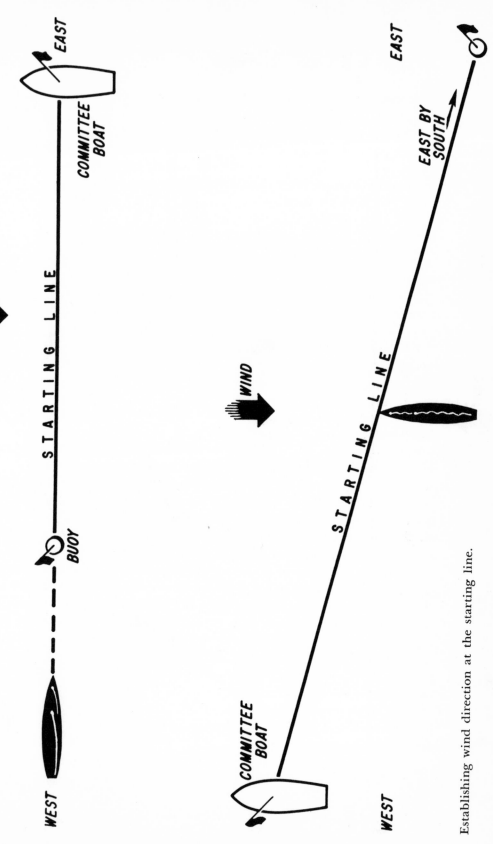

Establishing wind direction at the starting line.

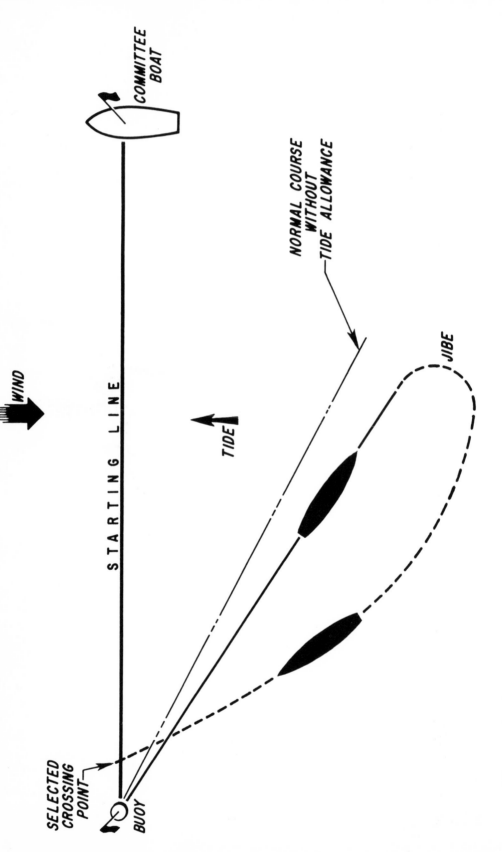

Allowance for tide at the start.

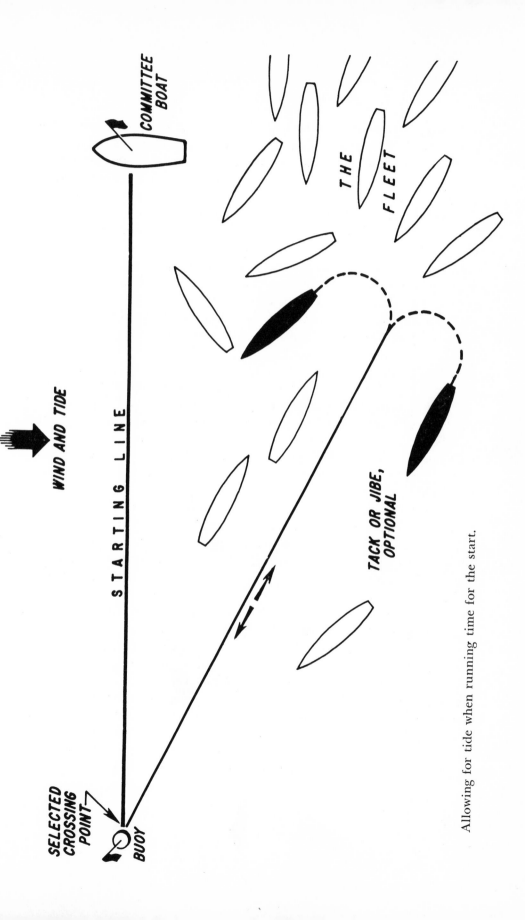

Allowing for tide when running time for the start.

For those unaccustomed to a quick reading of the compass, it is suggested that a compass rose be used for practice ashore by placing a pencil on the rose representing your boat and practice lining up the wind. Keep changing positions of the simulated starting line and become proficient in various bearings—that is, learn that the reciprocal of N/W is S/W, that of northwest by west is southwest by south, and so forth.

Having decided previously exactly where you want to be on the line at the gun, here is a suggested procedure for running time at the start. First, with your stopwatch, determine your tacking and jibing time from reach to reach. For a moderate-size boat (25 to 35 feet), I recommend that the normal run from the line back to the line be two minutes. It may be seen readily that if your total running time were one minute, you would meet the fleet heading for the line while you were endeavoring to tack or jibe for your return to the line. In boats 50 feet or larger, it is suggested that the total run be a minimum of four minutes, because of greater speed, longer tacking times, and need for maneuvering.

Presume your tacking time is ten seconds, reach to reach. You will be on the line, at the spot where you have chosen to cross, exactly two minutes before the starting signal, reaching (on the port tack), and you will continue on this reach for exactly 55 seconds. Then you will tack or jibe (ten seconds) reach up to the line for fifty-five seconds, and cross with the gun.

Naturally tide and sea must be taken into account in your runs. It is, therefore, vitally important to make several practice runs to learn what allowances should be made. A jibe is often preferable to a tack in returning to the line, especially in a fair tide. In this way you avoid a "barging" course. Furthermore, a jibe places your boat in a position to sharpen up and maintain rights of the leeward boat. In starts on the line away from the buoy or committee boat, the skipper must anticipate being smothered by weather boats on his approach as well as at the line itself.

It is also advantageous to have a tabulation for odd times in the event you are not free to leave the line at exactly two minutes before the start. For example, if you left your designated starting spot at a minute and 50 seconds before the actual start, your total seconds would amount to 110. With ten seconds allowed for tacking, your runaway would be exactly 50 seconds. With the various times tabulated on a card, the skipper will not have the problem of leaving his planned starting point at exactly two minutes before the gun, a difficult matter in a large class.

A few seconds can be life or death on a start. How often have we wished to speed up the committee's official watch when we are in the so-called coffin corner with too many seconds to dispose of. It is either over the line ahead of time, jibe and then be under the entire fleet on the port tack, or the third awful choice of hitting the committee boat. Walter Bowes, always a quick-witted sailor, found himself in this dreadful spot with eight or ten seconds to kill when sailing a 6-meter in France at Cannes. When he realized he was faced with the three equally unhappy alternatives, he observed a French sailor aboard the committee boat getting ready to pull the lanyard on the starting cannon. Bowes started a loud chant, "Cinq, quatre, trois, deux, un—Au feu!" As the sailor yanked the lanyard, Bowes crossed at the favored end of the line with a nice lead on the fleet.

SAILING THE COURSE

On the weather leg, the skipper must be continually alert to the trim of the sails. As a general rule, both the mainsail and the jib should be trimmed in flat, but take care that the jib is not so flat that it has insufficient drive. The jib *must* have lift and draft to pull the boat, especially in disturbed water. Skippers and crew are too often inclined to trim the jib too hard, subconsciously feeling this will make the boat point higher. The reverse is usually true.

One of the most vital items of racing equipment is the wind fly, or tell-tale, tied on the upper shroud, the one farthest outboard. Narrow pieces of ribbon are most frequently used, but ribbon flutters too much. My preference is for black thread, black being easier to see than white. However, if you haven't top vision and have difficulty seeing thread, use pieces of dark yarn—it doesn't flutter. The importance of the fly cannot be overemphasized. The keen helmsman will never let it out of his sight. *Absolute concentration* on this little guide rates A-1 in the list of must requirements for the skipper. It is also of equal importance off the wind and especially in light weather.

Of course the trim depends on conditions of wind and sea. If in a hard breeze the boat is burying her lee rail or carrying too much weather helm, ease the mainsheet a few inches. She must be sailed on her bottom. Adjustments should be continued as necessary. Always be sure the lee rail is not under and that sail is *not* trimmed too flat in rough water. Do not be too concerned about a luff in your mainsail. Remember that if the boat is overpowered, the mainsail must be eased to keep the boat on her bottom and the rail out of water.

Different tacks may require changes in the trim of the sails to meet wave conditions. On one tack you may have the sea at a better angle than on another, with the result that the boat will foot well with the sails trimmed in hard on one, but not on the other. On the latter, it may be necessary to ease the sails to give them pulling power to drive her through the seas. Changing the trim of the sails on different tacks is over-looked much too often.

When the breeze increases, attempt to feather your boat through the hard puffs. In other words, sail her a little finer as the puff strikes. This will keep her on her bottom, she will point higher, and she will actually not lose speed. Feel is a prerequisite for skillful feathering. The patient struggle through light weather is good fun and requires consummate skill, but for me there is no greater joy than sailing a well-tuned, well-equipped boat to windward in a very hard breeze.

On which side of the boat the helmsman should sit, whether to wind-ward or to leeward, is another much debated subject, but I doubt that it will ever be resolved, for either side may be the right one, depending on conditions. In a breeze I prefer to sit to windward; it's the natural place and the more comfortable. When you are seated to windward your weight is where it will help the boat most, and you can see the wind on the water before it strikes. Watching the seas, working her through them so they do not slow your boat down, is of great importance. Even when sailing before the wind, the skipper and crew should, in a good breeze, stay to windward, to keep the boat on her designed lines and ease her helm.

You must realize that you cannot force your boat to do the impossible. Merely guide her. Let her sail herself. Don't for example, try to sail her closer to the wind than she is capable of. You will sense and anticipate just before she is about to luff. You will similarly realize subconsciously that she is being sailed too wide. In disturbed water you will immediately feel that you are not giving her the necessary opportunity to get through the seas to her best advantage. Just remember that she can do it herself if you don't deprive her through poor handling.

Plan your approach to the weather mark long before you reach it. By all means be on the starboard tack if possible. Few maneuvers can be more costly than finding yourself on the port tack and meeting a solid wall of starboard-tack competitors. Never make the unpardonable mistake of overstanding the weather mark. Precious hard-gained distance you have earned is thrown overboard if you do. On the contrary, you may be able to improve your position by under-standing, especially if there is a current or tide setting you up to it. Whatever your tactics at the weather mark, you should be in a position to come in on the starboard tack or know you can cross ahead of the boats approaching with right of way.

The main halyard should be lowered a few inches on a run or reach to permit the headboard to be in the same plane as the sail. This will produce more draft in the upper part of the sail and is of great importance, especially in light weather. Slackening the tack downhaul is of secondary importance; it helps the lower but not the upper area. In drifting weather, the outhaul may also be slackened to advantage, and this is vitally important if your sail is flat. In light weather, when sailing to windward, you can use the spinnaker boom topping lift to take the weight off the main boom, thereby giving more draft to the sail. Off the wind, use the jib halyard when the spinnaker is set. Do not haul the foot of your mainsail beyond normal bounds; it merely distorts the sail, and gains no additional area.

A reach or run becomes, on some boats, a form of rest period, but very often it is these two legs that offer real opportunities for ground-gaining. On a reach, head no higher than the next mark, and if possible, steer to leeward of it so you are in a position to gain speed by reaching up. Again capitalize on the tide or current.

Everything must be set to hoist the spinnaker as you are approaching the weather mark, and by the time the spinnaker is two blocks it should be drawing. On many boats the spinnaker pole is set at the proper angle beforehand, and the sheet can be gradually trimmed in as the sail is hoisted. Be careful not to trim too fast, for if you do the spinnaker will fill and be difficult to hoist.

The great value of the boom vang is demonstrated on this leg. It should be set up before reaching the weather mark. The boom vang makes the sail and boom swing as a door, or, in other words, holds the sail in one plane. The sail can therefore be eased further off than would otherwise be possible. Without the downward pull of the vang, the mainsail will luff aloft first, and the entire sail must be trimmed to accommodate this condition. With the vang down, the luff occurs simultaneously along the entire hoist. The vang should be used with caution in light weather.

With the wind dead aft, and especially in light airs, a skipper should be aware that some advantage may be gained by tacking to leeward, by reaching up approximately a point or two to gain speed, and then jibbing over at the proper moment to maintain the equivalent course on the other jibe. In this way he also has a better chance of avoiding the fleet and keeping his wind clear.

At all times, whether on a run or on the windward leg, an alert skipper must make every effort to keep clear of his competitors. Avoid luffing matches on the runs even if to do so you must sacrifice your position. In the final score and in a large fleet, this precaution usually pays off. This also applies to private scraps on windward legs.

As in so much of life, there is really nothing new in sailing. Something appears to be new only because it was previously unknown. I have found that the more I learn the more I realize how little I know. Thus sailors who have had little or no experience in yacht racing may find more of interest in my comments than old timers will. As far as the experienced racing skipper is concerned, I can only hope that I have reminded him of at least one thing he knew but had forgotten. I hope that by applying that one new-old idea, he may win a race that otherwise he might have lost. I wish, too, that the ardent enthusiast starting to sail will some time give me the benefits of his learning. A great deal of my best instruction has come from juniors and beginners.

Index